Raiding on the
Western Front

In memory of Lucy

Raiding on the
Western Front

Anthony Saunders

Pen & Sword
MILITARY

First published in Great Britain in 2012 by
Pen & Sword Military
an imprint of
Pen & Sword Books Ltd
47 Church Street
Barnsley
South Yorkshire
S70 2AS

Copyright © Anthony Saunders 2012

ISBN 978-1-84884-485-8

Typeset in 11pt Ehrhardt by
Mac Style, Beverley, E. Yorkshire

Printed and bound by CPI Group (UK) Ltd, Croydon, CR0 4YY

Pen & Sword Books Ltd incorporates the Imprints of Pen & Sword
Aviation, Pen & Sword Family History, Pen & Sword Maritime, Pen &
Sword Military, Pen & Sword Discovery, Wharncliffe Local History,
Wharncliffe True Crime, Wharncliffe Transport, Pen & Sword Select,
Pen & Sword Military Classics, Leo Cooper, The Praetorian Press,
Remember When, Seaforth Publishing and Frontline Publishing.

For a complete list of Pen & Sword titles please contact
PEN & SWORD BOOKS LIMITED
47 Church Street, Barnsley, South Yorkshire, S70 2AS England
E-mail: enquiries@pen-and-sword.co.uk
Website: www.pen-and-sword.co.uk

Contents

Introduction

Raiding was a defining element of trench warfare on the Western Front during the First World War. And yet, so little has been written about the trench raid. While the subject is often mentioned in books about the fighting on the Western Front and features in many wartime memoirs, no single book has been devoted solely to trench raiding. *Raiding on the Western Front* aims to remedy this omission.

Raiding is as old as warfare. Indeed, it predates more formalised battles between arrayed armies. Up to more about the turn of the nineteenth century, light cavalry would engage in raids to harry an enemy, hitting supply lines, outposts and poorly defended places. The object was to cause havoc suddenly and quickly, then escape before retaliation could be organised. The trench raid, spawned by the immobility of trench warfare, differed substantially from this ethos of tip and run, partly because of the confined nature of the field of battle but nevertheless they bore similarities. The trench raid was not born of the First World War. The first operation recognisable as a trench raid occurred in 1863 during the American Civil War. The origins of the trench raid may be found in siege warfare when the besieged sallied forth from their defences in a sortie to impede the besiegers.

It is perhaps significant that some of the arms used by raiders during the First World War resembled medieval close-quarters weapons. However, it would be wrong to assume that raiding as practised on the Western Front, or, indeed, on any other front during the First World War since it was also a feature in other theatres, was medieval in form and execution. Although many of the early raids were ad hoc affairs, and while the fighting was often brutally close-quarters, no trench raid was ever meant merely to harry the enemy. Indeed, the purpose of raiding was more complex so that the arguments for and against its value to the conduct of the war are not easy to resolve. The question of success or failure of a raid, or of raiding as a whole, was and is not a simple equation that can be solved by inserting the appropriate figures to arrive at a definitive answer. For one thing, the criteria concerning success were not necessarily the same for the British, French or Germans, although outright failure was obvious. There were plenty of failures on both sides, some of them quite spectacular.

Raiding on the Western Front offers a clearer picture of the trench raid from an operational and tactical perspective as well as showing its wider strategic value. It looks at those who raided and those who were themselves raided. The main focus is on British and troops from the British Empire and Dominions (Canada, Australia, New Zealand and South Africa), and the Germans, but it also looks, to a lesser extent, at the French and the Americans. This book examines whether raiding changed how trench warfare was conducted on the Western Front. The nature of raiding, how raids were planned and executed and the consequences of successes and failures all form part of this book, along with an examination of how raiders were armed and trained. War diaries, official histories and some regimental histories and memoirs have been the principle sources of information.

Chapter 1

Genesis and Evolution of Raiding

On the morning of 9 November 1914, Captain R.E. Forrester led about twenty men of 2nd Black Watch, at that time attached to the Bareilly Brigade of the Indian Corps, in a daylight attack on a German machine-gun position located in a trench at La Bassée. The machine-gun had been causing the Highlanders a lot of trouble over recent days and the only way to silence it was to destroy it. Ten Germans were killed in the operation and the gun was put out of action with only two British casualties, both non-fatal, Forrester being one of them. This sortie was the first trench raid of the war. And it was a great success.

The night of the 9–10 November saw the second raid of the war, this time carried by the 1st and 2nd Battalions of the 39th Garhwal Rifles of the Indian Corps. Two fifty-man parties, one party from each battalion, entered a German trench that posed a real threat to the Garhwalis' positions, some 50 yards across no man's land, with the aim of making the trench unusable to the enemy. However, the German trench proved to be too well constructed, even at this early stage of the war, for easy demolition by mere infantrymen and the Garhwalis left without completing their task; they simply ran out of time. They managed to wreck part of the German position and succeeded in taking six prisoners. The Garhwalis' casualties were only slight despite a spirited rifle fire put up by the Germans. This was the first operation undertaken by the Garhwal Rifles, who had only been in France for only a month. The raid carried out by the Black Watch notwithstanding, the Garhwali raid of 9–10 November 1914 is usually considered to be the first trench raid of the war. There is no doubt that it set the pattern of future raiding operations as it was undertaken under cover of darkness, was intended to surprise the enemy, damage his defences and inflict casualties, without taking and holding ground except on a temporary basis necessary to carry out the operation.

Unlike the Black Watch's raid of the morning of the 9th, the Garhwalis' night-time raid was less conclusive, however. This was at a time when the

BEF and the Germans were constantly engaging in small-scale operations, of which the Black Watch raid and the Garhwali raid were indistinguishable from operations intended to improve the line in relation to that held by the enemy. The ground held by both sides was still contested in hard-fought little battles, each trying to secure better positions from which to dominate the enemy. The trench systems were incomplete and often rudimentary. Sapping forwards towards the enemy, a classic tactic of siege warfare, frequently resulted in battles and counter-attacks to deny ground or retake that which was lost to the enemy.

Two nights after the Garhwali raid, the Connaught Rangers became embroiled in operations to deny the Germans use of a trench they had dug within 35 yards of the Connaughts' positions that were adjacent to those of the Garhwalis. This involved raid, counter-raid and counter-counter-raid, all carried out over two nights. On the night of 12–13 November, the Connaughts attacked and took the new German trench, then lost it in a German counter-attack in which the Germans succeeded in entering the Connaughts' own positions but which were retaken by the Connaughts in a bayonet charge. To finish the business, the Connaughts mounted a raid on the German trench the following night, striking at midnight. Sixty men silently rushed the German position and killed the occupants. The raiders were supported by two machine-guns and they returned to their own lines with only five casualties.

It was under these circumstances that Major Taylor embarked upon a second raid on the trench attacked by the Garhwalis on the night of the 9th–10th. The object was to finish what they had started and emulate the success of the Connaughts. It was to prove an unwise decision. Alerted by the previous raids and all the fighting of the previous few days, the Germans were ready for them and the Garhwalis suffered as a consequence. It started to go wrong almost from the start.

This raid was ordered by General Keary, in command of the Garhwal Brigade of which the Garhwal Rifles were part. This was to be a bigger assault than the raid of a few nights' earlier. The raiders comprised six platoons of the 2nd/3rd Gurkhas, under the command of Lieutenant-Colonel Brakspear, and sixty men of the 2nd/39th Garhwali Rifles under Major Taylor. The object was to fill in the German trench and thereby deny them use of it. With this in mind, the raiding party included men of No. 4 Company Madras Sappers and Miners, and 2nd/3rd Gurkhas, whose task it was to destroy the trench once it had been captured. The raiders were split into three parties who approached the German trench from different directions. Only one of the three parties of raiders succeeded in entering the German trench, however, and they were soon in trouble. Brakspear returned to his own lines for reinforcements, despite heavy fire, and a new assault was made, but now the Germans had brought a searchlight into action and the cover of darkness was gone and German artillery was beginning to fire on them. The reinforcements were scattered. At midnight, British artillery was scheduled to fire on the German positions to cover the withdrawal of the raiders so the raiders had no choice but to leave.

The raid was a costly failure. Several officers were killed, including Major Taylor, and several more were wounded, while the Garhwalis alone lost thirty-eight men. Worse, the objective of the raid was not achieved. There were several reasons for this failure, not the least among them being German awareness of an impending raid, which highlighted the need for secrecy and surprise. Two raids carried out on the same positions within a few nights of each other, at a time when night-time operations were commonplace, were not likely to succeed. The element of surprise was completely absent in the second raid. Fighting spirit, courage and determination were not enough to carry the day, especially when the attackers shouted and hollered as they assaulted the German positions as they were trained to do in battle. The men had been warned not to do this, however. The failure also showed the importance of proper reconnaissance and good planning before a raid was undertaken. The dispositions of the new German trenches were not known to the raiders. Indeed, they were unaware that the Germans had dug new trenches since the first raid.

Undeterred by these costly enterprises, other battalions within the Indian Corps began to conduct raiding operations against the Germans soon afterwards. One hundred and twenty-five men of the 6th Jat Light Infantry, accompanied by sixty sappers of No. 3 Company Bombay Sappers and Miners, carried out a raid on the 16th. Unlike the Garhwali raid of few nights' earlier, however, this one was well planned and executed. Everything went to plan and no surprises awaited the raiders. This was more in the way of a small-scale night attack than a raid as it involved artillery support and the infantry advanced in open order as in a conventional night attack on prepared positions.

What is striking about these earlier raids is their resemblance to what might be termed conventional assaults. They were fought with the same weapons and with the same tactics as any other night operation, irrespective of whether ground was to be taken or simply denied to the enemy. The Indian raiders were armed solely with rifle and bayonet. At this stage of the war, grenades were largely unknown throughout all the elements of the BEF, although the BEF had first encountered German grenades on the Aisne as early as September. No trench mortars were involved in these raids as these, too, were unknown at this time. Indeed, the BEF had none whatsoever in the autumn of 1914. However, while the BEF had no hand grenades, the Germans were provided with them and, during the Jats' raid on the

16 November, a number of German bombs were captured and brought back to the Jat lines.

Although raiding became more sophisticated as the war progressed, the two raids carried out by the Garhwal Rifles and the others conducted by the battalions of the Indian Corps in the last two months of 1914 contained most of the elements that came to define raiding. Nevertheless, for the British, the notion of what constituted a raid was never made explicit by GHQ and, indeed, at corps, divisional, brigade or battalion levels no one made any attempt to define a raid. While raiding became part of the tactical doctrine of the BEF during 1915, it was only ever defined according to what a raid was expected to achieve, never in the manner in which the enterprise should be carried out. Thus, there was a lack of distinction between, at one end of the spectrum, fighting patrols and raids, and at the other, raids and enterprises that resembled small-scale battles, although the distinction between patrols and small-scale battles was perfectly clear to everyone involved. Even that distinction was to fade as the war progressed.

At the beginning of 1915, Field Marshall Sir John French, GOC of the BEF, decided to instruct the BEF to engage in raiding as a means of taking the fight to the enemy. Raiding was, by then, becoming established as an ad hoc tactical endeavour but had been restricted to the infantry of the Indian Corps and to those battalions of the British Army that were temporarily attached. On 5 February, Lieutenant General Robinson, Chief of the General Staff at GHQ, wrote to the First and Second Armies, the Cavalry Corps and the Indian Cavalry Corps telling them that:

> The Field-Marshall Commanding-in-Chief desires me again to draw attention to the importance of constant activity and of offensive methods in general in dealing with the enemy immediately opposed to us.
>
> 2. For reasons known to you, we are for the moment acting on the defensive so far as serious operations are concerned, but this should not preclude the planning and making of local attacks on a comparatively small scale, with a view to gaining ground and of taking full advantage of any tactical or numerical inferiority on the part of the enemy. Such enterprises are highly valuable, and should receive every encouragement, since they relieve monotony and improve the moral[e] of our troops, while they have a corresponding detrimental effect on the moral[e] of the enemy's troops and tend in a variety of ways to their exhaustion and general disquiet.

That the BEF was on the defensive, rather than the offensive, was of great concern to GHQ. There was a genuine fear of stagnation or even collapse should the troops remain in static positions for prolonged periods, especially when the whole ethos of the British Army was offence. Indeed, it was the abiding principle in all armies at that time and had been since the mid-nineteenth century. Like all the continental armies of the time, the British Army trained for attack, not defence. The spirit of the attack by the infantry was at the heart of all military doctrines. While the BEF was unable to engage in a major new offensive on the Western Front until the spring of 1915, smaller–scale operations seemed to be the ideal solution as they were not precluded by the lack of manpower or, indeed, by lack of equipment, both of which the BEF was already beginning to suffer from at the end of 1914. Such shortages became worse in 1915, although the manpower issue was partly overcome by the arrival of the Territorials, and later by Kitchener volunteers, coming to a head with the Shell Scandal of the middle of 1915. Lack of artillery and trench warfare munitions in the shape of grenades and mortars was not resolved until the second half of 1915.

The sentiment behind the GHQ instruction clearly reflected the BEF's need to attack the enemy rather than merely hold him at bay. After all, the enemy had taken control of large areas of France and Belgium and neither country was satisfied merely to wait out the stalemate. However, the instruction to take the fight to the enemy was not based on sound military experience. Indeed, the notion that morale would suffer if the BEF did not attack the enemy or that the troops would become bored by the monotony of trench warfare if they did fight tended to reflect a lack of understanding of the nature of trench warfare. That was hardly surprising since the British and, indeed, the French, Belgians and Germans had no experience of this form of warfare. They only had second-hand knowledge of trench fighting from the Russo-Japanese War, nine years previously, in which raiding did not figure.

There was no clear evidence that the morale of the enemy was adversely affected when raided any more than the morale of the raiders and the rest of their battalion was raised by a successful raid. The morale issue was largely supposition derived from enthusiastic reporting. As some of the earliest raids carried out by the Indian Corps showed, raiding could be very costly to the raiders, which was not conducive to raising morale. The idea that raiding exhausted those who were raided also seemed more fanciful than realistic. Indeed, the notion of raiding was viewed by GHQ in a decidedly one–sided manner as no one seems to have considered the possibility that the Germans would not only copy the British and take up raiding themselves but conduct retaliatory raids in response to being raided.

There was also the question of what raiding was expected to achieve other than harassment, which the GHQ instruction seemed to suggest was the point of raiding. Robinson's memorandum went on to state that:

Further, as you are well aware, enterprises of this nature constitute the most effective form of defence, since by throwing upon the enemy anxiety for his own security, they help to relieve our own troops from the wearying and demoralising effects produced by expected attacks on the part of the enemy.

That seemed to undermine the very point of raiding since it followed that the Germans would almost certainly retaliate. All the fighting so far had shown the Imperial German Army to be tenacious, determined and, in particular, very adept at counter-attacking. There could be little doubt that the Germans would respond if raided, especially when the reason for French's endorsement of raiding was the vigorous offensive operations being carried out by the Germans. French wanted the BEF to take back the initiative.

However, no one was expected to carry out a raid if there was not a 'reasonable chance of success', while the objective of such a raid had to 'be commensurate with the losses likely to be entailed' in achieving it. The real point of raiding was not simply to harass the enemy with random acts of violence but to achieve specific objectives. The trouble was that the 'specific objectives' were so vaguely expressed and the notion of 'commensurate losses' so ill-defined that the concept of a raid was open to very broad interpretation. This was only mitigated by the caveat: careful planning is essential for success. A more definitive description of the objective of a raid did not come until later in the war. The aim of any raid was to:

> enter the enemy's trenches by surprise, kill as many of his men as possible, and return before counter-measures can be taken. Special tasks may be added, such as obtaining prisoners for 'identification', damaging mine shafts, destroying a length of trench or post which is giving particular trouble.

But this aim and intention was not made clear in 1915. And the description still allowed a range of interpretations to be applied to the task according to the target under attack and the expectations of the officer ordering the raid.

During 1915 and 1916, raids were mostly instigated and organised at battalion level although sometimes they were ordered at brigade or divisional level. Thus, until February 1915, raiding was entirely local in concept and execution. Indeed, it remained little changed in this regard throughout 1915. Few battalions took to raiding, despite French's instruction. When he issued the order, only the battalions of the Indian Corps had taken to raiding. Throughout 1915, there was little enthusiasm for raids among most of the battalions of the BEF and few such enterprises were undertaken. This was largely due to lack of time. There was an overriding need to develop and maintain the trench system, a need not only felt by the BEF but by the French, Belgian and German armies as well. Until the beginning of 1916, more man hours were spent on digging, constructing, repairing and maintaining trenches, dugouts, saps and mortar and machine-gun emplacements, not to mention latrines, than on any other activity on the front line. This was made more demanding by the increasing need for greater depth in the defences and to improve existing works. Shelling and mortaring ensured that repairs were an unending task. Little time was available for taking the fight to the enemy by means of raiding.

By March 1916, the idea of what constituted a raid had developed considerably. A clearer definition of what such a 'minor enterprise' was supposed to achieve meant that raids could be more effectively carried out than hitherto. Moreover, the means by which the objectives of the raid were supposed to be accomplished were better understood. But this knowledge was limited to brigade, which was now the level at which raids tended to be ordered; there were less instigated than at battalion level compared to the early days of raiding. Extensive 'notes' on the subject of raiding were issued by GHQ, based not on theory but derived from direct experience, fully described in post-raid reports by raid commanders and submitted to brigade. There was now a clear understanding of the appropriate preparations and specific training required for a successful raid as well as an appreciation of the general principals of raiding. No rules were ever set out for conducting raids in the way that tactical schemes for offensive and defensive operations were set out in considerable detail in pamphlets issued by GHQ for platoons and divisions from 1916 onwards. Part of the reason for the lack of 'rules' was the varied number of men who might be involved in raid. Sometimes, it might be only half a dozen; other times, it might be 300 or 400.

By now, the BEF realised that success depended upon good reconnaissance of the target so that every detail of the approach, the attack and the withdrawal could be planned and rehearsed. This depended upon the effectiveness of the patrols sent out into no man's land. Indeed, effective raiding depended upon dominance of no man's land, which served the double purpose of preventing the enemy from discovering the intention to raid while preventing him from planning his own raid. Crucial to the entire enterprise was ensuring that the target was suitable for raiding, which meant establishing four criteria before any thought of a raid could be entertained, although failure to satisfy these did not always deter brigade or division from insisting on a raid still being carried out. Operational requirements, or what would be later termed 'the bigger picture', sometimes overrode other considerations. The viability of a raid was dependant upon:

The existence of a covered approach to some portion of the enemy's line
.... A lack of vigilance [by the enemy] discovered by our patrols ...
isolation of some portion of the enemy's line, so that it cannot easily be
supported or reinforced .... Facilities for supporting the operation by
artillery, trench mortar, or machine gun-fire.

Quite clearly, not every portion of the enemy's trenches was going to be
susceptible to a raid. Moreover, the sort of raids undertaken in November
and December 1914 by the battalions of the Indian Corps were no longer
considered to be acceptable; the targets would not have satisfied the criteria
of early 1916. The target of the raid could no longer be an enemy trench that
was simply too close to the British line or one that enfiladed part of the
British line if none of the four criteria were satisfied. In that case, other
means had to be used to deal with the threat. And by early 1916, there were
plenty of other means, such as trench mortars and rifle grenades.

Once an enemy trench had been singled out for a raid, those who were
going to carry it out, usually volunteers, had to familiarise themselves with
target, using, wherever possible, aerial photographs. By mid-1916, these
were becoming more plentiful. Reports from patrols, as well as information
given up by prisoners, along with intelligence gained with the aid trench
periscopes and from snipers, all contributed to the preparation of a plan for
the raid. While the orders for the raid came from brigade or division, the
plan for its execution was prepared by the battalion or company that had
been given the task of conducting the operation.

The raid had to have a specific objective and this had to be limited in
scope in order to make it realistic. While this was more of a concern for
division or brigade, nevertheless, the unit detailed to carry out the raid had
to ensure that its plan for the enterprise did not become over ambitious.
Equally, the choice of a night attack as opposed to daytime had to be made
by the raiders themselves. Raids during 1916 and 1917 mostly relied on the
cover of darkness. Moonless nights were too dark for anyone to find his way
with certainty or see his fellow raiders. There had to be some moonlight, at
least. As important was the amount of time the raiders spent in the enemy
trench. In order to reduce the risks of the enemy putting into effect his
countermeasures to nullify the raid, the length of time spent in the enemy
trenches needed to be kept to a minimum. The Germans, like the British,
rehearsed dealing with enemy incursions and had measures ready for dealing
with them.

With this in mind, the points of entry into enemy positions had to be
known in detail by the raiders, as well as the points at which the raiders
intended to leave the enemy positions at the appointed time. Remaining on
the target beyond the agreed time could result in being bombarded with

friendly mortars or hit by British machine-gun fire in support of the raid, not to mention artillery putting down a barrage to cover the withdrawal of the raiders. The actions to be taken by the raiders once they were in the trench had also to be planned, especially the timings. Each member of a party had to know exactly what his tasks were and how long each element of the raid took to complete. A raid was a precision operation with a specific objective, not an ad hoc sortie. Thus, all the raiders had to wear watches, synchronised several times over the days preceding the raid. Raiding helped to popularise the wristwatch, which, hitherto, had come a poor second to the traditional pocket watch. It was the huge demand for cheap and reliable wristwatches during the First World War that led to their widespread mass manufacture.

The composition of a raiding party varied considerably depending on the objective and the support from artillery, mortars and neighbouring units. Typically, a party might include: sub-parties detailed to cut wire; bayonet men and bombers to clear enemy trenches; bombers assigned to clear dugouts; parties to block the arrival of enemy reinforcements; rifle grenadiers, Lewis-gunners; a demolition party of Royal Engineer sappers for destroying dugouts, trenches and mortar emplacements; scouts; messengers (who might even bring a telephone wired to the British network); and stretcher bearers to bring back the wounded. In addition, some of the raiders might be given additional tasks, such as locating gas cylinders, which they were then supposed to drag back to the British line when they retired, a rather ambitious expectation even though those given this task were provided with ropes. Others looked for mine shafts; mining was a constant problem in some parts of the front. Locating and destroying enemy machine-guns was also a prime task on a raid.

To help make the raid proceed smoothly, some of the party were given various assault tasks that would enable the attackers to enter the enemy trench more easily. Apart from cutting wire with hand-held wire cutters, some men carried specially made mats, which resembled mattresses, so-called traverser mats 'made of a strip of stout canvas with wooded slates fastened across – proves quite efficient' that could be thrown across wire to allow men to cross without hindrance. Similarly, some men carried scaling ladders to help the raiders climb out of the enemy trench when it was known to be deep. Alternatively, potential ladder-carriers were given the job of cutting steps in the enemy trench to provide an exit.

The manner in which adjoining trenches were to be blocked and by whom, as well as the blocking points in the trench the raiders were going to hit, had to be well organised beforehand. A timetable had to be set and followed. The raiders had to be fully trained as bombers, that is, be thoroughly familiar with handling hand grenades. Until the end of 1915, that meant being familiar with up to twelve different patterns as well as with German patterns. With the widespread availability of the No. 5 Mills grenade from late 1915 onwards and the abandonment of all the stopgap grenades of the previous twelve months, the technical expertise required of a bomber was a little more manageable. He also had to be trained in the use of the revolver and pistol. And the raider needed to acquire nerves of steel so that he could stand stock still in the open whenever the Germans put up a star shell or a flare. Worse, he had to be able to cut wire by hand silently in the dark and crawl up to the enemy position across no man's land and 'lie up under the enemy's parapet' before retiring. Needless to say, they had to practise this on the ground over which they would have to move on the night of the raid and without alerting the enemy, otherwise the enterprise was a no-hoper.

Unlike some of the early raids in which more than one party of raiders entered the enemy trench, by 1916, only single parties were recommended because of the difficulties of good synchronisation between the parties. Nevertheless, it was acknowledged that more than one party might be needed for the raid. Each party needed to have its own password. And every member of a party needed to know the name of that party's leader. The raiders had to learn German phrases such as 'hands up' and 'come out', the latter being called into dugouts before grenades were tossed inside them. Equally, the raiders had to be aware of the possibility that the German defenders might call out commands in English or French, such as 'retire' or 'this way'. Cunning and subterfuge, although seemingly inappropriate in the middle of bloody fight, was not uncommon. It was as much for avoiding friendly troops firing on each other as the nullification of enemy ruses that such protocols were necessary. However, ruses to get close to an enemy position were not unknown. In 1918, German troops allegedly donned French Red Cross uniforms to fool US troops as a prelude to a raid.

All of this, of course, required rehearsal over ground made up, well behind the lines, to resemble the trenches about to be raided. About a week of training and rehearsal was reckoned to be advisable to secure success. Utmost secrecy of the operation was vital to reduce the risk of the Germans somehow gaining prior knowledge of the raid, which would allow them to prepare countermeasures. This could happen quite easily because documents that were not supposed to be taken into the front line sometimes found their way there, to be subsequently discovered during a German raid. Alternatively, a prisoner might be taken while on patrol and he might give up the information, or the enemy might simply deduce a raid was about to happen because of the unconcealed preparations in the British line. By 1916, raiding had become a complicated business. There was no substitute for complete surprise. That was the surest way of achieving success.

And while one of the objectives of any raid was now to obtain intelligence about the enemy in the form of documents and items of uniform by which the unit might be identified, the raiders were expected to leave behind anything that might identify them to the enemy should they be captured or killed. Thus, officers dressed like private soldiers, and all shoulder titles and badges of rank were removed prior to the raid. Everyone was instructed to reveal only name and rank should they be captured.

Such preparations were a far cry from the spontaneity of late 1914 and early 1915. A properly prepared fire plan for artillery, trench mortars and machine-guns was often needed in support of the raid both at its start and at its conclusion, the latter being intended to help the raiders retire. The 36th Machine Gun Company supported raids carried out by the 9th Royal Fusiliers in February and September 1917, for example, while the Light Trench Mortar Battery of the 19th Infantry Brigade, equipped with 3-inch Stokes mortars, supported a raid carried out by the 2nd Royal Welch Fusiliers in July 1916 and another Royal Welch raid the following month, both at Givenchy. In preparation for the Royal Welch raid, the battery dug twelve new emplacements for its Stokes mortars. On the evening of 5 July, the raid hit the Germans holding mine craters in front of the first-line trenches. Four mortars were operated at a slow rate of fire for 90 minutes between 10.30pm and midnight, maintaining a barrage on trenches south of the crater. Three mortars fired for 45 minutes on German support trenches behind the craters, while five mortars engaged enemy saps and front-line trenches. Altogether, the battery fired 2,345 rounds. On 21 August, the battery supported a raid on a German trench located at the west corner of High Wood but only fired 106 rounds.

The 5 July raid was also supported by five Vickers machine-guns of the 19th Brigade's Machine Gun Company, using indirect fire to shoot over the heads of the raiders. With the mortars, this was intended to isolate the Germans being raided from the rest and thereby prevent reinforcements coming to the aid of those under attack. The 36th Machine Gun Company's support of the raids carried out by the 11th Middlesex in daylight on the morning of 26 February 1917 and the 9th Royal Fusiliers the following September was similar to that provided to the Royal Welch by the 19th Machine Gun Company. Four Vickers guns fired for 70 minutes over the heads of the raiders to hit German communication trenches and potential forming-up areas for reinforcements. A total of 13,000 rounds were fired. In addition to the 36th Machine Gun Company, the raid was supported by three guns of the 76th and two guns of the 46th Machine Gun Companies, along with trench mortars and artillery.

When artillery was involved, its task was usually to cut the wire in front of the German position about to be raided but the mortars and machine-guns could be used in a number of ways intended to isolate the raided trench from the German flanks and rear by interdiction. The light Stokes mortar, an infantry-support weapon operated entirely within an infantry brigade rather than as part of the main artillery, provided very effective interdiction and tactical support for raids from 1916 onwards. They were very flexible in the sort of support they could provide and were used for fire suppression on the flanks of a raid. The raiders might also be supported by their parent unit firing rifle grenades. Whatever form the support took and irrespective of how simple the supporting fire might be, precise timing was necessary. This meant that nothing could be left to chance. Neighbouring units could provide suppression with rifle fire to prevent the enemy from engaging the flanks of the raiders. The converse of this was to populate flanking trenches with dummies so that their heads were above the parapet to draw German fire.

Support for a raid went beyond even these extensive preparations. One or more additional parties were positioned in no man's land on the night of the attack to provide covering fire during the withdrawal if needed, deal with hostile patrols should they happen upon the scene at the wrong moment and to act as liaison with the attackers as well as help to evacuate prisoners. A similar party might also remain in the British trenches, ready to act should they be needed, especially if the Germans launched a counter-attack. And to help the raiders return to the British line, white tape or calcium hypochlorite (a disinfectant in the form of a white powder) could be used to mark out the route home, a task usually allocated to one of the support parties.

Raiding did not become widespread until 1916, with the British, Australians and Canadians being particularly keen on this very aggressive form of domination over the enemy. The Germans were also keen raiders but never to the same extent, while the French were unenthusiastic, preferring instead the full-scale assault. The French thought raiding was ineffective and a waste of resources. In the five months between 19 December 1915 and 30 May 1916, the BEF raided the Germans sixty-three times. Forty-seven of these raids were regarded as successful. This meant that the objective had been achieved with only a few casualties. Failures, in which the objective was not achieved, were often very costly, with up to half a raiding force becoming casualties. Thus, the BEF suffered sixteen failures, that is 25 per cent of the raids failed. During this same period, the Germans only mounted thirty-three raids on BEF-held trenches, twenty of which were successful. That was a failure rate of nearly 40 per cent. Perhaps the French had a point, after all. Such a high failure rate does not suggest that raiding was an effective tactic. Costly though they could be, the value of successful raids outweighed the cost of the failures.

During the week preceding the opening of the Somme offensive in the summer of 1916, the Armies of the BEF flanking the Fourth Army, which was going to launch the infantry assault of the offensive on 1 July, carried out forty-three raids to mask the activities of the Fourth Army. The First Army made fourteen, while the Second Army made seventeen, seven of them by battalions of the I Anzac Corps, and the Third Army made twelve. It is questionable whether such raiding achieved very much, however, as the Germans were not fooled and the cost in casualties for the raiders was fairly high. The Germans mounted only six raids over the entire frontage of these three Armies during the same period, which might be construed as a success for the BEF if German raiding was actually suppressed by the activities of the three Armies, but levels of raiding tended to fluctuate for all sorts of reasons.

Between July and mid-November 1916, the period of the Allied Somme campaign, the three Armies increased their raiding rate and hit the Germans a total of 310 times. The raiding parties ranged from two platoons to two companies, with accompanying Royal Engineers who carried out demolition of the German trenches and dugouts. Of these raids, 204 were reckoned to have been successful. That is to say, the failure rate was 34 per cent. The Germans, on the other hand, hit back with sixty-five raids, of which only twenty-two were successful, a failure rate of 66 per cent, which was nearly twice that of the BEF. The question is whether their higher failure rate was due to effective Allied countermeasures or to inadequate planning, preparation and training by the Germans.

Following the cessation of the Somme campaign in November 1916, the level of raiding by the BEF declined. It picked up again in 1917. The British IX Corps mounted nineteen raids between 16 May and 7 June 1917, the three weeks preceding the Battle of Messines. The raiding parties ranged in size from twelve to 300. Again, the cost to the raiders was high; they suffered 172 casualties, although they took 171 prisoners and killed a number of Germans. In mid-November 1917, about 300 men of the German 184th Regiment raided trenches held by the British 55th Division, inflicting ninety-four casualties, more than half of whom were prisoners. During the winter of 1917–18, the BEF curtailed its raiding due to heavy losses during the Third Battle of Ypres, Passchendaele. The BEF needed time to recover and rebuild. Conversely, the Germans increased their raiding activities and between 8 December 1917 and 21 March 1918, they mounted about 225 raids on the Ypres salient alone. However, only sixty-two of these were reckoned by the British to have been successful. Given that the British were likely to bias any analysis of German raids in their own favour, this nevertheless represents an incredibly high rate of failure: 72 per cent. In this instance, for the British, a German failure meant a failure by the raiders to identify the British unit raided, which also meant that the raiders failed to get into the British line.

Several raids carried out on successive nights were sometimes mounted simply to secure prisoners. This occurred in August 1916, when the Highland Light Infantry were raided three times by the Germans, twice on the same night and again the next night. On the first occasion, the Germans had crawled through the long grass in no man's land to jump unnoticed into the British trenches. They had then tried to take two prisoners who, in resisting capture, were stabbed with *Nahkampfmesser* (trench knives). Having failed to secure a prisoner, the Germans tried again a few hours later but failed again. The next night, they bombed their way into the British trenches However, yet again, they failed to take a prisoner and suffered two fatalities for their trouble. To add insult to injury, as they returned to their own line, they were hit by 2-inch mortars, which dropped their big plum-pudding bombs among them. If this was an example of German raiding technique, it is little wonder their success rate was so low.

From these figures, it is clear that levels of raiding depended to a large extent on the wider strategic picture. The greatest number of BEF raids seemed to coincide with major Allied offensives rather than with the periods in between.[1] This rather belied the avowed intention of maintaining fighting spirit with raiding when the troops might otherwise lose their edge during quiet periods at the front. However, it is also clear that raiding was intended to be an act of aggression to dominate the enemy, prevent him from taking possession of no man's land and wear down his morale by keeping him on edge. Raiding was meant to have a psychological impact rather than just a physical one, although raids certainly helped in the gathering of intelligence about the enemy. However, from the intelligence-gathering perspective, patrols were probably a more effective and less costly means of doing this.

Raiding continued into 1918 and did not end with the German spring offensives of that year. Indeed, raiding persisted until the end of the war although it subsided with the return to semi-open warfare in the summer of 1918 and the Allied counter-offensives, which drove the German Army back beyond its original position at the start of the year. The Germans were still raiding in June, while some of the last British raids of the war were carried out in September by the 2nd Coldstream Guards and the 2nd Grenadier Guards. Raids were still being mounted in October and early November.

The practice of raiding had a legacy for the evolution of warfare in that the infiltration style of tactic employed on raids became part of the new assault tactics that evolved during the war. Indeed, the tactics developed by the German stormtroops came from those employed in raiding. The new infiltration tactics adopted by France, Britain and Germany, more or less independently of each other during 1917, were the tactics used in the battles of late 1917 as well as those of the 1918 offensives. Stormtroop tactics, a term that applied equally well to the new infantry tactics of the French and the

British as to those of the German Army, were very much those of the raider. In this sense, if in no other, raiding had a positive effect on the conduct of the war and contributed to the evolution of infantry tactics, which contributed to the evolution of a new form of warfare called deep battle and three-dimensional warfare.

Whether raiding on the Western Front can be traced to a raiding ethos in the tribal regions of India, the home of the Garhwalis, as some have suggested, is moot. There is no evidence to support that idea. After all, the first recognisable trench raid occurred in 1863, during the American Civil War.

Chapter 2

1915, the Rise of Raiding

Despite the instruction from GHQ in February for the BEF to engage in raiding as a means of taking the fight to the enemy because of all the benefits that would accrue to the British by so doing and all the consequent detriments that would fall on the Germans, very little raiding occurred in 1915. This was a year of harsh lessons for everyone about the nature of trench warfare. Despite the desire of Britain and France to push the Germans off French soil, the means to do it were not yet available. Tactically and technologically, as well logistically, the Allies could not complete the task they had begun in 1914. Neither could the Germans finish their invasion of France for that matter, as she was fighting on two fronts, a situation that Germany had anticipated. In 1915, German focus was in the East. The Allies had every expectation of finishing in 1915 what had begun a few months earlier, following the respite of the winter months, during which time losses would be made good and wounds healed.

The opportunities for the sort of battle that had dominated the first few months of the war were gone, although the Allies believed they could embark on big offensive operations and break through the German defences to emerge into the clear countryside, beyond where conventional open warfare could be resumed. If only sufficient destructive force could be brought to bear, it could be made to happen, was the belief behind the approach to resuming operations after the winter break. With this mind, the British and the French embarked upon a series of offensives at the start of 1915, beginning with the French Champagne offensive in January and February. The first British engagement of 1915 was the Battle of Neuve Chapelle on 10–12 March. The BEF went on to fight the Second Battle of Ypres between 22 April and 25 May, the Battle of Aubers Ridge on 9–10 May, the Battle of Festubert on 9–26 May and, finally, Loos between 25 September and 14 October. At the same time, the BEF was expanding at a considerable rate and taking over more sectors of the front from the French as it did so.

None of this is to suggest that the BEF fought fewer battles or less hard in subsequent years. Indeed, the BEF spent much of its time preparing for and engaging in major operations throughout the war. What sets 1915 apart from later years for the BEF is the novelty of the sort of fighting in which it was now engaged and, in particular, the huge task of providing trench warfare munitions in large enough quantities to meet front-line requirements, made more difficult by the lack of reliability in what was available because of the technical challenge all this presented to British industry. Added to this was a shortage of high-explosive shells and a dearth of large-calibre guns and howitzers, which was only remedied with the creation of the Ministry of Munitions in June 1915. This focused British attention on big battles rather than small enterprises that could do no more than irritate the enemy to no real benefit to the BEF.

Throughout 1915, the British believed that a breakthrough of the German line was possible. However, the Germans, who remained on the defensive during 1915, consolidated their gains and strengthened their lines, learning from their experience of the French Champagne offensive and, in particular, from Neuve Chappell, that a single line of trenches was not enough to hold back an Allied offensive. The Germans began the process of developing defences in depth, building a second line with a reserve line behind that, a process that was to culminate in 1916 with the Hindenburg Line, which had several lines to a depth of several miles.

Raiding was of little consequence for either side in the overall strategic scheme of 1915. There was little opportunity for it and a lack of belief in it as a tactic for progressing either the Allied or the enemy cause. So long as breakthrough was perceived as a realistic possibility by the British, the notion of raiding to harass the enemy was of little importance, save to bolster the fighting spirit of the troops. That it might need bolstering rather played to the old idea of soldiers doing as little as they could get away with in times of inaction, that is to say, when they were not engaged in fighting battles. Some commanders saw this as inevitable between battles when periods of lassitude, laxity and laziness would prevail, which only fierce face-to-face fighting could resolve. Not everyone in command was quite so out of touch as to imagine that nothing happened when battles were not being fought or were oblivious to the day-to-day demands of trench warfare. Life in the trenches was rarely a life of inactivity anywhere along the line, even in the quietest sector.

Experience of life in the trenches during 1915 showed that no soldier was ever left idle for long, even when out of the line. So much navvying was needed to build and maintain trenches, roads and light railways, as well as lay telephone cables, pump water, lay duckboards, dig sumps, latrines, bombing posts and listening posts, carry stores from one place to another or up the line, including rolls of barbed wire that had to be set out in no man's land. There were countless other tasks besides these. None of this changed, of course, in the coming years, but in 1915 it was all new and experience had to be gained about how to do it. And at the beginning of 1915, most of the digging had yet to be done. The trench systems of early 1915 were nothing compared to those of a year later. The trench line was never static. By 1917, it had grown and evolved, and by 1918, the front line was very different from what it had been three years earlier.

Nevertheless, some battalions in the BEF took to raiding early on in 1915 but the majority carried out none at all for the entire year. Even those that did take it up had few opportunities to raid. These battalions tended to have a policy of maintaining constant aggression towards the enemy and did not like to allow 'live and let live' to dominate on whichever part of the front they were stationed. It is instructive to compare the incidence of raiding in 1915 with sniping. While raids were few and far between, sniping was a constant. Indeed, it grew in intensity and became a problem for all soldiers in the front line, especially when new trenches were very shallow or badly made. Casualties from sniping were almost an everyday occurrence and far more troops were lost over the course of the month because of snipers than because of raiding. However, the importance of raiding began to change towards the end of the year, so that come 1916, raiding was taken up more vigorously as the benefits began to make themselves apparent. At the beginning of 1915, raiding was still a rather low-key local enterprise with a *Boy's Own* adventure flavour to it but by the beginning of 1916, any hint of amateurism was long gone. Now it was a much more hard-nosed and well-planned business.

The first raid of 1915 was carried out on the night of 2–3 January by the 1st Worcesters, near Neuve Chapelle. Again, as with the Garhwalis' first raid the previous November, they were reacting to the Germans digging a trench very close to their own line; it was a mere 50 yards away. Not only was this far too close – and at that time, German trenches were generally better constructed than British trenches so that they tended to afford greater protection, which increased the threat to the Worcesters – but there was every prospect of the Germans using the trench as a jumping-off point for an assault on the Worcesters. To forestall this, they raided it. The attack was swift and deadly. In effect, it was a bayonet charge, led by Lieutenant F.C. Roberts, who was subsequently awarded a DSO for the action, while three others of his party were awarded the DCM.

Roberts and twenty-five men took the Germans by surprise and killed the occupants of the trench for two casualties of their own, both fatal. While the courage and daring of Roberts is not in question – he later won the MC and the VC – nor that of his men, all of whom had volunteered for the raid, the action illustrates well the cavalier-like dash at the expense of method of the early raids. It was more in the manner of an eighteenth-century sortie than a twentieth-century assault. However, the German trench was too close to the British line to allow the artillery to bombard it without causing British casualties, while trench mortars were far too inaccurate at that time (even assuming they were available to the Worcesters) and they had no grenades to bomb it. A bayonet charge was really the only option. This was all to change during 1915, however. And such bravado would be severely punished by the defenders in the future.

Another early raid of 1915 was the first one carried out by Canadian troops. A party of Princess Patricia's Canadian Light Infantry, attached to a British brigade, raided a German trench in the darkness of the early hours of 28 February. Princess Patricia's Canadian Light Infantry was a battalion raised in August 1914 and funded by Hamilton Gault, a businessman from Montreal. It arrived in France at the beginning of January, well before the main Canadian contingent. Gault, with the rank of major, commanded the battalion. The raid by No. 4 Company, led by Lieutenant C.E. Crabbe, was assisted by a bombing squad of three commanded, by Lieutenant T.M. Papineau, and three snipers, under Corporal Ross, who was killed in the attack. They hit a German sap at St Eloi in the Ypres salient at 4.30 am, the occupants of which had been causing the Canadians a lot of trouble with grenades. In about 30 minutes, the raiders destroyed the sap but suffered several casualties as they fought off the Germans: five dead, eight wounded, Crabbe among them, and three missing. Their situation had not been helped by the fact that mud and battle damage had rendered useless all but one of the party's rifles during the course of the fighting. One of the missing was Lieutenant Colquhoun, who had disappeared when he had gone out to reconnoitre the target a second time before the start of the operation. He had already been out on a reconnaissance of the German sap and neighbouring trenches with Gault, who had been wounded.

By the time of the Battle of Neuve Chapelle in March, the notion of raiding had already begun to change. The 2nd Royal Welch Fusiliers, one of the more aggressive battalions on the Western Front, undertook a diversionary raid on 12 March to the north of the area being assaulted by the First Army. Twenty-two men, led by three officers, hit German positions in Bois Grenier. This was the first raid to have artillery support to protect the flanks of the attackers to help prevent a German counter-attack. Curiously, no mention of the raid appears in the battalion war diary. The raiders failed to capture or kill any of the enemy and did little damage to his works.

Captain Clegg-Hill directed operations from the British line while Lieutenants Mostyn and Fletcher took the twenty-two men in two parties from B and D Companies on the 'impromptu raid' at 10.00 pm. Passing close to a German listening post, the raiders had no choice but to rush it when fired on by its occupants, who then ran off. They no doubt warned the rest of the garrison of the enemy trench that the raiders were approaching. The Germans threw bombs at them when they got within range and the raiders had little option but to withdraw. Boxed in by the British barrage and enemy wire, they were lucky to get off as lightly as they did, suffering only one fatality and five wounded. Yet Brigade congratulated them on a job well done. If by that Brigade meant that the raiders had attracted a lot of German attention, the praise was well deserved because they had achieved very little else. They did not embark upon another raid until April 1916.

Raiding began to increase during the summer of 1915, but it was not until late autumn that it became significantly more frequent. This coincided with several developments, among them being the arrival of the Canadian Expeditionary Force, who enthusiastically took to raiding, the plentiful supply of reliable hand grenades in the shape of the No. 5 Mills, and an abundance of high-explosive shells for the artillery, along with more and bigger guns. Moreover, the BEF had increased in size so that while it took over sections of the front from the French, there were more troops available. So long as the BEF remained small in relation to the frontage it occupied it would always have insufficient manpower available for actions such as raids. As the year progressed, the BEF became better able to fight on a larger scale because it had the manpower, the guns, the ammunition and the logistical support.

This did not just mean engaging in battles but also minor enterprises such as raids. At the same time, of course, the Germans began to raid the British trenches but infrequently, at first. And like the British, they tended to send over small parties who tried to enter the targeted trenches by stealth rather than by force of arms. Typically, raids by both sides were against bombing posts or snipers, or to take prisoners rather than full-on fights against fully manned front-line trenches. The 2nd Lincolns undertook such a small-scale raid on the morning of 26 July. A small party crept up to a German sniper post at Bois Grenier, killed the sniper, then blew up the post with grenades before returning safely to their own trench.

On the night of 3 September, a small party from the 9th Royal Fusiliers at Houplines went over to the German wire and threw grenades into the German fire trench. Only four shots were fired at them in response. They repeated the exercise the following night and again on the 7th, and although they reported that throwing their ten bombs into the German trench 'caused much confusion' among the Germans, they also noted the lack of response to this, their third raid on successive nights. Not content with this, two parties went out on the 17th and each threw eight grenades into the German trench. 'Much scuttling was heard but no response was elicited beyond that of a sentry who fired 2 rounds high.' All this rather illustrated how thinly the

Germans were now holding front-line trenches to avoid unnecessary casualties from occurrences such as this. The Germans had opted for a thinly held front line since Neuve Chapelle, which had shown them the pointlessness of holding front-line trenches with strong forces. Put simply, it was waste of manpower because they only became casualties from shelling, mortaring or raids, although the latter were the least of their worries.

At the end of October, the British Second Army issued a directive that reflected the attitude of GHQ and was intended to encourage aggressive action against the enemy over the coming winter. Unlike the French, who, despite their unwillingness to concede another foot of French soil, were prepared to wait out the winter before renewing their attacks on the Germans in the spring, the British intended to make the lives of the Germans as miserable as they could during the winter with sudden artillery bombardments, continual sniping and, of course, raids. The belief that raiding sapped the enemy's morale and wore down his manpower was strongly held by British commanders but the evidence for this was somewhat lacking. While being subjected to a raid was unpleasant, shelling and sniping happened much more often and were much more dangerous than the sporadic raids of 1915. Raiding was far too infrequent to have much of an impact and raids on thinly-manned fire trenches were rather pointless if the object was death and destruction. The verbal response of 'English pigs' to one of the bombing attacks by the 9th Royal Fusiliers in September suggests that the Germans were more irritated than shocked by them, although the comment recorded in the war diary was probably a cleaner, less crude version of what was actually shouted at the time.

Everything changed in November. Now, raiding started to become more nightmarish for the Germans than hitherto as the enterprises became more brutal, bigger and better planned. The first of these new-style raids was carried out by the Canadians of the 5th and 7th Infantry Battalions. The Canadian Expeditionary Force, under the command of the British Second Army, were more than keen to take the fight to the enemy and they took the Second Army directive to heart. The first of the Canadian raids took place on the night of 16–17 November from positions on the River Douve, north of Ploegsteert Wood in the Ypres salient. It had been scheduled for the previous night but heavy rain had swollen the river, which rose several feet and forced the Canadians to postpone it. The torrent was simply too deep and too wide to cross using the specially made portable bridges with which the raiders had been training for the raid.

Two parties, each of four officers and seventy-seven men,[1] one from the 5th Infantry Battalion, the other from the 7th, both part of the 2nd Infantry Brigade, were given the three-fold task of entering the German trenches at two points in the salient to take prisoners, fooling the Germans into committing their reserves by making them believe the attack was on a much larger scale than it actually was so that the German reinforcements would present a good target for the Canadian artillery, and 'to lower the enemy's morale'. The principal target was La Petite Douve farm. This was the so-called left attack. The secondary target was the right attack. Those taking part, all selected from volunteers, spent a week preparing for the raid, having been 'excused all other duties'. The raiders also included bombing parties made up of men from the battalion bombing platoon from the Brigade Bombing Company. The composition of each party was made up of seven groups, each with its own specific tasks:

(1) Wire cutting party (Scouts)
    1 Officer and 4 NCOs
(2) Left Bombing and Blocking Party
    1 Officer
    2 Bayonet Men
    2 Throwers
    2 Carriers
    1 Spare Bomber
    4 Wire men (carrying 20 bombs each)
    2 Shovel men (carrying also 20 bombs each)
    Total: 1 Officer and 13 men
(3) Right Bombing and Blocking Party
    1 Officer
    2 Bayonet Men
    2 Throwers
    2 Carriers
    1 Spare man
    2 Wire men (each carrying spool of wire and twenty bombs)
    2 Shovel men (each carrying also 20 bombs; no rifles)
    Total: 1 Officer, [11] men
(4) Bridge Covering Parties
    Right 3
    Left 3
    Total 6 Rifleman
(5) Trench Rifle Party
    1 Officer (OC of Assault Party)
    5 Riflemen
    1 Telephonist with instrument
    1 Linesman
    2 Stretcher bearers
    Total: 1 Officer, 9 men

(6) Listening Post Support Party
   1 NCO and 10 men
   1 Telephonist with instrument
   1 Linesman
   Total: 13 men
(7) Trench Reserve Party
   2 NCOs and 20 men
   Remained in trench

TOTAL:	Assault Party	3 Officers,	[33] men
	Scouts and on Bridges	1 Officer,	10 men
	Support and Reserve		33 men

The raiders practised every aspect of the enterprise over ground that had been set up to replicate that which they would have to cross in order to approach the German trenches as well as replicating the German positions themselves, including the wire obstacle they would have to negotiate. The rehearsals included night work to ensure the raiders would not be disorientated by the darkness when it came to carrying out the operation for real. Aggressive patrolling over the preceding weeks by the 2nd Canadian Infantry Brigade had already established their dominance over no man's land. So there was little risk in taking small parties of the would-be raiders over the actual ground by the battalion scouts to familiarise them with the terrain in the nights before the raid.

In many respects, this raid resembled an assault in miniature and thus represented a departure from the sort of raids usually mounted. The parties were provided with portable bridges for crossing the river, scaling ladders for entering and leaving trenches, and so-called 'traverser mats'. Their purpose was to allow troops to cross barbed wire with relative ease. The idea, not a new one by any means, was that designated men threw themselves and their mats across the wire and thereby flattened it sufficiently to allow the other attackers to cross the wire obstacle. Similar mats, although of different form and construction (padded and quilted like medieval brigandines and jacks), had been the subject of experimentation earlier in the year for major daylight operations but handling such unwieldy objects was always problematical. Nevertheless, such mats were used from time to time on raids like the one carried out by the Canadians on the night of 16–17 November 1915.

The principal target of the two-pronged raid was the angle of trenches between the River Douve and La Petite Douve farm, which lay within a 500 yard salient that crossed the road that ran between Ploegsteert and Messines. This strong position was the objective of the 7th Battalion party. As a diversion, the party from the 5th was to hit the Germans south of the river, about 400 yards to the south-east. Both parties were faced by the 11th Reserve Regiment, 117th Division. Aggressive patrolling by the 2nd Brigade had forced the Germans to abandon their listening posts in no man's land, which, if manned, could have compromised the raid before the attackers ever reached their objectives. The targets had been chosen with care. Although La Petite Douve was a strongpoint, a covered approach along the right-hand bank of the river ensured the raiding party would be able reach it unseen.

On the morning before the operation, British and Canadian 18-pounders and 13-pounders bombarded the German wire in several places in addition to those points at which the raiders intended to cross it, while howitzers shelled communication trenches close to the raiders' targets. The German trenches at La Petite Douve were within range of the Canadian trench mortars and rifle grenades, which made the farm position an attractive target for a raid. Three screened routes by which the raiders could withdraw after the attack also made the objective an attractive target. In addition to the natural protection, the part of the salient that included the farm was only 75 yards long and could only be enfiladed from a nearby farm building. Moreover, the salient had been bombarded several times over the previous few days without an attack developing so the Germans would not be expecting one after the next bombardment.

In the afternoon before the raid, a trench mortar battery fired on the trenches and a machine-gun position at the farm. Canadian machine-guns were used for fire suppression on the flanks. Later in the afternoon and into the evening, rifle grenades were added to the barrage, while snipers became more active. Between 9.15 pm and 11.45 pm, the wire-cutting party set about making lanes through wire left uncut by the barrage. They wore out numerous pairs of leather gloves in the process. The bridging groups finished putting their 60lb bridges across the 10-foot width of the Douve by 2.00 am. While these groups were working, the bombing party established several grenade dumps along the route they would take. Irregular and sporadic rifle fire was kept up the whole time to hide the noise of these preparations, which, although kept as low as possible, could not be entirely eliminated.

The second, diversionary, target also provided a well-screened approach for the raiders as they could make use of ditches and hedges to avoid being seen. This, too, was a strong position in the enemy line and it was reasoned that the Germans would not expect an attack on it. There was the added advantage of the secondary target being so far away from the primary one that the enemy would be fooled into thinking that, when the raids hit them, the attack was over a much wider frontage than was the case. That misapprehension would serve to persuade the Germans to bring up their reserves.

The raid itself was scheduled for 2.30 am on the 17th. The raiders crossed the river using the bridges and negotiated the gaps in the wire but the party from the 5th Battalion ran into a serious obstacle in the form of barbed wire hidden in a water-filled ditch, which no one had discovered hitherto. This was immediately in front of the German parapet. In cutting themselves free, the raiders attracted the attention of the Germans in the trench on the other side of the parapet who, not surprisingly, fired on them. The Canadians threw grenades into the German trench in response and apparently silenced them. After half an hour of fruitless struggle, the party commander came to the conclusion they could neither cross nor get round the wire and water in the ditch so, reluctantly, he decided to withdraw his party.

The party from the 7th Battalion fared much better and took the Germans at the farm by surprise.

At 2.32 am the assaulting party entered the enemy's front-line trench, the officers leading and jumping in on a crouching sentry who was taking shelter from a shower of rain which had just started. This man was shot on the spot by the officer of the right party while the officer of the left party shot three more then turned and bombed down the trench for three bays till joined by his party, after which they pulled or bombed the Germans out of their dug-outs or drove them into communication trenches. The officer of the right party ... after shooting his first man and anxious to make prisoners seized the next man and taking his rifle clubbed a third, after which his party joined him and they started down the trench.

They took eight prisoners. Meanwhile, the blocking parties did their job and, altogether, the raiders held 40 yards of German trench after only a couple of minutes' work. The whole operation was over in less than 20 minutes and the prisoners, twelve including those taken by the left party, were escorted back to the Canadian line. They left behind about thirty German casualties, some of them dead. Remarkably, the Canadian casualties were only one dead, due to an accidental discharge of a rifle when one man stumbled, and one slightly injured.

The operation was a complete success. There is no question that this was down to good planning and careful reconnaissance, although that was not entirely without mishap as the experience of the 5th Battalion demonstrated. It was also attributed at the time to the way in which the raiders all refrained from whooping and hollering as they would in a daytime attack. Moreover, the thoroughness of the rehearsals over specially prepared ground that replicated that over which the raid would take place was crucial. In addition, the raiders were specially clothed and equipped for the enterprise, abandoning, for example, their Ross rifles, with which the Canadians were usually armed, in favour of the British SMLE. They left behind in their own line any other equipment that could identify them as Canadian and removed all identifying insignia before setting out so that, together with the British rifle, the fact that the raiders were Canadian was well hidden.[2] While the Ross would have certainly identified them as Canadians, the SMLE might have been substituted for another reason: reliability. The Ross was notorious for its poor performance in the wet and muddy conditions of the Western Front. It was not sufficiently robust for trench warfare. The Canadians eventually replaced it with the SMLE, starting in the summer of 1915. A year later, hardly a Ross remained in front-line service.

The artillery fireplan, which was designed to work in co-operation with the infantry assault, also worked well. During the operation, the guns had continued to fire on the German rearward trenches to isolate the target trenches but after the withdrawal the range was shortened to hit these front-line positions and catch any troops who might be assembling for a counter-attack. The heavy guns also fired on the approach roads at the rear to hit any reinforcements being brought up to assist in a counter-attack. This was the beginning of what would come to be known as a box barrage.

The response of the enemy was largely ineffectual and, initially, very disorganised, driven by a complete incomprehension of what was actually happening. The Germans in the La Petite Douve position simply gave up after making a weak bombing attack on the raiders, which was easily beaten off for no loss. The Germans then retreated to their support lines from where they fired rather aimlessly down the Messines road, apparently confused by the bombing attack at the secondary target as to the direction of the Canadian attack. It was not until 40 minutes after the raiders had returned to their own lines that the Germans launched a counter-attack. As they crossed their own front line, the Canadian artillery suddenly pounded the German forward positions and no doubt inflicted many casualties among the counter-attackers who were caught unawares. At this late stage, the German artillery now opened up on the area between the Canadian front line and support line in retaliation and in the mistaken belief that the Canadians were in the process of coming forward.

The careful preparations, along with a smooth execution of the well-rehearsed plan, were clearly instrumental in the success of the raid. Indeed, this raid became the model for future operations of this type by the battalions of the BEF, not just those of the Canadian contingent. The French commander, Joffre, was supposed to have been so impressed with the conduct of the raid that he circulated a description of the action to French troops. All the objectives of the raid were realised. The prisoners provided excellent identification of the regiment to which they belonged. They were equipped with a new type of rubber-faced gasmask not seen before, which provided very useful intelligence about German gas warfare capabilities at that time. In addition, much was learned about German methods of trench and dugout construction. And it was evident from what the prisoners said that the morale of the German troops was adversely affected by the raid, although it was hardly surprising the prisoners were subdued and unhappy. Nevertheless, the poor initial response of Germans to the raid indicated low morale.

In some respects, the great success of the raid was unfortunate as it led commanders to conclude that no useful improvement could be made to the structure, planning and execution of such enterprises. A degree of complacency overshadowed the achievements of the raiders. Not all future raids would be so successful, with so few casualties. Had this raid been less successful, greater effort would have been made to perfect the principles of raiding. That is not to suggest that no lessons were learned from the Canadian operation but they tended to be negative rather than positive, which did nothing to help develop the tactics of raiding. Clearly, raiding had a significant chance component and this needed to be recognised. Some flexibility needed to be built into the plan so that the whole thing would not collapse in the event of one of its elements going wrong due to unforeseen circumstances.

Another crucial factor in the raid's success was the enemy's poor discipline in maintaining minimum levels of security. They had allowed the Canadians to dominate no man's land before the raid and had failed to maintain contact with adjoining trench sections during the raid so that they neither knew the full extent of the assault nor were they able to mount a counter-attack until the operation had ended. The German troops had been poorly led and had lacked initiative. For the Canadians and Second Army to have concluded that the success of the raid could be replicated in future rather relied on the raiders facing equally indolent opposition. It is not unlikely that had the Canadians been facing a more resolute and better-led unit, the outcome of the raid might well have been very different.

Such caveats notwithstanding, subsequent raids also met poor opposition. On 13 December, the 2nd Grenadier Guards mounted a small raid. The object was to determine whether the Germans were busy digging a shaft for a mine as the Guards suspected. At 12.30 am, a lieutenant and eleven other ranks entered the German trench by stealth and explored it for 400 yards going west. They met no one. They returned to their own line without finding any evidence of a shaft. The exercise was repeated the following night, taking a sapper from a mining company with them. This time, they went east along the German line for 400 yards. And this time they met Germans, first a sentry post with three German soldiers, two of whom they killed silently, taking the third one prisoner. Then, they ran into a party of

Germans heading down the trench in the opposite direction and who immediately open fire on them but fell back as they did so. One of the Guards was killed but the rest returned to the British line unhurt. Again, there was no evidence of a mine shaft.

At the same time as the Grenadiers were exploring the German trench, a party from the 2nd Coldstreams entered the same trench at the same point as the Grenadiers and went 700 yards down the German line, but they, too, found no Germans. Although none of these actions was described in the war diaries as a raid, they had raid-like qualities in that the German trenches were entered, fighting ensued, then they withdrew. Had a shaft been located, a stronger party would almost certainly have been sent over to wreck it. Such excursions as these were becoming less common as the year came to a close, reconnaissance and observation being carried out by more covert means. However, the experiences of the Guards again illustrates how the Germans were now manning their front lines with only token forces and outposts during the night, the main force remaining further back to avoid unnecessary casualties.

Several British battalions carried out successful raids in December. Many of the raids involved only twenty or thirty men, while the taking of prisoners was often the primary objective. Three days before Christmas, a party of thirty-four men from the 1st Northumberland Fusiliers raided a German trench at Hooge in the Ypres salient. By stealth, they approached the Germans undetected, then threw 100 grenades into the enemy trench before returning to their own lines. They suffered only one minor casualty in the action. Some of these raids or bombing attacks were even carried out on Christmas Day, such as the one mounted by men of the 8th Royal Fusiliers. That sort of thing certainly discouraged a repeat of the fraternisations of the previous Christmas, which was no doubt one of their purposes. In the early hours of New Year's Day, the 10th Northumberland Fusiliers raided the Germans at Bois Grenier. This was not only their first raid, it was the first by any battalion in the 23rd Division. Such aggression set the tone for the BEF in the coming year, when raiding would come of age.

Perhaps one of the most significant raids of 1915 was a German assault carried out by Hauptmann Rohr against the French in the Vosges Mountains in October. Rohr was in command of an assault detachment, the Sturm Abteilung, the purpose of which was to develop new tactics. These were tried out for the first time on the Vosges raid. The operation, mounted by the 2nd Sturm Kompanie led by Oberleutnant Krafft and supported by a company of the 187th Infantry Regiment, took place on 12 October against the French positions on the mountain peak of Schratzmännle. Like the Canadians a few months later, the Kompanie practised the raid over terrain set up to replicate the ground over which they would attack, including the

German and French positions. Unlike the Canadians in December, however, the Germans proposed to make the assault in the late afternoon, although darkness would fall during the raid. And unlike the Canadians, the German raiders were merely a spearhead who would punch into the French positions, secure them, then withdraw to allow a conventional infantry unit to take over the newly won position. This was the birth of what were to become known as stormtroopers and with them came a new method of assault that dispensed with the conventional wave attack.

The assault opened at 5.29 pm, when six trench-mounted flamethrowers of the 3rd Guard Pioneer Battalion flamed designated positions in the French line and, 1 minute afterwards, the six assault groups of the 2nd Sturm Kompanie emerged from the sapheads that had been dug earlier and rushed the French positions, throwing grenades. French artillery on the flanks responded immediately but German counter-battery fire, including trench mortars, dealt with it very effectively. The initial action was over very quickly, with the stormtroopers in possession of the French trenches. At 8.30 pm, the French counter-attacked but failed to retake what they had just lost. Within half an hour, it was all over and the stormtroopers were on their way back to their own lines. They lost four dead and eleven others were wounded. The raid was a complete success.

While this raid differed substantially from the sort of raids carried out by the British and the Canadians in that they did not seek to take and hold ground, nevertheless, the German tactics were essentially the same as those used by the British and Canadians. Rohr was not content with raiding as an exercise in itself but proposed to employ it as a tactic within the broader tactical scheme of the assault as part of a major offensive operation. This he well demonstrated when the tactics he used in the Vosges were repeated on a much larger scale at Verdun the following year. While Rohr tended to emphasise many of the same desiderata for a successful raid as the British, he rather exaggerated the effect of determination of the attackers when it came to a contest between man and high-explosive ordnance. Although determination to see an action through is essential to any military operation, high explosive can never be overcome by determination alone, as the battles of 1914 and 1915 had already well demonstrated. The key to successful raiding was good reconnaissance, good planning and lots of practice. This would be born out by the raids of 1916.

Chapter 3

1916 up to the Somme

Raiding acquired a different imperative for the British in 1916, becoming part of a wider offensive strategy, while for the Germans it became a tactical tool wielded by a select group trained as raiders. The battalions of the BEF tended to take their turn at raiding, according to circumstances, some doing it more often then others, but those trained as raiders in the German Army were specialists. These were to become the assault troops of the German Army who spearheaded offensives. The British and French developed similar skills among their troops during 1917 and 1918 for offensive operations but not as raiders. For the BEF, raiding was a skill that everyone had to learn.

For both the Allies and the Germans, 1916 was the year of the big offensive. Each side embarked upon campaigns designed to destroy the enemy on scales not seen hitherto. For the British, 1916 saw the emergence of the doctrine of destruction whereby artillery attempted to obliterate the enemy before the infantry assaulted the destroyed enemy positions, a tactic that they employed on the Somme in the summer. For the Germans, a similar approach was used in their great offensive at Verdun, launched in February, although they applied it differently from the Allies. While the Allies went for long bombardments – the Somme opened with a week-long bombardment – the Germans opted for the short but intense hurricane bombardment – Verdun opened with a 21-hour bombardment that shocked the French. These offensives indirectly set the tone for raiding during 1916.

The Allies began planning their big offensive at the beginning of the year. The French were proposing to carry out several. These were all intended to be the means by which the German defences would be breached to allow the Allied armies to sweep into the countryside beyond and crush the enemy into defeat. The German offensive at Verdun, on the other hand, was intended to bleed the French to death. The offensives were intended to bring the war to a close before the end of the year.

As part of the Allied plan, the British and the French agreed that the Germans should be worn down in the preceding months. However, they could not agree on how this wearing down should be accomplished. The French favoured attacks by division-sized forces, attritional battles that preceded the main battle, but the British were unconvinced that this would not result in unsustainable Allied casualties and, hence, undermine their very purpose. Indeed, Field Marshall Haig, who had taken over command of the BEF from Sir John French in December 1915, was worried that such strong assaults that ended without exploiting successes would be perceived by both the Germans and the neutral countries as failed operations that could boost the morale of the enemy. Instead, Haig believed that raiding was a better answer as far as the BEF was concerned. He also argued that a succession of raids carried out at points well away from the area chosen for the main Anglo–French offensive during the two weeks prior to its start would fool the enemy into committing his reserves at locations distant from the frontage of the offensive. This would not only help to wear down the enemy but prevent him from bringing his reserves to the right place.

The raid now assumed a greater importance than hitherto. As a tactical policy, it was part of the overall scheme in the coming Anglo–French offensive. This policy not only dramatically increased the frequency of raids carried out by the BEF but also led to such enterprises being mounted on a larger scale. In March, GHQ issued SS107 Notes on Minor Enterprises, which set out how a raid should be organised and executed. This was the first time that the British had set out in print the principals of raiding. These principles were derived from experience and attempted to take account of the many forms that a raid might take, and emphasised flexibility as well as good planning. It was clear to everyone that the very nature of raiding precluded a dogmatic approach; planning and execution had to be specific to the objective, the weather and phases of the moon when the operation was carried out at night.

Between mid-December 1915 and the end of May 1916, the British carried out sixty-three raids. This amounted to eleven or twelve raids a month. For the most part, a battalion only mounted one raid so that this figure represents approximately sixty battalions, all of whom gained fighting experience from the raid. The Germans mounted thirty-three, six a month. On 27 May, GHQ instructed the BEF to increase the incidence of raiding over the next month as a prelude to the opening of the infantry-assault phase of the Anglo-French offensive on the Somme on 1 July. These raids were to be of at least company strength, if not greater, and aimed at the German front-line trenches. Each raid was to be provided with an intense preparatory bombardment by artillery and trench mortars. These, then, were to be battles in miniature. During the last week of June, the BEF mounted thirty-eight such raids outside the battle area of the forthcoming infantry assault.

One of the first raids of the year was that carried out on the night of 2 January 1916 by a party of about sixty-five from the 25th Battalion, 5th Brigade of the Canadian Expeditionary Force. They had opted to eschew artillery support and decided to use stealth to surprise the Germans. To achieve surprise, the raiders had to cut the wire by hand using wire cutters. They were rather too good at this and the party detailed to the task of cutting the wire finished long before the assault party was ready. In the time it took for the wire-cutting party to return and for the assault party to reach the German wire, a German working party found the lane that had just been cut and repaired it. By now it was nearly dawn so the raid had to be abandoned. Soon after this, the cutting of wire by hand became much more difficult as the Germans began using tempered steel wire, which was harder, tougher and more resilient.

The Canadian 28th Infantry Battalion of the 6th Brigade hit the German Spanbroekmolen salient north of Kemmel on the Messines Ridge at 2.30 am on 31 January. This was the 28th's first raid. The raiders were thirty volunteers led by Lieutenant K.C. Taylor and Lieutenant D.E. Macintyre, all of whom had been given specialist training in the handing of grenades and their tactical employment at the brigade's bombing school. Their principal objectives were the capture of prisoners and the killing of as many Germans as possible in the limited time the raiders could afford to spend in the German positions. This operation was intended to complement a simultaneous raid of similar strength by the 29th Battalion, also from the 6th Brigade, to the south of Kemmel. The night before the operation, two scouts went out into no man's land to cut lanes through the German wire.

The two raiding parties struck the German front trenches 1,100 yards apart. In the course of about 8 minutes in the enemy trench, the 28th Battalion raiders inflicted approximately thirty-nine German casualties for six of their own. Macintyre was rewarded with a promotion to captain. The raiding party from the 29th Battalion were hardly opposed during their brief sojourn in the German positions. In the space of a little over 4 minutes, they took three prisoners, threw grenades into several dug outs and left without loss to themselves. The reason why the Germans suffered more casualties during the raid by the 28th Battalion was entirely down to the chance timing of the operation. The 28th happened to enter the German positions just when a relief was in progress so that the trenches were much more crowded than would otherwise have been the case. Mills grenades produced a lot of fragments on detonation, almost all of them lethal at short range. None of the prisoners made it back to the Canadian lines, however, as they were shot down by a German machine-gun as they crossed no man's land. But otherwise, the double raid was a success and received recognition among British commanders as well as from Haig. The Canadian losses were two fatalities and ten wounded, although that was fairly high for a force only about sixty strong. That was 20 per cent of the raiders.

The 10th Yorkshire Regiment, a Pals battalion of the Green Howards, were in trenches opposite a German strongpoint called the Black Redoubt at the beginning of 1916. Forty-five men of D Company, led by five officers, raided the strongpoint on the night of 15–16 February with the intention of taking prisoners and ascertaining whether the Germans were setting up gas cylinders. The raid should have been postponed on account of the weather. Not only was the ground covered in snow, making the going harder than might otherwise have been, but it was so misty that they had trouble keeping to their route. Moreover, the snow made them stand out rather too prominently in their khaki. To add to their difficulties, the German wire was not cut. They did not get far before they were seen by the Germans in the redoubt. The German garrison showered the raiders with grenades, causing several casualties and forcing the men from D Company to withdraw having completely failed in their objective. Two officers and nine others were wounded. Three were unaccounted for when the raiders got back to their own lines. The snowy conditions should have been taken into consideration. The fact that the raiders had blackened their faces, a common practice to prevent pale skin from reflecting moonlight, did not help as that made them stand out all the more. By 1917, the BEF's specialised camouflage unit had devised snow suits, which were worn over the uniform to help raiders blend into the background but in 1916, nothing like that yet existed.

Some raids failed because the enemy detected the attempts by the raiders to cut the wire. Wire cut with cutters made a distinctive snapping sound, made worse by the ends of the cut wire springing apart with a loud ping. To made the process of cutting quieter, the wire was cut by two-man teams; one man operated the cutters while the other held the wire on each side of the cutter's jaws to prevent the wire springing when cut. Nevertheless, cutting wire silently was an almost impossible task. Minimising the noise required practice and patience. A raiding party from the 1st/5th Glosters, a Territorial battalion, were caught out when trying to cut wire by hand. This was towards the end of March, when they were in the Somme sector. Despite an artillery barrage that was intended to support the raiders, the Germans noticed them and fired rifle grenades at the wire-cutting party. This prevented them from completing their task, so the raid was aborted. The raiders withdrew without achieving anything. The raid by the Glosters on the night of 22–23 March, which was supposed to have been mounted in conjunction with another by a party from the neighbouring 143rd Brigade on the Glosters' left, had already been delayed by the tardiness of the 143rd Brigade, who were not ready on time. The artillery barrage was delayed by about 20 minutes because of it. Although casualties among the sixty-six-strong Glosters party were only slight, the whole operation was a washout.

During April, the Germans mounted several raids on the British trenches on the Somme held by the 1st Royal Welch Fusiliers. They preceded their attacks with artillery bombardments that caused several casualties. The timing of the raids was varied so that the Royal Welch would be kept on the back foot. However, the Germans failed to get into their British trenches. This was a very active sector during the months preceding the Anglo-French offensive in July, with constant bombardments by artillery, trench mortars and rifle grenades so that there was a steady trickle of casualties on both sides. The Germans also raided the 10th Royal Welch Fusiliers in the early hours of 5 May but were bloodily repulsed. Again, they failed to get into the British trenches. The CO of 76th Brigade, to which the 10th belonged, attributed the British success to the 'soldierly qualities' of the 10th Royal Welch.

In May, the Germans raided the 1st/5th Glosters. In the early hours of 9 May, Corporal Abel of D Company, in one of the company's listening posts in the Glosters' advanced trench, heard a party of Germans entering the trench at one of the barricades that was supposed to prevent such an occurrence. He immediately ordered his small party out of the bay they were currently occupying and take up positions in a bombing post behind. No sooner had his party vacated it when the Germans threw grenades into their former position, slightly wounding one of Abel's men. His party then threw grenades at the Germans, following up with rapid rifle fire, and drove them out. They then 'cleared the trench by orthodox bombing tactics'. None of the raiders appeared to have been killed as none were left behind when they withdrew and if any of them was wounded, they left no evidence of it. Similarly, the 3rd Coldstream Guards repulsed a German raid the same month. The Coldstreams realised a party of German raiders were trying to enter their trench in the early morning of 16 April but drove them off with grenades and a Lewis gun just before dawn. The Germans retreated without achieving anything.

Such episodes as these demonstrated the value of good training as well as the chance nature of raiding. In Corporal Abel's case, it is clear that his team was made up of men who had been trained as bombers. At that time, bombing was still very much a specialism in which relatively few infantrymen were fully trained. As the war progressed into 1917, more and more men became skilled as bombers so that by 1918, bombing was no longer a skill particular to a few but was universal among the infantry of the BEF. During 1916 and 1917, once men had been trained as bombers and having served a term in the battalion's or brigade's bombing platoon, these trained men went back to orthodox infantry companies to serve as conventional infantrymen once again, albeit with added bombing skills. In 1915, such skills were fairly rare and it was not uncommon for infantrymen to be confronted with the prospect of having to use grenades in a crisis when they had never seen one before. By 1918, most infantrymen were not only trained bombers but skilled with the rifle grenade and knew how to use a Lewis gun as well as the rifle and bayonet.

Bombing was not merely a question of throwing grenades. Indeed, bombing was carried out by a team, not one man, each member of which had a specific job and everyone in the team could do everyone else's should the need arise. Being part of such a team was a stressful and hazardous task, which was why bombers did not remain in the job indefinitely. Many became casualties so the need for replacements was relentless. Bombing was an essential element of many of the later raids. Bombing attacks on German listening posts, sentries and troops manning front-line positions at night, no matter how thinly, were prime targets for a bombing attack. The raids of late 1914 and throughout most of 1915 were, for the most part, of the more stealthy sort, however, in which bombs tended not to figure at all, largely because grenades were not available.

As far as the BEF was concerned, grenades were something of a problem until the latter part of 1915, when the Mills No. 5 became more widespread. Some troops had not seen one of these, let alone handled one, even as late as the spring of 1916. And without the Mills, night raids were much more hazardous and difficult for the raiders. Until the Mills was manufactured in very large numbers, the BEF had to make do with a range of stopgap grenades, none of which was really suitable for raiding. They all had serious drawbacks that militated against reliability and effectiveness. Not the least of the drawbacks was the way in which such grenades were lit. Commonly, a match composition or even the glowing end of a cigarette were the means of ignition, far from reliable and prone to misfiring, sometimes with fatal consequences for the bomber.

In the BEF, the evolution of the art bombing was dependent upon the development of reliable grenades and did not begin to emerge as a tactical method worth teaching until the second half of 1915. This coincided with the recognition by GHQ of the importance of training schools and the availability of the No. 5 Mills. Grenade tactics were firmly rooted in the handling procedures for the No. 5. While grenade fighting had been very much a case of out-throwing your opponent in a deadly game of catch until the autumn of 1915, subsequent tactical developments changed bombing from an enthusiast's pastime into a science. During 1916 and 1917, bombing squads became what in later times would be called all-arms tactical teams in which the hand grenade was but one tool in the armoury. While certain aspects of a bombing attack remained essentially the same in 1916 as they had been in 1915, others were quite different. Such skills became part of the tactical resources at the disposal of raiding parties. Thus, while the Germans developed stormtroop tactics from raiding, the British developed all-arms teams with tactical awareness, which had great flexibility to deal with most circumstances.

At the heart of bombing, of course, was the throwing of hand grenades. These were thrown from one bay to another so that the bomber had to acquire accuracy and precision so that he could always get his grenade into the bay that he was aiming at. He had to do this several times in quick succession. Grenade throwers came in pairs and they threw their grenades into successive bays simultaneously. At the same time, two bayonet man advanced down the same trench one bay ahead of the throwers but one bay back from where the grenades were landing. The job of the bayonet men changed subtly during 1916. While they were initially supposed to follow up the grenades to deal with any enemy who survived the explosions and fragments by bayoneting them, their role became one of leader rather than follower. Thus, rather than waiting for the throwers to act, the bayonet men advanced before any grenades were thrown and when they were unable to deal with whomever they met round the next bay, they retreated behind the one they had just crossed and called for the grenade men to throw their grenades. Immediately after the explosions the bayonet men advanced at the double until stopped again and the process was repeated.

Such attacks took place inside the trenches but by 1917, the process had evolved so that parties worked above ground as well as in the trench. The bombers above ground did much the same thing that the bombers in the trench had done previously. Thus, only bayonet men might be in the trench while the throwers were all above ground. At the same time, rifle grenadiers provided fire suppression by showering the enemy further away with rifle grenades. By the end of 1917, the role of grenade men had changed. At first, the grenades were intended to kill and injure as many of the enemy as possible before he could kill or injure the bombing squad. With the addition of Lewis gunners to the bombing team as well as riflemen, the object of the bombers was now to force the enemy out into the open, where they would be targets for the Lewis and rifles of the support team. A 3-inch Stokes mortar battery usually provided close support. A well-drilled team could work over an enemy position very quickly and efficiently, causing a great deal of damage.

Not all the grenades were intended for bombing up a trench, of course. Some were needed for dealing with the occupants of the dugouts who were sometimes given a command to come out, followed by a couple of Mills down the entrance if they did not respond quickly enough. Not all the grenades were explosive and deadly like the Mills, which produced several hundred lethal fragments on detonation, making it especially unpleasant in a confined space like a dugout. Some grenades contained lachrymatory, or smoke compositions, which were intended to force the occupants of dugouts to the surface by making it impossible for them to remain where they were. Some of those forced out were then taken prisoner but others were killed on the spot, depending on the objective. Clearly, to carry out a thorough sweep of an enemy position was not possible and only a relatively short section of trench could be worked up on a raid because of the time constraint. All raids ran to a strict timetable to minimise the risk of an enemy counter-attack. The raiders spent the least time possible in enemy positions, just enough to carry out the operation. Mostly, this amounted to no more than 20 or 30 minutes.

One of the essential objectives of any raid was to find material that identified the enemy regiment garrisoning the line at that location. Such material could come in a variety of forms, from items of uniform to identity discs. The First World War was the first war in which all soldiers wore such tags issued by the state and were intended for identification of the wearer should he be killed. The German Army was the first to issue them; the Prussian troops of the Franco–Prussian War of 1870–1 wore them. The French adopted them in 1881, while the British waited until 1906. Although the number and form of the tags varied – some were metal, others were made of compressed fibre – they carried sufficient information to identify the unit to which the wearer belonged and so were a prime 'souvenir' for raiders. Hence, it was not necessary to bring back a live enemy for purposes of identification, although prisoners were also searched for documents and could, of course, answer questions.

In October 1915, when raiding was beginning to become more business-like, GHQ issued SS381 Collection of Information Regarding the Enemy. While the identity disc worn by German troops was the favoured souvenir, all troops in the BEF were encouraged to look for the pay book, or *Soldbuch*, which was easy to recognise by its brown paper cover. Soldiers also tended to carry personal items such letters and diaries (although they were not supposed to keep diaries), from which intelligence could be gleaned. Raiders were expected to go through the pockets of those they had killed. In addition to these documents, officers might be in possession of orders, maps and other official material, which, for the most part, was not supposed to be taken into the front line. Such items had to be forwarded to division immediately, with an account of whether the documents were taken from prisoners or the dead. So seriously was the matter of captured enemy documents taken that

anyone hanging on to some he had acquired was liable to be court-
marshalled as, indeed, was anyone who took such documents into the front
line. At the beginning of May 1916, Battalion Orders for the 1st Royal Welch
Fusiliers stated:

> 16. Captured Trophies, Arms, etc.
> Attention is again directed to General Routine Order No. 549. The desire
> to collect "souvenirs" has frequently hampered the success of operations,
> and the danger this reprehensible practice is to be made clear to all ranks.
> Special articles, such as anti-gas appliances, letters, identification marks
> and discs, may be of the utmost value to the Intelligence Department and
> must be sent at once to Hd.Qrs. of formations. Strict disciplinary action
> will be taken with anyone found in unauthorised possession of such
> articles while proceeding on leave.

Every official document had a printed caveat on its cover, which stated
plainly just how far forward the document could be taken. Mostly, they were
not to be taken beyond brigade or battalion headquarters as they contained
secret information. If they were taken into the front line, there was every
possibility of their being captured in a raid as, indeed, they were from time
to time. GHQ issued translations of captured German documents, from
which a great deal of intelligence could be gathered about arms and tactics.
Some of these documents included detailed accounts and analyses of recent
operations that would provide valuable tactical and operational insights
about the enemy.

Much information could be gleaned from the uniforms. Until about 1916,
the German army wore the 1910 pattern uniforms, which had insignia and
braiding that identified the regiment of the wearer. Shoulder straps –
epaulettes – in particular, carried regimental numbers or monograms while
the edges of the tunic, its cuffs, epaulettes and collar were all braided in a
colour specific (*waffenfarbe*) according to the branch of the army in which
the wearer served, such as, for example, infantry, artillery, trench mortars or
engineers. Although a uniform that bore none of these identifying insignia
was issued in late 1915, the 1910 pattern continued to be worn until the end
of the war, although it became much less common. The caps, which became
less common in the trenches from 1916, also had the regimental number
stencilled inside them. While the British and Commonwealth uniforms
never carried the same sort of insignia as German uniforms, nevertheless,
they still bore shoulder titles, collar badges and other insignia from which
battalions and divisions, as well country, could easily be identified. Such
identifications became more widespread among the troops of the BEF as the

war progressed so that British and Empire troops wore more of them on their uniforms in 1918 than they had in 1914.

Often, German units also marked their equipment with regimental numbers. Typically, cartridge belts, rifles and bayonets were so marked. Besides identifying the unit to which the enemy troops belonged, captured equipment could also provide technical data. Shell fuzes were always of particular interest. Technical knowledge about enemy equipment, especially new munitions, was almost invariably derived from unexploded ordnance and captured equipment. Bringing back so-called souvenirs from raids was one way of keeping abreast with new developments in enemy munitions. This, of course, worked both ways so that the Germans copied some Allied munitions while the Allies used captured German equipment to devise new munitions of their own. Raids also allowed intelligence about the construction of the enemy's trenches and dugouts to be acquired provided, of course, the necessary information could be gathered quickly by men who knew what they were looking at, such as sappers. Early British raids were a little demoralising because the raiders discovered just how well German positions were constructed. They were more substantial than they expected.

In April, the 2nd Royal Welch Fusiliers carried out several raids. The first was a small affair mounted on the 2nd near Auchy. Second Lieutenant Coster and eight men 'went out at 2 a.m., and bombed enemy sap east of MIDNIGHT CRATER. The raid was successful as groans were heard and the party returned in safety.' The next raid was not so successful. In the early hours of the 9 April,[1] three raiding parties, made up of volunteers from A, B and D Companies, left the Royal Welch trenches under the cover of an artillery barrage. The objective of the B party was an enemy sap and the intention was to kill or capture its garrison. With this in mind, the trenches to the left and right of the sap were the targets of the two other parties. While the sap extended into no man's land, the trench from which it originated was behind the German wire. For the A and D parties to hit their objectives, they had first to get across the wire. The role of the artillery was to cut it for the A party, while the party from D Company was going to use the then new Bangalore torpedoes to blast their own lane through. The idea was to test the effectiveness of the torpedoes on this raid.

The Bangalore torpedo was a metal tube filled with the explosive ammonal (a mixture of ammonium nitrate, TNT and powdered aluminium), fitted with a detonator. Several lengths of such tubing could be screwed together and the whole thing pushed under the wire without anyone having to approach the wire. It was an invention of Major R.L. McClintock of the Bengal Sappers and Miners, dating from 1912. At about the same time, he had also invented a hand grenade and a rifle grenade. While the former may have been the origin of many of the improvised grenades used by the BEF up to about the autumn of 1915, his rifle grenade did not see service on the Western Front. The Bangalore torpedo, on the other hand, saw widespread use from about mid-1916. When the torpedo detonated, it blasted a lane approximately 5 feet wide.

The A and D parties could not penetrate the German wire. The artillery failed to make a path through it because it was so dense. Although the A party found lanes that had clearly been cut by the Germans, they were not prepared to risk entering these lanes in case they were traps on which machine-guns and trench mortars were targeted. Rather than do nothing and return to their own line with their grenades, they decided to throw them into the German trench from where they were. The D party faced a different problem; they could not explode their torpedoes. The devices given to them by the Royal Engineers failed to work so they, too, could not penetrate the German wire and, like the A party, had to throw their grenades into the German trench from beyond the wire, a far from satisfactory outcome. The B party managed to rush the sap but the Germans in it caught wind of what was happening and ran for it before they could be bombed. The entire operation was a washout. To add insult to the failure, the Germans fired a small mine, which fortunately did little harm. The previous day, the British miners had fired a camouflet of their own but it had clearly done little damage. The battalion war diary recorded: 'Two small raids were carried out simultaneously. The right one, under 2nd Lieut F.R.C. Barrett bombed an enemy sap, and the left one under 2nd Lieut E. Coster did likewise.'

The next raid was no more successful and was more costly. Mounted at Cuinchy on 24 April, this was a two-party affair against a re-entrant of a small salient, involving eighty men and four officers from B and C Companies. It was:

> carried out in two places on CUINCHY Right. The right party under Lieut D W Morgan and 2nd Lieut RH Morris, 30 Other Ranks. The left party, 2nd Lieut C R J R Dolling, 2nd Lieut J R Conning and 25 Other Ranks. Both parties left the line at 10 pm after a 15 minutes bombardment. The Northern party entered the enemy trench a few yards South of LA BASSEE Road. This party captured a German anti-gas apparatus and a rifle, and accounted for several of the enemy. The Southern party was held up by enemy wire and only a few of the party entered the trench.

The raiders suffered a number of casualties, including all the officers and eighteen of their men who were all wounded. A further three of the raiders did not return to the Royal Welch line, 'believed killed'.

The war diary entry was terse and failed to describe just how the raid had gone wrong from the outset. The B Company party came up against uncut wire and were 'enfiladed by a machine-gun' which killed at least one of their number. He was Sergeant Joe Williams who, earlier in the day, had been in the custody of the military police for striking one of the Red Caps who had called him a 'Welsh bastard'. He had been released just so that he could take part in the raid. This machine-gun was supposed to have been suppressed by two Stokes mortars, which were still relatively new at this stage of the war. Unfortunately, the mortars misfired and became inoperable so that the German gun remained intact. Although both the B and C parties managed to get into the German trench, the Germans who had occupied it had gone by the time the raiders arrived.

Worse, they were now hit by the Germans in the positions behind them. And to cap it all, not only was no identifying material found but another two men, both NCOs, were killed. A post-raid analysis by the Royal Welch officers led them to the conclusion that the Germans had been expecting them, waiting in their second line to hit the raiders, and that the wire-cutting of the previous night had probably alerted them to the attack. Raiding always required a degree of cunning in this respect. The raiders and the raided tried to outmanoeuvre each other before the raid was mounted. And it was this as much as alertness of sentries and carelessness of raiders that contributed to the failure of some of these enterprises.

The 1st Royal Welch Fusiliers mounted a raid on the night of 25–26 May. Lieutenant Stansfield led a party of twenty-five, split into five sections of four led by an NCO. Their objective was to hit a loop in the German trench positioned on the edge of a mine crater, then work up the right and left sides to enter Kiel Trench at two points, then take prisoners, kill Germans and bomb the dugouts. Two sections went to the left and two to the right while the third evacuated the wounded, escorted prisoners and handled 'loot'. The raid began well enough with the party departing from the British line at 11.50 pm. It only took them a couple of minutes to negotiate the first line of German wire located just inside the crater's edge. The loop was unoccupied. Further down the crater was a thick belt of concertina wire that they had not known about. They had to work their way round it. Stansfield noticed what appeared to be a gap and they made for that but were spotted by the Germans in Kiel trench, which was no more than a few yards away. Snipers opened up on them and grenades were thrown at them. The raiders threw Mills back. After about 25 minutes of this, the party was forced to withdraw as they had suffered one killed and eleven wounded, including Stansfield. Second Lieutenant Siegfried Sassoon, who was serving with the 1st Battalion at the time, won the Military Cross for his part in bringing in the wounded under fire, going out into no man's land several times to do so.

Courage was not infrequently shown during a raid. Raiders were invariably volunteers and none of them lacked fighting spirit, no matter which side they were on. It took a cool head to work under the noses of the enemy and steel-like nerves to jump into an enemy trench in the dark, not knowing whether an enemy was waiting or whether he was taken by surprise. Such actions as those of Sassoon and Second Lieutenant Baxter of the 1st/8th (Irish) Battalion, The King's (Liverpool Regiment), although very different, were taken in the full knowledge of the possible consequences. When the 1st/8th (Irish) Battalion mounted a raid on 17 April, Second Lieutenant Edward Baxter won the Victoria Cross for his actions but he was killed in their execution. On 26 September 1916, *The London Gazette* reported:

> Prior to a raid on the hostile line he was engaged during two nights in cutting wire close to the enemy's trenches. The enemy could be heard on the other side of the parapet.
>
> Second Lieutenant Baxter, while assisting in the wire cutting, held a bomb in his hand with the pin withdrawn ready to throw. On one occasion the bomb slipped and fell to the ground, but he instantly picked it up, unscrewed the base plug, and took out the detonator, which he smothered in the ground, thereby preventing the alarm being given, and undoubtedly saving many casualties. Later, he led the left storming party with the greatest gallantry, and was the first man into the trench, shooting the sentry with his revolver. He then assisted to bomb dug-outs, and finally climbed out of the trench and assisted the last man over the parapet.
>
> After this he was not seen again, though search parties went out at once to look for him. There seems no doubt that he lost his life in his great devotion to duty.

The fighting that occurred on a raid was not quite the same as any other sort of fight, although the combat that ensued when two aggressive patrols met in no man's land was of similar ferocity. Trench warfare was not always close when a major operation required troops to advance above ground but when operations allowed the attackers to get into the trenches, craters and posts occupied by the enemy, such as on a raid, the fighting was at a much shorter range. A raid was a mixture of close combat, bombing and short-range shooting, fought with grenades, pistols, daggers and clubs. It was often brutal, with no quarter given. A raid was no place for a faint heart.

At the beginning of May, the 20th Royal Fusiliers carried out two small raids on an enemy sap and a listening post with the support of a Stokes mortar battery. The post was unoccupied but the enemy was still in the sap and a grenade fight ensued. They suffered four casualties. These sort of bombing raids were encouraged. Unlike raids on enemy front-line trenches, attacks on saps and listening posts did not usually need wire to be cut beforehand. Moreover, these posts tended to be somewhat isolated from the main line of defence and were vulnerable to hit-and-run attacks. Such bombing attacks helped to give dominance of no man's land to whichever side took the more aggressive stance. However, militarily, such raids did not achieve much and were no more than an irritation. They became increasingly commonplace during the first half of 1916. A post belonging to the 1st Bucks was bombed just before dawn on 22 April, resulting in six casualties who could not be evacuated until the following night. This was in a very active sector near Hébuterne. During this period, the 1st Bucks alternated front-line duty with the 1st/5th Glosters. Shelling and mortaring were common day and night. There was an unrelenting attrition.

A raid did not always result in retaliation, although it often did, especially if the raid was successful. The response might be immediate in the form of an artillery or trench mortar bombardment but this was more in the nature of a counter measure than retaliation. Similarly, the troops flanking a raided trench might fire off rifle grenades to attack the raiders. Tit-for-tat raiding was a common response. This could be counter-productive, however, as the raiders were usually prepared for a return raid. And there was a limit to how far tit for tat could be taken before it became an all-consuming vendetta. Raiding needed good planning and thorough rehearsal for success. Failure to heed these principles was to run the risk of a costly mistake. So long as aggressive-minded battalions in a sector faced a similarly robust enemy, the competition to take and maintain control of no man's land was often a fierce contest that manifested in regular patrolling and raiding as neither side wanted to concede dominance. And while raiding maintained the offensive spirit and helped to give front-line troops experience of trench fighting as well as working cooperatively with artillery and trench mortars, it could also disturb the peace of an otherwise quiet sector to no useful purpose. Such disruption occurred whenever an aggressive battalion took over trenches in a quiet sector.

Raids were a constant concern during 1916, for the BEF as well as the French and German armies. The incidence of raiding went up as the year progressed. With every German raid came the possibility that they would gain intelligence of the forthcoming Allied offensive. This became a real concern during May and June. There is no doubt that the Germans on the Somme discovered the date of the offensive from raids they mounted in the preceding weeks. However, General Eric von Falkenhayn, Chief of the German Imperial Staff, was not persuaded by the evidence provided by the raids. He believed the offensive would come somewhere else. He was fooled by the false evidence provided by the big rise in raiding by the BEF in the sectors not involved in the offensive. In this, Falkenhayn was on his own because none of the other German commanders were fooled by the subterfuge. They were well aware that the evidence from their raids not only made it clear where the Allied offensive would happen, but when. However, Falkenhayn, who had initiated the Verdun offensive, had the final word as Chief of Staff. His reluctance to heed the intelligence provided by the German raiders contributed to his fall from grace in August. He was replaced by Hindenburg.

Chapter 4

Two Raids

On the evening of 11 April 1916, a raiding party of thirty made up of men from the 110th Reserve Infantry Regiment and Pioneers from the 1st Reserve Company, 13th Pioneer Battalion, led by three officers of the 110th, raided a trench known to the Germans as the Spion held by the 1st Royal Irish Rifles at La Boisselle. Nearly a fortnight later, at 9.30 pm on 23 April, a party of twenty from the Royal Irish raided the Germans. Both operations were planned meticulously. However, the outcome of the first enterprise was very different from that of the second. These raids took place on a part of the front line where the Somme offensive would be launched a few months later.

Planning for the German raid began five days before it was scheduled for execution, when the 12th Company of the 110th Reserve Infantry Regiment received regimental orders to mount the operation. The orders ran to ten pages of typescript, including three pages of tables devoted to the artillery fireplan. Emphasis was placed on the fire-suppression roles of the artillery, mortars and machine-guns. Thirty-seven copies of the orders were prepared, including five spares, and sent out to everyone involved in the enterprise from division down to the infantry companies and machine-gun sections. Part of the operation was a feint to be made against another section of the British line a little further to the south of the target, just north of La Boisselle cemetery. This included a bombardment of the British wire in front of the false target. The objective of the raid had two aspects, primarily to take as many prisoners as possible and secondly to collect arms and equipment, including trench mortars, machine-guns, rifle grenade stands and filled packs. The second aspect was stated more in hope than expectation, however, because the small size of the party would make the manhandling of heavy equipment difficult.

The raiding party given the task of entering the British trench was to be no more than thirty strong and led by three officers, although the entire raiding team comprised fifty-seven men and five officers. The trench party was split into three patrols of ten men, each led by an officer. A support team of twenty-four and one officer was available to the raid commander to use as he saw fit according to circumstances. The raiders were expected to spend exactly 25 minutes in the British positions, after which time they were to withdraw.

The artillery fireplan was very detailed and involved seventy-three guns and mortars of various calibres from 77mm field guns to 150mm howitzers and 210mm trench mortars. The number of rounds to be fired on each target and the duration of each shoot was specified for each gun. This included some gas shells. There were twenty-seven targets in all. Registration of the guns for these targets was to be concealed by a bombardment on the morning of the day of the raid together with the detonation of a small mine, all designed to mislead the British. In order to help conceal the registration further, the process of registering all the guns was to be spread over several days. Whenever possible, batteries involved in registration did so in conjunction with distant batteries unconnected with the raid as well as in conjunction with retaliatory strikes on British trench mortars. Timing was to be irregular to avoid each shoot being connected with every other one so that they appeared random. In addition, machine-guns were to engage targets behind the British front line during the entire operation to hinder any preparations for a counter-attack.

7. The machine-gun officer will arrange that, during the whole time of the raid, the enemy's rear trenches in Target-sectors 76–81 are kept under a constant fire, with a view to causing him all possible loss, and, at the same time, to safeguard our patrol [raiding party] against counter-attacks.

8. The Officer Commanding 1st Reserve Company, 13th Pioneer Battalion, will arrange for a gallery of the left-hand minefield to be ready charged by the morning of the day before the raid, and for a gallery of the right-hand minefield to be ready charged by the evening of the raid. The former will be sprung at the conclusion of the feint bombardment, the latter as an introduction to the feint bombardment.

A number of trench mortars were given the task of cutting the British wire before the raid, then assisting the feint bombardment on the evening of the raid. Other mortars were to bombard the British machine-gun positions. A so-called Albrecht mortar was given this task. These were large-calibre weapons improvised from wood wound with wire for strength. Two medium mortars were to maintain a desultory fire on the British wire throughout the night prior to the raid and during the next day, the day of the raid. One heavy and two medium mortars were supposed to cut a gap 50 yards wide for the raiders on the evening of the raid. In addition, other mortars, including light mortars, were to take part in the feint bombardment.

The timetable for all the elements of the raid were set out to the second and no aspect was left to chance. Nevertheless, the orders were changed by division at the last moment, increasing the number of mortars tasked with wire cutting and delaying the moment one team of ten raiders left their positions to attack the Royal Irish to avoid them becoming casualties from their own artillery bombardment.

According to the war diary of the 1st Royal Irish Rifles, at 6.55 pm on 11 April:

> A very heavy bombardment from guns & howitzers of all calibres & trench mortars etc broke out on our lines & also on the battalions on our right & left. It was most intense on our centre held by A Coy. Some uncertainty still exists as to what actually happened, but a German raiding party, estimated at about 40 men entered our trenches & took some prisoners … it is thought that the enemy entered the trench on left of sector X.20.3 and right of X.20.4 as 27 grenades were found there. All quiet by 8.15 pm.

The war diary noted that nine Royal Irish were killed and thirty-nine wounded, while twenty-eight were missing. The casualties were attributed to shellfire rather than to the raiders.

The raiding party rehearsed the operation well behind the lines in the five days since receiving the orders for the raid so was not garrisoned in the front line trenches from which the raid was to be mounted. At 4.00 pm on the afternoon of the operation, the party marched from Martinpuich via Pozières to the regimental line between Lattoff Trench and Krebs Trench, then assembled in the assigned dugouts ready for zero hour. The preliminary artillery bombardment opened up at 8.00 pm.

> Shortly after fire was opened, the whole of the enemy's position from Windmühle to Besenhecke was wrapped in greyish-white smoke, which the wind drove back over Sap No. 3 into our lines.

Sap No. 3 was adjacent to a position called the Hohlweg, which was the jumping-off point for the raid. Some of the smoke was, in fact, gas. Many of the German shells had either K or T gas fillings, both lachrymatory compounds, both very unpleasant with the potential to incapacitate, but non-lethal. Two hundred of the K and 178 of the T shells were fired into a relatively small area of the British line so that the density of the gas was fairly high. Nevertheless, only a small proportion of the gas shells fell on the trench line because it curved away from the barrage line.

Within 10 minutes of the smoke/gas drifting over the raiders, it became impossible for them to remain in the affected trenches without wearing their gas masks. Yet, they were still in the dugouts. By 8.20 pm, it became clear that the gas was not going to disperse. The raiders moved up to the Hohlweg adjacent to Sap No. 3 and when, 5 minutes later, the raid section leaders all signalled they were ready to move off, the Royal Irish line was completely obscured so that it was hard to tell if 'our own shells were still falling on the point of entry or whether our artillery had already lengthened their range.'

The pre-raid bombardment of the British wire and entry point to the Royal Irish line went according to plan. It only evoked a weak response from the British guns while the feint bombardment drew their attention instead. As a consequence, no British shells landed anywhere near the raiders or their jumping-off point during the entire raid. The German trench mortars, completely destroyed the British wire for 44 yards in front of the raiders' intended entry point.

At 8.27 pm, the raid commander, Hauptmann Wagener, ordered the patrol under the command of Leutnant Stradtmann to move off by crawling forward. At the same time, Leutnant Boening led out his six stretcher bearers, who then followed Stradtmann's patrol. As they went forward, the stretcher bearers posted markers for the other patrols to follow. Each marker was fitted with a shielded red signal lamp, which could only be seen from the German line. Exactly 1 minute after Stradtmann set out, Wagener ordered Leutnants Dumas and Böhlefeld to lead out their ten-man patrols. They followed the markers to the entry point into the Royal Irish trench. When they got there, Stradtmann's patrol had already taken 16 yards of trench and three prisoners. These three Royal Irish had emerged from a dugout just as Stradtmann's patrol entered the trench and although they came out with bayonets fixed, they were instantly disarmed.

From the point of entry into the Royal Irish trench, Leutnant Böhlefeld and his patrol immediately turned right, while Dumas and his patrol went left. Within a few yards, Böhlefeld reached three dugouts, one of which had been very badly damaged in the bombardment. All its occupants were either dead or wounded. Those in the two undamaged dugouts surrendered to Böhlefeld when he warned them to come out. He sent his prisoners back under the escort of eight of his men, leaving him to defend the captured section of trench with the remaining two.

Dumas and his men had a little more of a fight on their hands as they went along the trench in the other direction to Böhlefeld. First they came upon one of Stradtmann's men digging out a partially buried Vickers machine-gun, then, as his patrol continued down the trench, they reached a destroyed dugout. He had sent three of his patrol over the ground to reach a communication trench that joined the front-line trench at the destroyed dugout. As they entered the communication trench at a point about 11 yards from that junction, the three Germans came up behind several Royal Irish who were endeavouring to reach the front-line trench and engage the Germans. The Royal Irish were surprised and bayoneted before they could do anything. While this was happening the rest of the Dumas patrol fought their way down the trench, passing two more dugouts, one of which had been destroyed and contained only dead. Before they could clear the undamaged one, a party of Royal Irish came down the trench from another communication trench. A short, sharp scrap then followed with grenades and pistols. The Royal Irish withdrew having suffered a number of casualties. The Germans were unscathed and succeeded in taking more prisoners.

All this had taken no more than 3 minutes. Firing and grenade detonations could still be heard by Wagener who had remained in the German line with his reinforcements to direct operations. It was the Dumas fight he could hear. Wagener now sent out five men under Elb to reinforce Dumas. They were accompanied by the adjutant, Leutnant Erb. Before they reached Dumas, however, the sounds of combat ended. The raiders had gained the upper hand at every point. Wagener now decided to reinforce the patrols with an extra fifteen men under Leutnant Freund who was ordered to attack the British position at the Spion from behind. The Spion was a little further to the north from where the raiders had entered the Royal Irish trench. He also sent over another four men under Vizefeldwebel Wölfle to reinforce Böhlefeld.

Wagener had now used up all his reserves, which left him with no flexibility to respond to any newly developing situation. Fortunately, he had foreseen this eventuality and that afternoon had warned the neighbouring companies that they might have to provide reinforcements at short notice. He now exercised that option.

The next phase of the operation now developed as Leutnant Freund followed the Royal Irish trench, going in the direction of the Spion. Crossing an adjoining communication trench his patrol reached the trench that led directly to the Spion and they jumped into it, taking the occupants completely by surprise. According to Wagener's after-action report, they took ten prisoners 'hardly without a struggle and secured several rifles and articles of equipment'. Those who did fight back were bayoneted. Those who tried to run off were shot dead. None of this was going well for the Royal Irish. One of the patrol found an improvised mortar so firmly secured in the trench that it could not be moved. Vizefeldwebel Wölfle destroyed it with several grenades and, bizarrely, 'pistol shots'.

Two patrols now combined to act in cooperation as they worked down the trench. These were Böhlefeld's and Freund's, the former already reinforced by Wagener's drafts. As they advanced down the Royal Irish trench they came across several destroyed dugouts 'which were filled with dead. Individuals standing about in the trench were killed by the patrol or made prisoner'. It is evident that the raiders showed no mercy if surrender was not immediate and without hesitation. Not everything went the raiders' way, however, as a party of at least twenty-five and perhaps as many as thirty Royal Irish got away from the raiders. As this party tried to escape, they were caught by the German bombardment that was intended to isolate the British position and they 'now came running towards Stradtmann's patrol'. Not surprisingly, Stradtmann perceived this as part of a British counter-attack and responded accordingly. His men opened fire. A close fight ensued as shooting was replaced by bayoneting. The raiders had the upper hand in this and those who failed to surrender were shown no mercy. However, the Royal Irish had now recovered from the initial shock and they all put up a spirited resistance.

Dumas and his patrol were in the Royal Irish positions for longer than the others and were involved in more of the fighting. By the time Erb reached Dumas, the fighting had flared up again although it had not actually stopped since the first patrol had entered the Royal Irish trenches. Resistance to the incursion grew as the raid developed and the fighting became more fierce with hand grenades and pistols as the principal weapons. According to the post-action report by Wagener, Dumas's patrol was responsible for killing more than twenty Royal Irish and wounding a great many more. Remarkably, the raiders suffered only minor injuries in all this and only one of them needed treatment; his forehead had been cut by a grenade splinter. The other raiders all returned on time but Erb, Dumas and the rest of his patrol did not and Wagener feared they had all been killed or become prisoners. He ordered Stradtmann and Boening to take several NCOs to go back into the British position and search for the missing patrol. They met them as they were returning, apparently unhurt. The last man was back in the German lines by 8.50 pm. The bombardment of the Royal Irish trenches that the raiders had just left opened 1 minute later and continued for about 10 minutes.

As the German bombardment came to a close, a heavy British battery shelled Sap No. 3 for a couple of minutes. The raid was officially declared over at 9.05 pm. The raiders took twenty-nine Royal Irish prisoners, five of whom had been wounded in the action. They had seized a Lewis gun, one sniper rifle, twenty rifles and a great many steel helmets, ammunition belts, packs of various kinds and some gas helmets.

Wagener's assessment of the raid was that it was a success. His was not the only report of the operation as Oberst Freiherr von Vietinghoff, the regimental commander, also wrote a report. He had issued the original orders for the operation. The bombardments and feint aside, as far as the raid itself was concerned, it is evident that the gas fired on to the part of the

British line about to be raided had a huge effect on the Royal Irish and their ability to fight. Gas masks were essential and, indeed, even the raiders of the first patrol were obliged to put on theirs while waiting to set out because the gas was blown back over the German line by a strong breeze, which no one seems to have anticipated from weather forecasts. At least three men in the first patrol were severely affected, including Stradtmann, one collapsing, the other two being violently sick, although all three quickly recovered. The gas had the same effect on the Royal Irish, of course, and they, too, had to don their masks. Nevertheless, it impeded their ability to fight as they were disorientated by it. Indeed, a good many were incapacitated, which enabled the raiders to gain access and take control. That was, of course, the point of the gas shells.

Most of the Royal Irish put up a serious fight despite being gassed. Although Wagener claimed in his report that some had offered little resistance it is evident that the Royal Irish platoon commanders were not prepared to give ground easily and that they led their men with considerable courage against the raiders. What is less clear is why they inflicted so few injuries on the Germans. Much of the fighting involved grenades being thrown by both sides. A grenade exploding in the confined space of a trench was lethal to anyone within 30 yards of it. The Mills was probably the most lethal hand grenade of the war because of the large number of fragments it produced when it exploded and it had only a 5-second fuze, which meant that it could not be recovered and thrown back by the enemy. According to Vietinghoff, the 'Royal Irish Rifles created a most favourable impression, both as regards the physique of the men and their mode of repelling an assault'. Wagener also stated that the majority of the Royal Irish fought hard and did not simply give up.

The casualty figures provided by the Royal Irish do not quite match those suggested in Wagener's report. His report implies that the Royal Irish lost a lot of men, firstly to shellfire, then to the raid itself. Whereas the number of prisoners taken coincides with the number of men missing following the action, there is no suggestion in the Royal Irish diary that many men were killed or wounded directly by the raiders. Despite the close fighting in the trenches with grenades, pistols, bayonets and rifles, as described in the after-action report, the Royal Irish recorded no losses attributable to the raiders. This implies that the Germans' perception of the action differed from what actually happened. In other words, Wagener's report puffed up the effect of the raid, although he was accurate about the number of prisoners. There is no question that those involved in an action tend to describe the events in bigger terms and ascribe greater losses suffered by the enemy than a more dispassionate appraisal would assign to the events. No doubt some of those described as killed in the report were, in fact, only wounded, while the war diary has combined the casualties suffered under the bombardment with those of the raid. However, it is clear that the Royal Irish losses were substantial and the raid was a German success.

Vietinghoff believed that had it not been for the gas, the raiders would have had a much tougher fight on their hands. Indeed, the operation might well have failed but for the gas. The conclusion was that shelling a position with gas was a prerequisite for a successful operation as this ensured that the enemy could not put up an effective resistance. From this, he concluded that the best way to carry out a raid was to inflict similar damage on the enemy beforehand, using both high explosive and gas, which not only would ensure a large number of the enemy were killed or wounded but the very sight of the casualties would lower the morale of the survivors to such a level that they would be unable to fight. This was the destruction strategy at the heart of major offensives in 1916 such as the one being fought by the Germans against the French at Verdun at the time of this raid. In other words, his conclusion vindicated strategic policy. However, reality did not reflect theory. As the British were to discover in a few months time on the Somme, this was a dangerous approach to take as the ideal could never be realised no matter how long and how intense the preliminary bombardment might be.

Vietinghoff understood that the gas combined with the high explosive incapacitated the Royal Irish to such a degree that they were overwhelmed when the raiders struck. Their ability to fight had been curtailed only temporarily but for long enough to allow the raiders to complete their mission without serious interference. It was the reduction in the ability of the Royal Irish to fight that enabled the raiders to succeed, not the level of destruction wrought by the bombardment. However, Vietinghoff thought that more high explosive was needed on future operations in case the raiding force was too small, which rather begged the question: why then mount a raid? Since the aim of nearly every German raid was the taking of prisoners, killing everyone in the front line beforehand with a highly destructive bombardment would have been counter-productive. However, his intention was that the raiders should only be confronted with isolated groups of demoralised defenders.

Significantly, he realised that incapacitating the enemy meant that the attackers could penetrate more deeply into the British lines and go at least as far as the second line, if not the third, without meeting serious opposition. He was not suggesting that the same raiding party should attempt to go that far but rather that fresh assault troops should take over from the first patrols once they had secured their objective. This kind of leapfrogging infiltration of the enemy lines, already practised in an embryonic form by the new stormtroop battalions, was a tactic that would be developed further in 1917. But in order for infiltration to work, the firepower of the artillery had to subdue and disorientate the enemy, rather than attempt to destroy him, something that no side appreciated fully at this stage of the war. Vietinghoff almost grasped that point but was rather too attached to the notion of destruction as a means to provide easy access to the enemy lines. For the BEF, the significance of disorientation rather than destruction began to be appreciated in the mid to late summer of 1916.

Vietinghoff also made the point about the limitations of using gas on such an operation: the unpredictable nature of the wind made gas unreliable. A sudden unfavourable change in wind direction after the gas had been released would mean that the raiders had to wear masks to avoid becoming casualties themselves. The practical difficulties of fighting at close quarters while wearing a gas mask made their use unpopular for raids, although German troops like the British were trained to fight in them. Nevertheless, a gas mask inhibited vision and made breathing difficult when doing vigorous exercise such as engaging in a grenade fight. This raid was not only a success in that a number of very useful prisoners were taken for no loss and who divulged information significant to the 110th Reserve Regiment when questioned, but it also provided valuable tactical insights for future raids as well as for major offensive operations.

In contrast to the German raid of 11 April, the Royal Irish enterprise eleven days later was far less successful. There can be little doubt that it was mounted in retaliation for the earlier raid and, like the German operation, an artillery bombardment preceded it, fired by its own divisional artillery in conjunction with that of the divisions to their left and right so that a significant length of the German front line was heavily shelled prior to the raid. However, only selected targets along the German line were targeted, which would have disguised which German trench was about to be hit by the Royal Irish raid. The bombardment opened at 9.30 pm and was of short duration, a hurricane bombardment that was not intended to destroy the enemy trenches but to subdue their garrisons so that their ability to fight was reduced. This was the equivalent of the German use of gas in their raid of the 11th. A twenty-man Royal Irish raiding party led by Second Lieutenant Muir left their own lines under cover of the bombardment and made for the German wire. This had already been cut and the raiders soon reached the enemy trench. They took the occupants by surprise. However, things started to go wrong very quickly as the raiders were suddenly caught by the fire from two machine-guns that had not been disabled by the bombardment so that they were prevented from entering the German trench. They began to have casualties and the raiders had no choice but to withdraw. Four men were wounded and, when the raiders reached the safety of their own lines again, one of them was missing, presumed killed.

They returned empty-handed. They had not even managed to identify the regiment they were raiding as there had been no opportunity to take any identifying tags or papers. By 10.45 pm, it was all over and the front had settled down once again. This raid was the antithesis of the successful German raid of ten days earlier. Whereas the Germans achieved all their objectives, the Royal Irish achieved little more than killing a few Germans before they were hit by machine-gun fire, which forced them to retire. The 1st Royal Irish Rifles did not attempt another raid until October. In the meantime, they were heavily involved in the fighting on the Somme from 1 July.

That the Royal Irish raid did not succeed was not due to bad planning, nor poor execution, but rather to a series of little things that together added up to failure. Perhaps the principal reason for the German success was a combination of good fortune, a well-executed diversionary bombardment and, more particularly, the use of gas shells. Although gas in itself was not a guarantee of success since effective gas masks mitigated against high casualties, nevertheless, it led to the Royal Irish being overwhelmed at the critical moment because their ability to fight was severely, if only temporarily, reduced. Such a reduction in fighting ability did not occur among the Germans when the British fired a hurricane bombardment as a prelude to the retaliatory raid. The reasons for that were probably poor target location rather than anything else. Simply put, when the artillery fireplan was drawn up, no one may have known of the existence of the two machine-guns that ended the Royal Irish raid. This came down to either a lack of recent aerial photographs of the area or clever camouflage by the Germans, which prevented their detection. It is more than likely that the guns were located in positions between the lines, not actually in them, where they were much easier to detect.

There is no doubt that raids could be very unpredictable in how they played out. The outcome of the German raid could have been very different, irrespective of the use of gas shells. The Royal Irish could have mounted a serious counter-attack had circumstances been slightly different but chance constantly played into the hands of the Germans on that occasion and they escaped with practically no casualties. There is also the strong likelihood that the Germans were on higher alert than might have been the case had not the Germans raided the British line ten days earlier, whereas up to that point the Royal Irish had had no reason to be on greater alert than they were usually. Hence, surprise favoured the Germans rather than the Royal Irish on both occasions. Surprise carried a huge advantage. When it could be achieved, surprise was far more potent than an artillery bombardment, which took away the element of surprise to such an extent that it had to be contrived by subterfuge and cunning, taking up more time to plan and more resources to execute. If anything could lower morale, it was being raided without warning.

Surprise had always been the ideal strategy for raiding but the widespread use of artillery and trench mortars to disrupt the enemy prior to a raid made it almost impossible to achieve. Even the raid of 11 April did not achieve surprise. The Royal Irish were overwhelmed rather than surprised, although the outcome was much the same. During the months preceding the Somme offensive and during the months that followed, raiding was the art of battle in miniature. Now, the purpose of the raids, certainly as far as the BEF was concerned, was not merely to gather intelligence but to cause mayhem among the Germans who were already reeling from the battles of the offensive – they suffered very high casualties – and keep them off balance. It was during the fighting in July that the account of the German raid on 11 April was captured.

Chapter 5

The Australians: June and July 1916

The Australians launched their first raids on the Western Front in June 1916, having only been in France since March. The very first Australian raids coincided with Haig's instruction of 28 May for an increase in raiding as a prelude to the offensive on the Somme. Haig's order to the First, Second and Third Armies to 'take steps to deceive the enemy as to the real front of attack, to wear him out, and reduce his fighting efficiency'. This included the mounting of:

> raids by night, of the strength of a company and upwards on an extensive scale, into the enemy's front system of defences. These to be prepared by intense artillery and trench-mortar bombardment.

However, the decision to carry out raids had already been taken by the Australian Imperial Force (AIF). The Australians had been frustrated by their run of back luck in trying to capture a prisoner despite aggressive patrolling in no man's land. The solution was to mount a raid. This decision was all the easier to reach because two enterprising Australian officers had already made a thorough reconnaissance of the German wire near Armentiéres, the sector in which they were currently stationed. What they found suggested that this was a good place for a raid.

Captain Foss of the 7th Brigade, AIF, was not content to wait for opportunities to arise but preferred to make them for himself. This was how he came to be out in no man's land on the night of the 30 May, going along the German wire yet again. He and a fellow officer, Lieutenant Gill, the scout officer of the 28th Battalion, had already scouted much of the wire and it was on the strength of the intelligence they had gathered that the 7th Brigade was given the opportunity to carry out the first Australian raid on the Western Front. Foss's solo reconnaissance trip paid dividends because he discovered a way through the wire and he got within 15 yards of the German trenches without being detected. In this area, no man's land was 400 yards deep. He had been able to get so close because he had made use of ditches that hid him from view. Better still, the German wire was in a poor state of repair at the point he now found himself. This was a perfect place for a surprise raid.

Because both the 26th and 28th Battalions of the 7th Brigade identified this point as a target for a raid, they were given the task of planning and executing a joint raid. This enterprise was to be one of stealth; there would be no artillery preparation and no support from trench mortars. While this allowed the Australians to use surprise to shock the enemy, the Germans were by now well accustomed to such raids and were less easily taken unawares compared to a year or even six months earlier. This meant that complete surprise was essential for success otherwise the raid would be a costly disaster. Artillery and trench mortar bombardments helped to knock the enemy off balance, if only temporarily, which made the trench fighting a little easier for the raiders. Without artillery and trench mortar support prior to the raid, the fighting would inevitably be harder. On the plus side, however, the raiders would not have to negotiate damaged trenches and it would be easier for them to secure prisoners, or so the theory went.

Gill and five of his scouts had the task of cutting the enemy wire immediately before the raid. Foss was given command of the enterprise. The raiding party was made up entirely of volunteers, six officers and sixty other ranks. The party was split into two groups so that the target could be approached from two directions during the attack. As with all raiding parties, the men in each group were divided into sections that were given specific tasks. These included blocking the enemy trenches at given points to prevent a counter-attack, intelligence gathering and fighting up the enemy trenches. The fighting parties were made up of two sections in each group. One party in each group was to attack up the left branch of the trench while another went up the right branch. Telephone operators along with linesmen to lay telephone cable into the enemy trenches were to ensure communication was maintained with the Australian line during the operation. Scouts, runners, stretcher bearers and parties to man the enemy parapet (or rather the parados so that they faced the German rear rather than the Australian front line) were also part of the raiding party.

Training for the raid was carried out over a period of two weeks under the supervision of two Canadian officers, Lieutenant Kent and Lieutenant Conners. It is evident they were borrowed for the purpose because of the widespread belief that the Canadians were the masters of the raid. As had become standard practice by now, a replica of the enemy positions was constructed behind the lines. For this to be as accurate and up to date as possible, reconnaissance flights over the German line had brought back several photographs. Once these trenches had been dug, the raiders rehearsed their attack time and again until they were thoroughly familiar with their tasks and the enemy ground. The only thing missing from the practice runs was the enemy himself.

Although the artillery was not going to fire a preparatory bombardment, it was going to provide a box barrage once the raiders were in the enemy trenches. This would help prevent the Germans developing a counter-attack. The barrage would isolate the trenches from the rest of the German line. To this end, the guns had to fire registration shots in the week preceding the raid in such a way that their true nature was disguised. By 5 June 1916, the preparations were complete and the raiders and artillery were ready. The raid was scheduled for that evening.

While one of the objectives of the raid was to gather intelligence about the German regiment facing the 7th Brigade, the Australians had no intention of providing similar information to the enemy in the event any of the party were killed or captured in the German position. With this in mind, all the raiders were issued with British uniforms in place of their Australian tunics; and these lacked all identifying insignia. Each man wore a white armband to identify friend from foe once they were in the German position. Until the raiders jumped into the German trench, the band remained covered by a black one. The raiders blackened their hands and faces and painted their bayonets so that no light would reflect off bare skin or shiny metal.

They were armed with a wider range of weaponry than was customary for normal front-line trench duty or, indeed, participation in a major assault. The additional weapons included knobkerries constructed from pickaxe handles. The helve was already provided with a metal collar on to which a corresponding socket in the pickaxe head was slid to form a firm friction fit. It was designed so that the pickaxe head and the helve could be carried separately for ease but be quickly assembled when needed. The knobkerrie head made use of this facility. It had been designed in the Second Army Workshops, operated by the Royal Engineers but commanded by an officer from the Sherwood Foresters, Captain Henry Newton, a remarkable inventor of simple solutions to the demands of trench warfare. The flanged knobkerrie was his design. It resembled a medieval mace. It was not popular with Australian officers, who quickly dispensed with it. The knobkerrie was intended for silent killing but, surprisingly perhaps, its effective use required more than aggression and intent. The bombers, scouts and runners were all armed with the knobkerries and revolvers rather than the customary rifle and bayonet with which the rest of the party were equipped.

The drawback to raids in the summer was the length of the day. It remained light until about 9.30 pm while the night was short; the sky began to lighten less than five hours later. Thus, the period of complete darkness during which a raid might be carried out was very short. Not only the assault on the enemy trench but the approach and withdrawal all had to be in darkness to avoid detection. The length of time the raiders could safely spend in the enemy's trenches before they had to withdraw was determined by the time it took for the approach and the withdrawal. Thus, all elements of the raid had to be efficiently executed while the schedule was followed precisely. In this operation, the attackers were aided by the long grass that had grown up in no man's land due to the inactivity in the sector. There had been no artillery bombardments of no man's land because neither the Allies nor the Germans had mounted an offensive operation here since the front line was established in the autumn of 1914.

At 9.30 pm on the evening of the 5 June, Gill's wire-cutting party set out from the Australian line, crawling towards the Germans in two lines of three. It took them 45 minutes to reach the ragged and unrepaired German wire. As they began cutting their way through it, the rest of the raiders set out following the same line of advance and in strict order: the two trench parties, the two blocking parties, then the parapet party with the covering party bringing up the rear. Gill had developed a technique for cutting wire that prevented the characteristic and very audible 'click' and 'ping' when a strand was severed with a conventional wire-cutting tool. He had adjusted the bite of his cutters so that they did not completely sever the strand but weakened it enough to allow the strand to be broken by hand and, hence, without the tell-tale noise.

Gill and his team made excellent progress, moving forwards on their backs as they cut the wire, until they were almost through it. Then, the operation began to go wrong. Gill, who was working with Corporal Tozer, noticed they were almost on top of a German listening post they had not noticed before. Although the sentry had clearly heard something – his attention was directed towards the wire-cutting team – he had not, in fact, seen them. Gill and Tozer lay still for 10 minutes, then slid back the way they had just come, rejoining the cut strands as they went. It was now 11.30 pm and the raiders faced a dilemma. While alternative plans had been made prior to the operation to deal with difficulties such as this, time was not on their side. They could try to press on regardless with the attendant risk of discovery before they got to the German line, call in a bombardment on the wire or abandon the enterprise altogether. A bombardment was not really viable given the raiders' proximity to it.

The decision to abandon the raid was taken by Brigadier Paton, who had come up to the front line and established a temporary headquarters for the raid. A message explaining the raiders' problem reached him at 12.30 pm, by which time it was far too late to adopt any alternative plan since any revised orders would not reach Foss until about 1.00 am at the earliest, which would leave only 90 minutes of darkness to carry out the raid and withdraw. Paton decided to reschedule the raid for the following night but, rather than repeat the stealth approach, employ a short bombardment by 2-inch medium trench mortars in the morning to destroy both the wire and the evidence of the previous night's activities. That way, the path would be clear for the raiders and the Germans would not be alerted to the forthcoming raid by the sight of cut wire in front of their positions.

Artillery played a bigger role in the second attempt than during the first. At 11.15 pm, the guns and trench mortars of the Second Division, including some of the heavies, fired on targets north and south of the raider's objective. The intention was to misdirect the Germans so that they would, hopefully, remain unsuspecting of the true target. After a 10-minute shoot on these targets, the artillery switched targets and bombarded the raiders' objective for another 10 minutes before switching again to fire a box barrage around the objective to isolate it from the rest of the German line.

While the artillery was busy, the raiders moved out into no man's land and occupied a line of disused rifle pits located about halfway across. Here they waited until the artillery began its box barrage. Mortar bombs landed quite close to them. Although the Australians had had little experience of working with barrages, the sudden increase in range of the guns and mortars was immediately obvious and they rushed forwards to take the German front trench. The wire had been completely destroyed by the bombs of the medium mortars, which were very effective at this task. After the start of the artillery bombardment of the Somme offensive, the mediums would become even more effective at removing wire entanglements because of the wider use of a fuze, which allowed the bomb to detonate on the ground surface rather than under it. The No. 110 fuze was not widely used before the Somme for fear that the Germans would discover the British had a very effective wire-cutting fuze. It is possible this fuze, also designed by Henry Newton, was fitted to the bombs fired on the German wire for the Australian raid.

The Australians took 2 minutes to cross the ground and reach the German parapet. Had any of the enemy remained in the trench and alert, the raiders would certainly have been spotted and fired on. But none remained alive in the trench and the assault groups, made up of the trench parties and the blocking parties, were able to approach the parapet and lie down along it ready for the final assault. In the meantime, the covering party, commanded by Lieutenant Phillipps,[1] set itself up along the German wire ready to give fire support should it be needed. Foss gave the command to attack and the lead raiders jumped into the German trench. It was empty. More worrying was the fact that the layout of the trench bore no resemblance to the replica over which they had practised so hard. In fact, this was not even a trench as it had no parados but was open at the back. Indeed, what had been interpreted from the aerial photographs as a trench was, in fact, little more than a breastwork in which dugouts had been constructed.

None of the German front line was made up of trenches as such but consisted of similar works, including the communication trenches, which were no more than sunken paths with hurdles along the sides. As the raiders worked their way along these works and formed blocking parties as practised, hardly a German was seen. It was as though they had vanished. In fact, most of the garrison were sheltering in the dugouts where they had retreated once the bombardment had opened up and they had yet to emerge; a fatal error of judgment. As the raiders reached each dugout, a grenade was tossed inside. Whoever was inside was very likely killed or mortally wounded by the grenades. In the confined space of a dugout, the explosive force combined with the fragmentation of the grenade on detonation proved to be deadly. No Germans emerged from the dugouts. The few who were encountered above ground were either shot or bayoneted before they could do anything. So far, only one prisoner had been taken, a youth who had been hiding alone in the first dugout encountered by Foss in which the latter had rather foolishly entered using his torch.

The operation was over in 7 minutes. The raiders had cleared the enemy trench 30 yards each side of the point of entry, bombed dugouts, killed the six Germans they had encountered all within that time and captured three men belonging to the 231st Reserve Infantry Regiment. Foss fired a green flare from his Very pistol, the signal to retire. No rifle or machine-gun fire had been directed against the raiders from the German second line during the assault, largely because of the effectiveness of the box barrage. Indeed, the Germans failed to mount a credible response to the Australian incursion at any time showing how ill-prepared they were in this sector, an error they would not repeat in the future.

In the meantime, Gill's scouts had set out a luminous-taped return route for the withdrawing raiders to follow. By means of the tape, they made the rifle pits in one dash, then, after a brief pause, made a dash for the ditch in front of the Australian line, where they had waited before the operation got under way. However, German artillery was now shelling up and down the length of the Australian line and the raiders could not get through it to the relative safety of their own trenches. This bombardment was in response to the shelling of their own lines. It was not specifically targeted at the raiders because the German artillery had no knowledge of the raid at that stage and the shelling had hit different positions up and down the line. Nevertheless, it was a major obstacle for Foss and his party. He had no choice but to wait in no man's land. All communication with Paton's headquarters had been lost because the shelling had severed the telephone cable that the linesmen had laid out during the advance to the German position.

As they waited, the raiders began to suffer their first casualties. Artillery was always the biggest killer of men in the First World war, not so much because of the explosive force of the shells but rather because of the fragments[2] from the shell casings, which could travel a long way, much further than hand grenade fragments. A shell landed among the raiders and killed two, injuring four. The Australians manning the front trench also suffered under the shelling. Twenty of them were killed or wounded, largely because of the paucity of adequate shelter. Had not the garrison been reduced in number in expectation of German retaliation, the casualties would have been far higher. Whereas German front-line positions were usually provided with deep dugouts in which troops could shelter during shelling and thereby reduce casualties, this practice was not universal in British trenches. The reason for this was the belief at GHQ in the early days of trench warfare that shelter of the sort favoured by the Germans would encourage a defensive mentality among British troops that ran counter to GHQ's policy of aggressive dominance of the enemy parapet. This policy with regard to dugouts was later amended as a matter of practicality.

Thus, while the raid was a success, the consequences were costly. At the time of the raid, the Australians were very new to the conditions of the Western Front and the nature of the fighting. The Australians were especially keen to take the fight to the Germans but before the raid they were anxious about engaging the enemy in close fighting. It is worth noting that the employment of bombers working above ground to throw grenades into the objective trench rather than having them work in the trench moving forward one bay at a time was very much a new development in bombing tactics at that time. It was a practice that would not become widespread for another six to nine months.

After the raid, the Australians, although already confident of their own fighting abilities, were boosted so that their morale rose. This had a rather unfortunate and unforeseen consequence. The press, always eager for a good story, especially when it came from a source other than the official one, took up the success of the not only the Australian raid but other actions carried out by the Anzacs on the Western Front and exaggerated their prowess. Not surprisingly, perhaps, those British troops who had been in France for two years and fighting under very trying conditions were not overly enthusiastic about these accounts. This led to some resentment. The British and the Indians had fought through 1914, 1915 and, in 1916, the months preceding the arrival of the Australians and New Zealanders, acquiring the experience and expertise that contributed to the evolution of tactics, both of attack and defence. The Anzacs benefited from their knowledge as well as from that acquired by the Canadians. However, the relish for these exaggerations was not shared by the Anzacs themselves. On the contrary, they were nonplussed by them and were at pains to disassociate themselves from the news reports.

The next Australian raid was mounted a week later in the early hours of 13 June. This time, the 6th Battalion of the First Division provided the raiding party. Their target was a section of trench between two strongpoints, the Lozenge and the Angle, located to the west of Le Bridoux, near Armentiéres. And once again, this target had been selected because of the poor state of the German wire in that area. This time, the issue of stealth did not arise and 2-inch medium mortars were given the task of destroying the wire prior to the operation. The shoot was carried out at 5.00 pm on the day preceding the raid. The Australian artillery had orders to put down a 10-minute bombardment on the target before the raiders entered the German trench. As before, the artillery fired on a number of other targets at the same time to mislead the Germans about the true target.

The fifty raiders were selected from 400 volunteers. That so many volunteered was an indication of the fighting spirit of the Australians and the effect of the successful raid of a week earlier. The raiders were split into various groups, principal among them being two so-called trench parties. Each of these comprised three bayonet men, two bombers, two carriers, three 'salvage scouts' and a sergeant. One party was led by Lieutenant A.J. Hyde, while the other was under the command of Lieutenant A. Laughlin. Essentially, these parties were bombing squads. In addition to these, were scouts, a party of so-called parapet bombers, and a covering party of twenty-two. These men trained for the raid at the Divisional Bombing School over ground that had been dug to recreate the German positions about to be raided. Unlike the previous raid, the bombers were to take the lead role in the enterprise. This was very much a bombing attack.

While during the first raid the Australians had trained to enter the target trench before engaging the enemy, the tactical approach for this raid was quite different. The so-called parapet bombers were given the task of moving along the parapet, above ground level, throwing grenades into the enemy trench ahead of the trench party who was advancing along the trench. These bombers would be provided with covering fire by the covering or support party in no man's land. The enemy could not come upon the raiders in the German trench by surprise.

The raid did not start well. It was a rainy night after the half moon set at 12.30 pm, while the blackness of the night was so deep the raiders had great difficulty in seeing where they were going. Nevertheless, they left their own line and crawled across no man's land until they reached a slight rise about halfway across, a distance of some 110 yards. It took them 20 minutes to reach this position, where they had to wait while Australian artillery shelled their objective. From some way to their right, roughly in front of the Angle strongpoint, came the noise of a German wiring party hammering stakes into the ground. Fortunately, the party remained unaware of the raiders. The Germans stopped work as soon as the bombardment began. The bombardment only lasted 10 minutes before the guns lifted to another target 100 yards beyond the German front trench. This was the signal for the raiders to move forwards.

Now, they came upon a serious obstacle. Unknown to anyone until that moment, a wide ditch extended the length of the German parapet and just in front of it, created by the removal of earth to form a breastwork against which the parapet abutted. The Germans had then filled the ditch with barbed wire, some of which was staked while some was fixed to knife rests. Since this obstacle had not been known to the gunners, it had not been specifically targeted, with the result that much of the wire remained intact. Laughlin had not noticed this obstacle when he had reconnoitred the German wire prior to the raid. In the darkness and being below normal ground level, the wired ditch had been effectively invisible. This now held up the raiders, who bunched up at the wire unable to cross it while, all the time, the Germans were sending up flares on their flanks, which inevitably illuminated the raiders.

Laughlin forced his way through the wire and reached the parapet, whereupon an alert sentry shot him in the leg. The rest of his party now pushed their way through the wire and reached the parapet. When they had all lined up along the line of the parapet, Laughlin gave the order to leap into the trench. Lieutenant J.D. Rogers, who had led the raiders to the German wire with the aid of a compass, had done so with great skill for they found themselves at precisely the correct point of entry. The trace of the German trench was instantly familiar; the replica over which the raiders had practised was identical with that of the trench the raiders now entered.

The trench bays were provided with dugouts for accommodation and shelter from shelling. The German garrison was clearly sheltering in these or had run away because the raiders encountered only one German soldier, who immediately fled. Even examination of some of the dugouts did not uncover any Germans, apart from, curiously, an elderly man in one and a scared soldier in another, both of whom were made prisoner and bundled over the parapet to be quickly escorted back to the Australian line. The dugouts had doors and, in at least one instance, the doors were locked from the inside indicating that Germans were hiding there, but the Australians made no attempt to blow open the doors and, instead, moved on. The raiders who had turned left as they had entered the enemy trench found much the same situation as their companions who had turned right. In one dugout, the doors of which were open, a light could be seen so a grenade was tossed inside. When it exploded the light was extinguished but quickly relit. Several more grenades were thrown in. They all exploded but the effect of these multiple detonations was not investigated as the signal to retire was given.

In the course of the raid, the Australians found a trench mortar, which they tried to disable with grenades, and a machine-gun, which they tried to take back with them across no man's land, but the heavy gun and its mounting proved too much of a burden and it was abandoned. The German Maxim of 1908 weighed more than 40lb. At least it could no longer fire on the Australians.

The raid was a success with six prisoners being taken and twelve of the enemy being killed in the course of the operation. The only serious casualty among the raiders was a stretcher bearer who was hit by rifle fire from the Angle strongpoint as the raiders withdrew. However, for all the careful reconnaissance, planning and rehearsal that had gone into the preparation for the enterprise, serious mishaps had still occurred. These required quick on-the-spot thinking to resolve. The Australians had remained in contact with headquarters during the raids but the delays in communication complicated matters and ran the risk of compromising the operation to such an extent that the raiders were put at risk simply because they were waiting for fresh orders. Fortunately, the telephone communications set up by the raiders of the 13 June remained intact so that the Australian artillery could be instructed to avoid hitting them as they returned to the Australian line. And although the German artillery had replied in both of these raids, the casualties in the first raid had arisen more by chance than by good preparation by the Germans. To some extent, this good fortune derived from the poor planning of the Germans for dealing with raids and it misled the Australians into thinking all future raids might be equally successful. However, the Germans quickly learned from their mistakes. In future, they would be better prepared, more vigilant and more aware of the signs that presaged a raid.

The 7th Brigade was ordered to mount another raid on the 18th but this was cancelled during the preliminary bombardment. Despite the shelling, two German machine-guns had continued firing without hindrance and it was clear from the bullet strikes on the wire in front of the German trenches that they had been sited to provide crossfire into the area the raiders would have to pass in order to reach the German line. This could not have been coincidence. Rather, it was clear anticipation of a raid based on intelligence. How the Germans had acquired the prior knowledge was open to question but consideration of what had become standardised raid preparations, such as wire-cutting by medium trench mortars and artillery registration, was certainly enough to raise suspicions. Although the German artillery response to the preparatory bombardment was apparently haphazard and weak, that was not evidence of poor preparation since it is highly likely that the guns would have hit no man's land when the Australian bombardment lifted to the next target and caught the raiders in the open. Since the raid was cancelled during the preliminary bombardment, the German guns did not get the opportunity to put into operation plans to shell the raiders at their most vulnerable.

The New Zealanders of the I Anzac Corps were the next to try their hand at raiding. This raid was unlike those recently untaken by the Australians, however, as it was less about taking prisoners and gathering intelligence and more about pinching out an enemy incursion into no man's land as the Germans set about straightening their line. The Germans wanted to eliminate a re-entrant in their line but had the New Zealanders permitted the Germans to carry out this modification unmolested, the new line would have brought the Germans much closer to the New Zealanders. As far as the New Zealanders were concerned, not only was this straightening operation unwelcome but it might have been the first step in the preparation for a major assault on the Allied line. In other words, the straightened line might have been intended as a 'jumping off position'. There was already photo-reconnaissance and other evidence to support this conjecture: new trenches behind the front line. The British were well aware of this sort of operation because the Germans had mounted several of them in the Ypres salient.

The raid was scheduled for 17 June. The raiders rehearsed their attack behind the front line in replica trenches and they were well rehearsed by the time of the raid. The New Zealand artillery provided a 20-minutes bombardment of the German trenches before the raid went in but the Germans were now much wiser and better prepared than they had been with the earlier Australian raids in the same sector. Either the raiders were too keen to get among the enemy or the guns were slow in lifting from the German parapet but as the raiders ran forward to reach the German trench, two officers, Lieutenant White and Captain Alley, were hit by fragments from one of their own shells. Alley, the raid commander, was mortally wounded. Another officer had already been hit before the raiders had even set off from their own line.

The New Zealanders managed to get into the German trench without further mishap and dealt swiftly with the two Germans they met by bayoneting them. They met no other Germans. The purpose of this raid was to determine whether the new trench was, indeed, part of the preparations for a forthcoming assault. In this respect, the raid was not successful. The trench was still under construction and provided no clues about future operations that might be mounted from it and, without prisoners to interrogate, the raiders failed to provide an answer to the question that had set the raid in motion. The three officer casualties were a high price although the uniforms of the dead Germans showed that they belonged to the 24th Saxon Division. But that was about all the raiders learned and such intelligence could have been gathered by more covert means. Indeed, had more care been taken over the intelligence that was already available, far from strengthening the sector in preparation for an attack on the Anzacs, it would have become apparent that the Germans were, in fact, removing the heavier of their guns from the area and moving them to the Somme, where the Allies were about to launch a major offensive. They would not have done that had they been planning an operation in the now thinned out sector.

Chapter 6

Wearing Down and Deception

A raid mounted by the 14th Welsh Regiment on the night of 4–5 June at Farquissart was unsuccessful with a number of casualties. Two small parties entered the German trenches but only one met any Germans, which resulted in an exchange of grenades. The action forced both parties to retire, however, leaving behind one dead and one missing, presumed killed. This raid had been planned before Haig's order to increase raiding to wear down the enemy but, if his intention was to be realised, raiding needed to be more effective than this. That is not to suggest that this particular failure was due to bad planning or poor execution by the 14th Welsh. Sometimes, success eluded raiders because the enemy was more aggressive in defence than the raiders were in attack.

The next raids mounted by the Australians were in direct response to Haig's order.

Anzac Corps headquarters issued instructions to the infantry brigades under its command for mounting as many raids as possible 'between the 20th and 30th of June' and to try to mount a raid on the corps' front every night of that period. This amounted to three raids by each division of the I Anzac Corps. These raids were all carried out after the start of the week-long artillery bombardment that marked the opening of the Somme offensive. Indeed, these raids were continued after 1 July.

The artillery shoots that preceded all the raids undertaken at this time were intended to serve several purposes, not the least of which was the creation of paths through the barbed wire by which raiders could reach their objectives. At the same time, the bombardments were meant to harass the enemy and prevent him from intervening during the raids. Such bombardments were intended to isolate the positions being raided. Some of the bombardments were feints and in cooperation with these, dummy paths were cut and sometimes paths for raids yet to be launched were cut. Wire cutting was a major task of medium trench mortars but sometimes it had to be cut by hand. Alternatives were tried. On a raid carried out on the night of the 28–29 June by fifty-eight men and four officers of the 1st Battalion 1st Australian Infantry Brigade, a Bangalore torpedo was intended to be used to cut the wire instead of the medium trench mortars. For this to be possible, a longer artillery bombardment was necessary to allow time for the torpedo to be put in place. However, the artillery commander vetoed the plan because he was concerned that the longer period of shelling would give the Germans ample warning of the raid. Unfortunately, the mortars then failed to cut the wire properly and the raiders had to cut their way through it by hand.

The first of these deception and wearing down raids took place on the night of 25–26 June. Two operations were carried out on this night by two different brigades of the I Anzac Corps at Armentiéres, the 5th Australian Infantry Brigade and the 3rd New Zealand Infantry Brigade. The size and composition of the raiding parties was similar but not identical. The Australian party was made up of nine officers and seventy-three other ranks while the New Zealanders included three officers and seventy-two other ranks. The Australians hit a German position south-east of Bois Grenier and inflicted thirty fatal casualties, of which ten were caused by the Australian guns, and captured four men of the 231st Reserve Infantry Regiment. A further twenty-five Germans were wounded in the raid. Against this, one raider was killed and thirteen men were wounded, most of whom were hit by German artillery in no man's land as they were withdrawing. The raiders did well to avoid more casualties because the Germans were well prepared for them.

The raiders came up against a ditch containing uncut wire, a feature that seemed to be rather more common than anyone realised. Again, as in previous enterprises, it had not been detected prior to the raid. At least one machine-gun was traversing the area in front of the German trench but the elevation of the gun was slightly too high so that, by keeping low, the raiders were able to keep below the region being swept by the gun. Yet again, once the raiders were in the German trench, they found it almost deserted because the garrison had taken refuge in the dugouts as soon as the bombardment hit their trench and did not come out again when the shelling ceased. The raiders destroyed two grenade stores before they withdrew. Despite the apparent unwillingness of the garrison to fight the raiders, a counter-attack was quickly mounted, suggesting that this was pre-planned rather than an extemporised response, although that does not explain the reluctance of the garrison to fight. However, the timing of the counter-attack was off. The raiders were already recrossing no man's land when the enemy started bombing along their own trench to deal with the Australian incursion.

This raid stood out from most others because of the actions of Private William Jackson of the 17th Battalion (the volunteers for the raid had come from all of the battalions of the 5th Brigade). Still in his teens, he captured a prisoner and took him back to the Australian line, then, when he realised that several of his fellow raiders had been wounded and were still in no man's land, he went back out to help them. He brought back one man, then went out again. Sergeant Cambden, another of the raiders, and Jackson were in the process of bringing back Private Robinson when a shell exploded close to them. Cambden was knocked unconscious by the blast and a shell fragment ripped off Jackson's right arm below the elbow. He managed to reach his own line, where an officer tourniqueted his arm. Yet, despite this apparently incapacitating injury, he went back out into no man's land to look for more wounded. He spent half an hour searching before he returned. For this selfless act, Jackson was awarded the Victoria Cross.[1]

The German description of the events differed somewhat from the Australian version. According to the German account, at midnight, the 229th Reserve Infantry Regiment pushed back two twenty-strong Australian raiding parties with grenades and, 2 hours later, the 231st Reserve Infantry Regiment drove off a wire-cutting party. However, another party of raiders managed to get into the German line and take four prisoners.

The New Zealander raid was on a trench east of Pont Ballot. For the loss of two dead and eight wounded, the raiders hit the Germans of the 133rd Regiment hard and killed about thirty of them, wounding another nine, all above ground. The number of casualties inflicted on those who remained in their dugouts was probably comparable but the New Zealanders had no way of knowing the extent of the German losses in the dugouts without entering them to count the dead and dying, which they were not about to do. Again, the Germans had anticipated the raid because of the wire-cutting that had preceded it. When New Zealand scouts went out into no man's land at the start of the raid, they could hear a working party repairing the cut wire. A 15-minute preliminary bombardment re-cut the wire.

When the raiders jumped into the target trench, the enemy was present in considerable numbers but, surprisingly, failed to put up much of a fight. These were shot and grenaded rather than taken prisoner. Unofficial orders were to take only three prisoners. While in the trench, they discovered a mine shaft, which they blew up. After 15 minutes, the raiding party withdrew. Once again, the Germans failed to inflict any casualties on the raiders while they were in the trench. The New Zealanders looked as though they would escape entirely unscathed but a German stick grenade being carried back by one of the raiders detonated as they approached their own line. The man carrying it was killed and three others were wounded. Nevertheless, this was another successful raid that fulfilled the substance and spirit of Haig's orders.

Another Australian raid was carried out the following night. This was mounted by a party from the 18th Battalion of the 5th Brigade of similar size to those of earlier raids. They hit a trench south-east of Bois Grenier. This raid, unlike the others, involved hard fighting as soon as the raiders reached the German parapet. It is evident that this garrison from the 230th Reserve Infantry Regiment was prepared to repel the raiders and did their best to defeat them. The preliminary bombardment consisted of two periods of shelling, each lasting only 5 minutes. The short duration of the bombardments was due to a sudden change in plan at the eleventh hour because of a German bombardment on the Australians, which prevented trench mortar ammunition for the raid being brought to the mortar battery on time. This led to a postponement of an hour and a half so that the first bombardment was fired at midnight instead of 10.30 pm. This concealed the wire-cutting by the mortars. Another hour and a half later and the artillery fired on the trench for another 5 minutes. Thus, an insufficient weight of ordnance landed on the German trench to aid the raiders in their enterprise. The 5-minute bombardment was favoured because it prevented the Germans from realising a raid was about to hit them but at this stage of the war the so-called hurricane bombardment had yet to be developed. This was one of short duration on a small area with a very large number of guns so that the defenders were completely overwhelmed.

As this second bombardment was in progress, the raiders, led by Captain H.L. Bruce went forward but they discovered that the wire had been only partially cut. They had to spend some minutes snipping their way through. The Germans were waiting for them and forced the raiders back with grenades. The party fell back to the safety of the ditch in front of the parapet then attacked again. This time, they succeeded in overcoming the defenders and got into the trench. They threw grenades into the dugouts as they advanced along the trench. A German counter-attack that was developing in the open to the rear of the raided trench was thwarted by the raiders throwing grenades and killing the officer leading the counter-attack. They spent nearly 10 minutes in the trench before withdrawing.

Despite the fighting and the liberal use of grenades on both sides, the Australians only suffered fourteen casualties, none of them fatal, and one man was taken prisoner. The Germans, on the other hand, lost thirteen dead (the Australians claimed as many of sixty fatalities),[2] while a further twenty-three were wounded. The Australians took four prisoners. So, again, this was a successful raid.

On the same night, a party of sixty-two volunteers, including four officers, from the 25th and 27th Battalions of the 7th Australian Infantry Brigade took part in a big raid on the Germans near Ontario Farm, west of Messines. This, of course, was not part of the Anzac Corps' sector of the front but on the part of the front held by the British 24th Division, V Corps.[3] The Australian contingent constituted one of three parties, the other two being from the British 17th and 72nd Brigades. While the raid was successful, with four prisoners being taken by the Australian party and few casualties being inflicted by the Germans when the raiders were in the enemy positions – one dead and five injured among the Australians – the German counter-bombardment as the raiders returned to the British line led to twenty-nine more casualties. This raid was scheduled to be preceded by the release of poison gas (from cylinders) but weather conditions forestalled this part of the operation and the raiders had to make do with a 10-minute artillery bombardment. A raid was cancelled a few nights later when, once again, gas was to be released immediately before the assault but the weather conditions were unfavourable for such action. On another occasion, the use of smoke to cover a raid was also cancelled due to unfavourable weather conditions.

In the Anzac Corps' sector, the 6th Infantry Brigade mounted a company-sized raid on German positions held by the 231st Reserve Infantry Regiment south-west of the Armentiéres–Wavrin railway line on night of 29–30 June. The raiders came from the 22nd, 23rd and 24th Battalions, comprising 240 men and eight officers. They were supported by a covering party of sixty-one men and three officers of the 21st Battalion. This was a much more complex operation than the smaller raids the Australians had carried out hitherto. Indeed, of all the raids mounted by the Anzacs in this period immediately preceding the infantry assault phase of the Somme, this one was most significant. There is no question that the fighting during this raid was much tougher than the Australians had experienced on their earlier smaller enterprises. The expenditure of artillery shells and trench mortar bombs was very high. Around 8,000 shells and 1,000 mortar bombs were fired.

The operation to destroy the wire prior to the raid was itself a complex process. Not only did this involve an initial artillery shoot on 20 June, which was incorporated in a feint for an entirely different operation, but the artillery then fired shrapnel on succeeding nights, between 20 June and the 29 June, in order to keep open the gaps that had cut in the wire by the initial bombardment. This was aided by the firing of Vickers machine-guns into the wire as the shrapnel was fired. The idea behind this rather complicated fireplan was to prevent the Germans from repairing their wire prior to the raid. Needless to say, the Germans were under no illusion that a raid was imminent. However, the preliminary bombardment to the raid deviated somewhat from the norm in order to wrong-foot the Germans. It lasted a mere 4 minutes before the guns began to lift to the next target. Rather than all the guns changing target simultaneously as was customary, they did so individually over 1 minute so that the lift was not immediately apparent to the Germans. Such a short bombardment was clearly intended to disrupt the defenders rather than obliterate them. From the response of the Germans, it seems that the bombardment failed in its purpose.

The raiders were split into three parties so that, in effect, the raid became three that attacked three points simultaneously. The raid did not go entirely to plan. The common problem of uncut wire almost prevented the right-hand party (23rd Battalion) from reaching the enemy trench. The medium mortar bombs had overshot the wire so had failed to damage it even slightly. The raiders had to cut the wire by hand. Fortunately, they were able to cut a way to a listening post in no man's land at the head of a sap that lead back to the German front trench. Had they been forced to cut their way to the trench itself, they would have been detected. Indeed, they would have been forced to abandon the enterprise long before they reached the trench. When the right-hand party reached the parapet of the German trench, they were showered with grenades. The Germans had been waiting for them because they had been alerted by the occupants of the listening post, who had redrawn as the raiders approached. Nevertheless, the raiders forced their way into the trench and bombed the four dugouts they found. They remained in the trench for 5 minutes, then withdrew having killed and wounded a number of the enemy.

The centre party from the 22nd Battalion faired slightly better but still found the wire in front of them was only partially cut and a path through it had to be finished off by hand. When they got closer to the enemy line they discovered that the trench, like so many others, had a ditch filled with staked wire in front of the parapet. Half the party managed to get through this obstacle and into the trench after 5 minutes of hard work. Like the right-hand party, the 22nd Battalion raiders bombed the dugouts and tried to take prisoners. Meanwhile, the left-hand party from the 24th Battalion also had to negotiate a wire-filled ditch, and this one was full of water. As they crossed it, some of the Germans began to throw grenades at them. The raiders fought their way into the trench but due to some confusion caused by someone giving the signal to retire, the raiders withdrew before time. When the mistake was realised, they rallied and got back into the trench. They bombed dugouts against rifle fire from an adjoining communication trench that overlooked the raiders. Four of the party were killed.

The raiders also tried to blow up several concrete pillboxes, all of which housed machine-guns, but they were only partially successful in what was a very difficult task. Reinforced concrete is surprisingly resistant to destruction by explosive.[4] By the time the raiders returned to their own line they had taken five prisoners from the 231st Reserve Infantry Regiment on whom they inflicted thirty-two fatal casualties and a further seventy-three injuries during the raid, although the Australians claimed to have killed more than eighty. Indeed, the party from the 24th claimed to have killed fifty in the action. The party ensured that no wounded raiders were left in the enemy trench or in no man's land. They searched until daybreak. Twenty-one of the raiders were wounded in the action.

While the operation was a success, it is evident from the rising number of casualties that such enterprises were taking a steady toll on the battalions of the I Anzac Corps. The Australian official history states that:

> Whereas in the last week of April the casualties of the I Anzac Corps had been only 118 as against an average of 563 for each of the four other corps of the Second Army, those for the week ending July 2nd were – I Anzac, 773; average in the other corps 533.

However, in the succeeding week, the Anzacs suffered 880 casualties when they mounted two raids and the Germans hit them with two. Regular shelling was, of course, a major reason for the losses. Nevertheless, raiding provided the Anzacs with valuable experience of fighting the Germans, who probably suffered even greater losses. Against that, the level of tension among the Australians and New Zealanders rose as such operations were very stressful, made worse by the number undertaken by the Corps. The opening of the infantry assault phase of the Somme offensive saw no let up on the raiding. Between 30 June–1 July and 2–3 July, the 1 Anzac Corps mounted four more raids before this intense episode was concluded.

None of these raids was on the same scale as the 29–30 June operation. Perhaps the most effective and best executed raid of this period was that carried out on the night of 1–2 July by 144 men and four officers of the 9th Battalion, 3rd Australian Infantry Brigade. This was against a position held by the 21st Reserve Infantry Regiment south of Fleurbaix and north-east of a kink in the line known as the Sugar Loaf Salient. It was led by Captain Maurice Wilder-Neligan, a pugnacious and fearless soldier. Unlike all the other raids mounted by the Anzacs at this time, there was no preliminary artillery shoot to subdue the enemy. Indeed, the approach and assault were silent operations in which stealth was the key factor. Medium trench mortars cut the wire and a diversionary artillery bombardment was fired on the German line some 450 yards away on the right flank of the raiders' objective to deceive the Germans about the intended target.

Given the lack of artillery support and the size of the raiding party, the planning had to be meticulous and the execution precise. The Germans had a machine-gun position in the Sugar Loaf Salient and it was particularly troublesome. The silencing of this gun was the principle objective of the raid. The raiders were divided into three parties and the intention was for each party to hit the German line at the same time at three points 200 yards apart. The purpose of this separation was to minimise the effect of enfilade on the raiders. The left party of forty-six was commanded by Lieutenant H.T. Young, the centre party of fifty-eight was commanded by Lieutenant J.P. Ramkema and the right party of forty-six was commanded by Captain C.E. Benson, the overall commander being Wilder-Neligan, who was aided by a small headquarters group comprising two runners and two telephonists so that he could keep contact with his subordinates as well as with the brigade commander, Lieutenant-Colonel Robertson.

The composition of the parties included twelve different roles from bombers, bayonet men and ladder men to men assigned to cut wire and experts in machine-guns (see Table 1). The 'salvage men' had the task of locating and bringing back enemy arms and equipment, while the 'mat men' carried wire-crossing mats. Ladders made the task of exiting the enemy trench easier than would otherwise be possible. As on other raids, telephone line was laid as the raiders crossed no man's land but it was always vulnerable to shell fire, hence the precaution of having men specifically tasked with carrying messages. The experts in machine-guns were there to deal with the German guns when they had been captured.

The mats were always of questionable value when it came to their principle function, namely to help men cross barbed wire obstacles. In many ways, they were more of an encumbrance than an aid. But they did come in very useful in one unintended way. When it came to bringing back captured equipment, especially heavy items such as trench mortars, machine-guns and their mountings, the mats were invaluable as they enabled the equipment to be dragged rather than manhandled, which was a much more difficult task. In this operation, a captured machine-gun and its mounting was recovered in this way.

Table 1: Composition of raiding parties for enterprise against Sugar Loaf Salient

	Left party	*Centre party*	*Right party*
Bayonet men	7	11	7
Blocking men	6	4	5
Bombers	8	14	8
Engineers	1	1	1
Ladder men	2	2	2
Machine-gun experts	1	1	1
Mat men	4	4	4
Runners	2	2	2
Salvage men	8	10	7
Telephonists	2	4	2
Wire cutters	4	4	4 (+ 2 reserve)

The date and time of the operation was not revealed to those taking part until they were actually proceeding to the start line in the evening of 1 July. They were told they were about to undertake a final rehearsal but when they were taken by bus to 'an old house near the firing line' they realised this was no practice run. Hitherto, of course, all rehearsals had been undertaken behind the lines over ground that replicated the terrain they would be crossing on the operation and the layout of the trench they were to attack. Their faces were blackened and each man was given a piece of chewing gum.[5] Chewing the gum stimulated saliva and hence prevented a dry mouth, which could lead to coughing and give them away. Absolute silence during the approach was essential.

The Australians had already dug a sap towards the Sugar Loaf but away from the intended target. Not surprisingly, the Germans detected the sap and inspected it but they made no attempt to disrupt its construction. On the afternoon preceding the raid, medium trench mortars fired on the wire in front of the sap and in the evening the artillery shelled that part of the German line to deceive the Germans who knew something was afoot. This part of the line was not the objective, of course. As the bombardment got underway, the raiders set out for their objective. It took the three parties 90 minutes to get approximately halfway across no man's land, 200 yards from their target. It was now 12.45 am. Two Australian Vickers machine-guns now opened up, not so to provide fire support but to make a lot of noise in order that any sound made by the approaching raiders would be masked by the gunfire. It took the raiders another 90 minutes to move forward another 100 yards, which brought them up to the wire, which was already cut.

The raiders now advanced another 50 yards. While the left-hand party got through the wire without hindrance both of the others experienced varying degrees of difficulty. By 2.00 am the centre party had lost touch with Wilder-Neligan, the raid commander. However, the three parties escaped detection. Wilder-Neligan now gave the signal, by telephone, to the artillery and machine-guns to fire a support barrage and thereby isolate the target from the German rear and flanks. Within 30 seconds, the machine-guns were firing on the flanks and 90 seconds later the artillery began hitting the areas behind the raiders' objective. As this fire support came down, the raiders stood up and rushed the last 50 yards to the German trench. The bombers led the way over the parapet. By 2.12 am, all three parties were in the trench. The raiders were immediately involved in heavy fighting.

The fighting had started before the Australians even reached the trench. Wilder-Neligan had come upon an observation post occupied by three Germans. He shot two of them but the third threw a grenade at him. Wilder-Neligan was seriously injured by grenade fragments, which hit him in head and upper torso. Despite these injuries, he remained in command of the operation throughout and was awarded the Distinguished Service Order for his action. The fighting in the German trench followed in the same vein. An unexpected consequence of the artillery bombardment further down the line, which was intended to fool the Germans about the intended target of the Australian operation, was that those troops who should have been manning that part of the line being bombarded sought refuge by moving down the trenches to what they thought was a safer location but what, in fact, turned out to be the target of the Australian raid. Hence, the trenches were full of Germans, far more than might have been expected to be present in a front-line trench at night.

Meanwhile, the left-hand party pushed the Germans in that section of the line towards the centre, bombing and bayoneting their way along until they reached one of the machine-guns that had been causing the Australians so much trouble before the raid. Private D. Mahoney disposed of the crew with grenades. The gun was manhandled over the parapet and brought back to the Australian line along with its mounting using one of the wire-crossing mats. Ramkema's party discovered a dugout holding twenty-one Germans who fired at the raiders but every shot missed. Ramkema fired his revolver into the dugout and killed several Germans, then demanded that the rest surrender. They did and with the assistance of Sergeant Kenyon he 'drove the 15 towards the Australian line'. The prisoners tried to resist and four of them were shot dead for their trouble. Eleven prisoners eventually made it to the Australian trenches.

The right-hand party led by Benson managed to get into the German trenches entirely undetected. They immediately set about the enemy, killing a large number of them and capturing four. Benson was killed as he helped two wounded raiders out of the German position. Among the three parties there were seven Australian fatalities and a further twenty-six were wounded, most of these occurring during the furious 5 minutes of fighting that took place once the raiders entered the enemy positions. All but two of the dead were recovered. One badly wounded man was left behind and he was subsequently made a prisoner. These three casualties provided the Germans with the identification of their attackers. The Australian incursion had been brief but ferocious. The 7th Company of the 21st Reserve Infantry Regiment took the force of the raid. The Australians left behind at least fourteen dead from this company – the raiders claimed more than fifty Germans had been killed in the operation – and another forty Germans were wounded. They captured twenty-one although the 21st Reserve Infantry Regiment reckoned to have lost another four. These may have been killed as they were not taken prisoner.

On the night following the successful raid on the 21st Reserve Infantry Regiment, 2–3 July, the 11th Battalion of the 3rd Australian Infantry Brigade carried out a much smaller raid on a position known as The Tadpole, near Cordonniere. This was perhaps the antithesis of the earlier larger raid since the preparatory artillery bombardment completely destroyed the trenches held by the same Bavarian regiment and killed all but one of the garrison, who, having survived the onslaught, was unlucky to be bayoneted by the raiders. Hence, there were no survivors from whom to take prisoners. In all, at least thirty-eight, perhaps as many as fifty, Germans were killed in the bombardment. Not surprisingly, the raiders suffered no loss in the enterprise. Curiously, the German regimental report of this raid described the action in quite different terms and called it:

> a renewed enemy enterprise against the 7th and 8th Companies, again very well prepared by artillery. On account of their experience of the day before, these companies were already prepared, and inflicted on the enemy a bloody repulse, although not without loss to themselves.

Clearly, they failed to recognise the operation for what it was, a raid.

On the same night as this Australian operation, the Wellington Battalion of the 2nd New Zealand Infantry Brigade raided positions south of Frelinghein. Unlike the Australian raid, in which sixty-two other ranks and five officers took part, the New Zealanders' raiding party was the strength of half a company, some 104 men led by four officers. The raid was something of a disaster and resulted in the deaths of twelve of the raiders, a further thirty-six of them being wounded and five of their number becoming prisoners. Three of the four officers became casualties. It is evident that the Germans were anticipating the attack and were well prepared for it. Not only had they evacuated the target trench but they had blocked it so that the raiders were contained within it. The preliminary bombardment of the German positions occurred a mere 10 minutes before the raiders attacked but had no effect because of the German preparations. The moment the raiders began crossing no man's land they were engaged by rifle fire. When they did manage to get into the German trench they were trapped. The Germans threw large numbers of grenades at them from behind the barricades they had constructed as well as from support trenches. The raid commander, Lieutenant H.J.D. Sheldon, ordered a retreat. As the surviving raiders escaped through a narrow gap in the wire, the Germans continued to throw grenades at them.

Whether these raids, and others like them carried out by the three Armies not involved in the Somme offensive, achieved the object of wearing down the enemy or deceived him about where the Allied offensive was going to take place is questionable. It is also doubtful that German morale was in any way lowered by such raids. Too often, the Germans knew about the operation because they had noticed the preparations and correctly interpreted them for what they were. They were also well aware of the forthcoming offensive. The defenders then gave the raiders a bloody reception. During the last week of June, the BEF carried out thirty-eight raids while the Germans only mounted six. A raid by B Company of the 2nd–4th Oxfordshire and Buckinghamshire Light Infantry was carried out on the night of 29 June. It failed because of uncut wire and unsubdued German machine-guns. Eleven of the raiders were killed.

Raids mounted by the Fourth Army on the frontage of the forthcoming offensive immediately prior to 1 July certainly provided useful information about the effectiveness of the artillery bombardment on the German wire and trenches. From these, it became apparent that the results of the bombardment varied enormously along the enemy line, from complete destruction of wire and trenches in some places to practically no impact on either wire or trenches in others. Indeed, some raids failed because the wire was intact and could not be penetrated by the raiders, while on other occasions they failed because the trenches were too well defended by troops who occupied undamaged positions. On the night of 25–26 June, the Fourth Army carried out four raids.

> North-east of Carnoy, the 18th Division found the enemy trenches empty and much damaged; north of Maricourt the 30th Division found them lightly held, but captured only one prisoner; south of La Boisselle, the 34th Division found them strongly held and failed to get in; opposite Ovillers, too, the 8th Division reported the trenches full of men, but managed to capture one prisoner.

On the nights preceding the infantry assault by the Fourth Army, the other three Armies carried out many raids. The Third Army mounted twelve, the First fourteen, and the Second seventeen. Seven of the latter were carried out by the I Anzac Corps. In nearly every raid, the Germans were alert and met the raiders with grenades and rifle fire. Casualties were consequently high. It was that kind of price that raised questions then and subsequently about the value of raiding.

Chapter 7

The Kensingtons – A Farce in Diverse Acts

The Kensingtons (1st/13th London Regiment) landed in France on 4 November 1914, and soon afterwards took up positions in the British line near Estaires. The Battalion participated in the Battle of Neuve Chapelle in March 1915 as well as the attack on Gommecourt at the start of the Somme on 1 July 1916. Not only did the Kensingtons have battle experience but they had done much front-line service in the trenches before they carried out their first raid. This took place a fortnight after the bloody fighting at Gommecourt.

The raid was against enemy positions near Hébuterne. It was something of 'a tall order' to undertake the raid 'so soon after their experience on that day', by which was meant the attack on Gommecourt. Nevertheless, the men chosen to undertake the raid were happy to do so. Accordingly, the battalion's 'best bombers' were selected and the operation was carefully planned and rehearsed. The night of the raid was exceptionally dark, 'the night having fallen like a thick black blanket,' in the words of the Battalion's war diarist. And it had begun to drizzle, which did nothing to improve matters. The raiders reached the laying-up point beside the German wire without incident, lay down along it and awaited the signal to attack.

Unfortunately, as they waited, something spooked a German sentry and he threw a grenade towards where the raiders lay concealed by the darkness. The thrower was luckier than he ought to have been because the grenade landed where one of the Battalion's officers was lying. Luckily for him, the time-fuzed grenade thrown by the German arrived in front of the officer before its fuze had burned down to the detonator and not only did he have the presence of mind to pick up the grenade before it exploded but he had time to make the conscious choice to throw it further in same the direction in which the German had tossed it in the first place. It exploded harmlessly. As the German got not reply in the form of a few Mills, he evidently decided nothing was amiss and he took no further action. It had been a close call.

After this narrow escape, the supporting bombardment opened up and although it was not heavy, it appeared to do the job of hitting the enemy parapet. However, the Germans responded by firing trench mortars in salvoes on the area in which the raiders were waiting. Clearly, they suspected a raid. Some artillery also began firing and a machine-gun joined in, all shooting across or into the same area. While this caused the raiders a great deal of concern, they escaped injury. The intensity of the bombardment on the raiders became too much and it was perfectly obvious that they stood no chance of even reaching the enemy trenches let alone completing the operation without serious loss. The raid was abandoned. One NCO was not content by this outcome, however, and went in search of the enemy with a hobnailed trench club, well suited to a handy brawler. He returned safely, having found what he was looking for.

This first raid by the battalion was more of an object lesson in how not to carry out a successful raid although, in all fairness, the Germans were clearly alert to the possibility of a raid and had made appropriate arrangements to deal with any attempted incursion. In this, the enemy was successful as the raid was driven off. The next raid by the Kensingtons was not much better than the first. As the war diarist recorded after the event 'in its execution became more of a comedy than anything else'. This raid was an ad hoc affair carried out 'on the Laventie front' – part of the line held by the First Army – which the diarist rather laconically referred to as 'that "home from home"' because the battalion had been stationed there before.[1]

The raid was the pet project of one (unnamed) but well-known officer who had a reputation for 'harebrained tendencies'. The objective of the raid was to put a stop to the:

> nightly peregrinations of a certain bearded old 'dug-out' whose special job it was to go to certain points along the enemy front line to fire a Very Light and pull a string which was connected to all the MGs on his front.

The raiders included a covering party, a Lewis gun section, who had to set up their gun in a swampy piece of ground in front of a ruined house. Needless to say, they were not very happy about it. The assault party made its way towards the enemy trenches, negotiating paths through great masses of old wire that was in considerable disrepair. These were not freshly made paths but had come about over time. One NCO became lost. Indeed, he had been running rather than walking cautiously. The consequence was that he fell into the wire and became trapped in it, held fast by its barbs. However, no one went to his aid and he was left to his own devices. He continued to call out for several hours without anyone taking any notice. Luckily for him, no German took a shot at him, either, no machine-gun fire came his way and no enemy patrol found him. Eventually, he pulled himself free and made his way back to the British line, none the worse for his ordeal. Afterwards, 'When asked why he had been running he explained that the vision of Raiders' Rum, which he was afraid of losing had urged him on'. Desperation drives men to strange acts.

The rest of the small raiding party reached their objective without incident. They crept stealthily through the mire up to the enemy parapet and waited for the signal to go, then jumped into the German trench only to land on a mat of wire. The mat was not so much intended to keep out raiders – this party still found their way into the trench – but to prevent hostile grenades from landing in the trench. Having found their way into the trench, the raiders proceeded to explore it and found various dugouts and shelters and a machine-gun emplacement. The latter they 'salted' with explosive charges they had brought with them and ran a fuze out into the open. They withdrew to a safe distance to light the fuze[2], only to realise one of their number was missing (besides the errant NCO). Moments later, he came hurrying towards them. As he reached them he called out in a whisper, 'There he comes!' (presumably the bearded object of the officer's ire that had led to the raid) and trod on the burning end of the fuze, promptly extinguishing it. For reasons that were not made clear in the subsequent account, no one in the party seemed to possess another means of re-igniting the fuze so that put 'an end to the blowing up business'. The raiders threw two grenades at the approaching 'he' and immediately withdrew. Whether the bearded German was hit or dissuaded from further peregrinations was not explained. So ended an absurd charade of a raid, not so much a military operation as a caper from *The Boy's Own Paper*.

While the next raid undertaken by the battalion was a much more serious affair, luck still did not favour the 1st/13th Londons. This operation was against German positions near the Mauquissart Crater in the region of Neuve Chapelle. A Company commanded by Captain Clarke undertook this endeavour some time after the abortive raid against the bearded German.[3] It was mounted at a time when quite deep snow lay on the ground so the raiders were issued with snow suits to prevent their khaki uniforms from standing out against the snow. The company practised the raid over a replica of the trenches they would be attacking and were well prepared by the night of the operation. They raiders made their way out into no man's land to await the preparatory artillery bombardment, which had long since become the customary tactic for raids.

Almost as soon the British artillery opened up, the Germans responded with a counter-bombardment while the German troops facing the raiders and on their flanks opened up with rifle and machine-gun fire across the area of no man's land occupied by the raiders. They stood little chance of reaching the enemy parapet let alone getting into the front trenches. Nevertheless, the bombers among them evidently gave a good account of themselves. One NCO lost his life on his third attempt to get into the trench, killed right on the parapet. The raiders had to admit defeat and withdraw without achieving anything. They were harassed by gunfire the whole time as they recrossed no man's land. This did not let up when they reached their own lines and rifle fire followed them up their own communication trenches. Luckily, the Germans were poor shots and few casualties resulted.

All their efforts came to naught. Indeed, they were almost comical in their ineptitude, a parody of raiding devised and presented by Fred Karno's Army.[4] No element of their three raids could be described as anything but failure. The Kensingtons did not attempt another night raid until almost the end of the war. Instead, their next raid was a daylight operation. Now, at last, fortune began to favour them and their daytime enterprises were much more successful. The first of these was against 200 yards of German trenches at Windy Corner at Neuve Chapelle. This was the largest daylight raid undertaken so far by the division and was carried out by 150 officers and men of the Kensingtons.

The morning of the raid dawned misty and the raiders took advantage of the unexpected weather conditions to take up their jumping-off points in no man's land. The supporting bombardment hit the German front trenches as the raiders again moved forward in the mist. When they reached the jumping-off point, the bombardment lifted to the German support lines and flanks. By this time,[5] British infantry were being trained to get as close to barrages as possible to help them win the race to the enemy parapet before the Germans could get out of their dugouts and shelters and defend their trench as the bombardment lifted. With the creeping barrage introduced in 1916, infantry were expected to follow very close behind it for the same reason. There was some risk of being hit by friendly fire if they got too close but most of the explosive force and shell fragments went forwards in the direction of the shell trajectory rather than backwards so it was possible to get closer than prudence might suggest. However, on this occasion, one of the raiders was unfortunate to be hit by fragments from a British shell.

Almost as soon as the bombardment lifted, the raiders were in the German trench. They proceeded along it, bay by bay, but without meeting many Germans. Six were found in a concrete dugout, their arms and equipment hanging off the exterior of the structure. A couple of grenades thrown into the shelter persuaded the surviving four to come out and surrender. After collecting up the papers from the dugout, they were examined in the trench but found to be inconsequential. Then, a group of the raiders had a narrow escape when one of them dropped a Mills grenade from which the pin had been removed. A corporal quickly picked it up and tossed it over the parapet. It exploded without doing any harm a couple of seconds later.[6] That, too, was a lucky escape that took a cool head to bring off.

While one party of raiders dealt with the front trench, a second party made its way to the support trench but failed to reach it before the signal to withdraw was heard (a bugle call). When the raiders reached the British line, they did not stop but continued all the way back to the support line, moving above ground rather than along trenches, in anticipation of a German counter-bombardment on the British front trenches timed to coincide with their return. This precaution prevented any casualties arising from the German shells. A curious postscript to the raid was the squad drilling a warrant officer gave to the four German prisoners after they had been escorted to Battalion HQ. When they failed to execute his barked-out orders – clearly, they did not understand English – the warrant officer was beside himself with anger and nearly laid them out with his fists.

While it is unclear whether the Kensingtons undertook many other raids, daytime or at night, during the rest of the war, they undertook at least one more raid before the war ended. This was in the spring of 1918, the time of the German offensives. The operation was at Oppy, north of Arras. The enterprise was very similar to the raid they had carried out at Neuve Chapelle a couple of years earlier. The raiding party was limited to only fifty, including two buglers and two officers. The raiders were sent to the British camp at Roclincourt to rehearse the operation over replica trenches. The rest of the battalion were told they were 'a working party' but it is doubtful this rather pointless ruse fooled anyone. Aerial reconnaissance photographs provided detailed up-to-date information about the enemy positions. At the same time the raiders were learning and practising, the artillery was cutting the wire in a gradual and random progression intended to avoid alerting the Germans. In case the Germans noticed the damage that was being done to their wire and sent out repair parties to deal with it, several Lewis gun sections were positioned in no man's land, which, at that time, was covered in long grass. By the time of the raid, the wire had been almost completely destroyed.

It was inevitable that the Germans would notice how damaged their wire was becoming as the artillery progressed with its work. Over the last three or four nights preceding the raid, the Germans grew increasingly nervous and constantly fired off flares throughout the hours of darkness. Their sense of safety seemed to return with the dawn and they were far less vigilant during the day than they were during the night. By this stage of the war, daylight raids were not uncommon so the Germans had no reason to assume that any assault on their trenches would happen at night.

The raiders arrived in their own front trench several hours before zero hour, which was set at 6.45 am. They slept for those hours so that they would be fresh for the operation. At 6.40 am the raiders were in position. In the meantime, the artillery was bombarding the German line about a quarter of a mile away. Not one shell was fired at the raid objective. At 6.45 am, the raiders moved off in two parties and complete silence, the long grass of no man's land helping to hide them from any Germans opposite who might have been looking out over their parapet. One party reached the enemy parapet quickly without a shot being fired. As the second party crossed a communication trench, they were seen by the crew of a machine-gun in the German support line and they opened fire. The gun was silenced by the return fire from the second party's Lewis gun. Before it was silenced, however, the machine-gun hit three of the raiders, three of the four casualties suffered in the raid.

The second party worked its way to the rear of the front trench, then, in unison, the two parties closed in on the Germans in the front trench and cleared it using grenades in cooperation with bayonet men, riflemen and the Lewis gunners. Tactically, this was a well-established procedure by this stage of the war. The bayonet men advanced along the trench ahead of the bombers who worked both in the trench and above ground on the flanks to deal with more serious opposition than the bayonet men could cope with on their own. This was an all-arms tactical system in which all the infantrymen involved had the training and skills to undertake any of the tasks, from bomber to bayonet man. The notion of a specialist bomber who only threw grenades had gone out the previous year. Now, every infantryman was trained in the use of grenades, specifically the Mills No. 5 and the Mills No. 23, an improved version of the No. 5. The bombers' task was not so much to kill the enemy as in 1915 and 1916, but to force him into the killing zone of the riflemen and Lewis gunners.

The raiders took four prisoners, who were sent back to the British line as quickly as possible, then the signal to withdraw was blown by one of the buglers and:

> the whole party vanished as if by magic. The whole business was over in seven and a half minutes from start to finish, including the fetching back of the wounded men and the settling up with about 25 of the enemy.

There was one other casualty besides those shot by the machine-gunner, a fatality. An NCO tried to carry the dead man back but he was too heavy and the ground too broken so the attempt had to be abandoned. A great deal of useful intelligence was gathered by the raiders and from interrogation of the prisoners. A forthcoming German attack was comprised by this intelligence so that, when it came three weeks later, the British were prepared for it. This well illustrated just how useful a raid could be.

The battalion mounted one more raid before the war ended. This was carried out on 1 June 1918 at Arras by C Company against a German division astride the Cambrai Road in front of Estaminet Corner at Tilloy. The German offensives had not yet ended and the Allied counter-offensives had yet to start. Although the German advance had been severely blunted by the end of May, they had not been halted. At Arras, the lines had not changed much because it was at a hinge in the German advance. No man's land was several hundred yards wide at Arras and, at Tilloy, contained several abandoned trenches and gun pits that had fallen into disrepair. Active patrolling by C Company allowed the Kensingtons to reconnoitre these disused trenches and the enemy listening posts in no man's land over a long period. From their awareness of the derelict trenches, came the idea for a raid. Nearer the date of the operation, aerial reconnaissance and 'ground observers' kept a constant watch on these old positions and the listening posts.

The reason for the interest in the disused trenches and pits was simple. The company intended to use them as the jumping-off points for the raid. On 31 May, the company went out to these positions and waited. The company also set up a headquarters, including signallers, linked by telephone to the British line. Unlike nearly every other raid by this stage of the war, the raiders used only their knowledge of the enemy line from patrolling as a guide for the operation. They did not practise the operation over a replica of the ground. Indeed, they did not practise it all. While this may have looked like a risky approach to adopt, especially in light of their raiding history, in practise, it prevented early detection of the raid – German reconnaissance flights could photograph the practise ground from which the target could be determined by skilled interpretation – and preserved the element of surprise. Surprise was helped by the poor state of the enemy wire so that the artillery did not need to cut it.

For about 24 hours, the 100 men of C Company lay up in no man's land and remained as quiet as possible to avoid detection. They succeeded because the Germans never realised they were there. Zero hour was just after dusk on 1 June. Two minutes before that moment, 'the enemy started one of his storms of whizz-bangs[7] and for that short time everyone's heart was hammering at the top of his throat'. This bombardment was not in response to the impending raid, however, but a regular, if random, occurrence: it did not follow a timetable. Nevertheless, it was a potential threat to the raiders although, fortunately, none of the shells were aimed at no man's land.

The operation went well. The raiding parties reached their objectives by separate routes without incident, then worked their way up the trenches. In the meantime, they were given machine-gun support, which saturated the flanks and German support lines. Significantly, the emphasis on grenades for working up a trench was no longer evident in the tactical scheme taught to British troops. Rather, the prominence of the bayonet men now stood out as the vanguard of an attack, as was the case in this raid. Grenades were now only a resort when all else failed. The fighting, as ever, was fierce but over very quickly. Some thirty prisoners were taken, some of them surrendering very readily, while the raiders suffered fewer than twenty casualties. Several dugouts and two machine-gun emplacements were destroyed. One of the Lewis guns fired off 'nearly 700 rounds without a stoppage', a fairly unusual occurrence since the Lewis was prone to stoppages. On the signal to withdraw, the raiders returned to the disused trenches and gun pits in no man's land and awaited the German retaliatory bombardment to hit the British front trenches, which were unoccupied in anticipation. Once the shelling had ceased, they returned to the British line.

The raiding experience of the Kensingtons was not a microcosm of the experience of the many small enterprises carried out by the BEF as a whole during the course of the war. While some of the Kensingtons' more absurd exploits were due to lack of expertise in the planning and tactical execution of small enterprises and may have been unique to them in the detail of the debacles, nevertheless, such failures were a wider phenomenon and not limited to one battalion. The Fred Karno element of one or two of the Kensingtons' raids was to be found in other raids carried out by other enthusiastic thrusters in other battalions. And there was a darker side to that comedy. Some individuals went out into no man's land after dark to conduct almost private wars of their own.

Success or failure of such an enterprise did not, of course, depend on only one side in the business. Well-prepared and well-executed attacks tended to favour the attacker in these enterprises but well-prepared defenders who executed a well-practised defence to small-scale incursion could easily defeat an otherwise good raid and make it bloody for both sides.

More importantly, perhaps, the way in which raids were executed as the war progressed reflected the changing tactical skills required of infantrymen within an all-arms tactical team or platoon. The raiders of 1915 and, indeed, 1916, often showed a *Boy's Own* approach, whereas by late 1917 and in 1918, greater tactical skill was applied as a matter of course so that the enthusiastic extemporised enterprise was no longer even considered.

From this point of view, the experience of the Kensingtons offers an insight into the changing perception of the raid as a military tactic, a change that began in the second half of 1916. Although raiding had long since acquired approval from GHQ, it was not until the Somme and its aftermath that raiding acquired a more cold-blooded strategy. Nevertheless, it had been heading that way since the beginning of the year. While the Somme offensive continued – it ended in November 1916 – raiding was less actively pursued but as the campaign wore itself out, raiding was taken up again with renewed aggression.

Chapter 8

Operation *Wilhelm* –
A German Raid, July 1916

On 19 July 1916, the 229th Reserve Infantry Regiment carried out a raid against a small salient in the British line, known to the Germans as the Bastion, near Rue du Bois. It was held by the 2nd Battalion New Zealand Rifle Brigade. This salient extended 140 yards out from the rest of the line and was approximately 250 yards wide at its base. No man's land in front of the head of the salient was 100 yards deep, while on the flank on which the German raid took place it was 250 yards deep. By pure chance, the raid took place 500 yards down the line from a section of the German line raided 2 hours earlier by the New Zealand Division, who had hit the 229th's neighbours, the 231st Reserve Infantry Regiment, leaving behind thirty-three German dead. Unlike the New Zealanders' raid, however, the German operation was far less successful. At the time, it no doubt served as an object lesson to the Germans on how not to plan and execute a raid.

At 11.15 pm, two parties of raiders from the 229th attempted to get into the New Zealanders' trenches in the salient. The northern party succeeded but withdrew almost immediately, leaving two of their number dead and another wounded. They also left twelve demolition charges and a lot of their equipment. They were in and out before a counter-attack could be mounted by the New Zealanders, of whom one was killed, three were wounded and another three were missing. According to the German report of the action, the raiders took seven prisoners but five were shot when they 'ran away or would not accompany their captors'. The southern party faired less well. They were denied access to the salient by the New Zealanders, who fought them off with grenades.

Orders for the raid were sent out by 50th Division HQ on 12 July, giving a week's notice of the operation. The orders did not set the date for the raid or even the target trench to be raided, leaving such details to the judgement of the 229th Reserve Infantry Regiment to whom the orders were sent. The orders also left the size of the raiding party to the discretion of the regiment. Indeed, no aspect of the proposed raid was defined by the orders. In effect, the orders merely stated that a raid was required and instructed the regiment to organise it according to their own expectations and knowledge of the enemy trenches opposite them. Neither the purpose of the raid nor the particular reason it was required at that time was made clear. Once the regiment had planned its operation, a detailed written proposal was to be submitted to 50th Division HQ. Strict secrecy was required so that no mention of it was to be made on the telephone[1] and the other regiments in the division would only be informed on a need-to-know basis.

Two days after receipt of the orders, a written proposal for a raid was sent to the divisional HQ. The author of the proposal set out, item by item, the details of the proposed operation. This was not, of course, the definitive plan and so far no operational order had been issued. The submitted proposal included the request for a 'conference ... on the 14th, at 5 pm, at regimental headquarters, at which will be present the commander of Artillery Group I, the commander of Engineer Company No. 15. The commander of the Trench Mortar Company and the officers concerned of the regiment.'

The scheme worked out by the regiment set out the time and date of the raid, its size as well as the specific target and the timetable of the whole operation. The scheme also detailed the objectives, a tactical requirement on which division had left to the regiment to decide, although the objectives had to receive divisional approval before the operation could go ahead. 'The regiment suggests the night of the 19–20th of this month for the raid; it is going to be relieved on the night of the 20th–21st'. That the raid should have been set so close to the relief of the regiment by another seems rather poor planning on the part of divisional HQ. Should a postponement have become necessary for whatever reason, the raid would have had to have been cancelled. In addition, being so close to a relief, the raid would have been treated with a lot less enthusiasm than might otherwise have been the case. That sort of thing did nothing to help promote morale.

Regiment proposed that the raid should be made by a party comprising 'three officers, twelve non-commissioned officers and forty men' from the infantry and 'one officer, three non-commissioned officers and fifteen men' from the engineers.

Proposed Course: From 10.40 pm to 11.30 pm shooting of artillery and trench-mortars for effect; from 10.55 to 11 pm cease fire on the front and support trenches. The object of this pause is, that if the enemy holds the front trench lightly only, he will, on the cessation of fire, occupy the front and support trenches in expectation of attack, and thus suffer heavy losses when bombardment is resumed.

That was the theory. It was certainly true that by this stage of the war it was becoming common practice not to hold the front or fire trenches in strength because that way casualties were minimised in a bombardment. It was more common among German regiments than British battalions in 1916. Whether troops would immediately rush forward to take up positions in the front trenches when a bombardment ended in anticipation of an assault was something of a gamble on the part of the Germans, however, as they had little evidence to support the assumption the troops opposite them would do that on this occasion. A successful counter-attack to an incursion was not so easily mounted if the front positions were reoccupied then pounded by artillery and overrun in an immediate assault. There was every likelihood that the New Zealanders would remain in the support line until the German intentions were clear, preparing for a counter-attack.

That the objective of the raid was not given to the regiment by divisional HQ but left to the regiment to propose was not the usual way of proceeding in the German Army any more than it was in the BEF. While battalions might offer unsolicited suggestions about suitable targets for a raid because of local knowledge of a specific situation or problem, division did not merely order a raid on some unspecified target, without providing at least a desirous objective. The 50th Division HQ seems to have arbitrarily ordered it. In none of the orders or subsequent reports of the action was any clue provided about the reasoning behind 50th Division's order. The objectives the 229th Reserve Infantry Regiment proposed in the submission to divisional HQ was to 'Search for possible presence of gas cylinders, signs of mining, take prisoners, capture material. The party will return after remaining 15 minutes in the enemy trenches.' The proposal also set out the geographical limitations of the objective. However, none of these objectives was in the least specific to this salient. Indeed, the notion of gas cylinders or mining in such a tiny area of ground was, frankly, ridiculous, as the authors of the proposal were no doubt aware. The list of objectives looks very much like the response to an examination question: set out the objectives of a raid.

The suggested codename for the operation was *Wilhelm*. This carried a hint of irony that seems to have escaped divisional HQ as the name was approved. It was also adopted as the password for the operation.

German bureaucracy and the randomness of the order to carry out the raid were all too readily expressed in the way divisional staff then interfered with the proposal and subsequent plans for the artillery shoot to support the operation. It is evident that the fussing over irrelevant details by the staff irritated Oberleutnant Werner, who took part in the raid and wrote an after-action report, as well as others in the regiment. One of the criticisms by the staff was the high officer to other ranks ratio. In short, there were too many officers and not enough men. The regiment was forced against its better judgement to increase the size of the raiding party by another twenty men, that is, half as many again. This was not only pointless, because there was no operational justification for the increase, but it made the party less manageable and, hence, made it more vulnerable to being compromised on the night.

The staff insisted on several other unnecessary changes to which, for the sake of peace and quiet, the regiment acquiesced. One of the more absurd issues with which the staff interested itself was how the raiders would be dressed for the operation. While some elements of how raiders dressed for an operation were always of some importance, the question of whether the raiders wore a white armband for the purposes of identifying friend from foe in the dark should have been easily settled. However, the staff seemed unable to recall their earlier directives so that they ended up contradicting themselves, first stating none should be worn, then stating one should be. Regiment informed the staff, in writing, that as of the 14 July, the staff had already stipulated that the raiders should have:

> No white armband, but a white cotton band, to be obtained from the regimental engineers post; cap, no shoulder straps, hand-grenades, wire-cutters, shovels, trench clubs, pistols, dagger, electric torch. Everyone will chose the weapon he prefers.

The list of weapons from which the raiders might choose according to their own preference shows how trench fighting was very close and brutal. What is missing from this list, of course, was that most essential of tools, the fixed bayonet. The Germans did not share the British love of the fixed bayonet although there is no doubt that it was very much a decider in trench fighting. Used with skill and determination, it was much more effective than clubs or daggers and far more intimidating. The inclusion of shovels in the list was not indicative that the raiders should dig during the operation. On the contrary, the shovel was used in the manner of an axe to cut down the enemy.

The divisional staff wanted the raiders to assign one officer to the task of examining and making notes on the British trenches: 'an officer should be detailed to examine minutely the condition of the enemy's position'. The regiment was unimpressed with divisional HQ's notion that such a complex task could be carried out by one officer. The regiment responded by stating that:

> Four infantry officers have been specifically instructed to examine the condition of the enemy's trenches. The regiment believes that such a task is too much for one officer alone, and if he became a casualty, the execution of the task would not be ensured.

Clearly, regiment did not have a high opinion of the abilities of the staff officers at 50th Division HQ but had no choice but to listen to their instructions. It is evident that the staff had little idea of the practicalities of trench raiding.

The pre-raid conference was held on the date requested by the raid planners and all those required to attend did so. The issue of how the artillery should support the raid was an important one since a raid succeeded or failed according to the effectiveness of the artillery support. The regiment would have preferred to have avoided a preliminary bombardment of the New Zealand positions because it gave warning of the impeding assault. However, as they were well aware and the artillery representative was at pains to emphasise, the enemy positions that were the target of the raid were too strong and too well wired for the raiders to attempt a stealthy silent approach with any expectation of success. Surprise would have to depend on hitting neighbouring sections of the British line with bombardments to deceive the New Zealanders and conceal the true target of the raid.

With these criteria in mind, the artillery fire plan had three main objectives. The first of these was the neutralisation of the New Zealanders in the target area of the salient and in the neighbouring sections of the line. The second objective was the neutralisation of the enemy's ability to hit back with machine-guns, trench mortars and artillery. And third was isolation of the trenches being raided from the support lines and flanks by means of a box barrage. At this period in the war, the German artillery was beginning to focus on neutralising the enemy's ability to fight rather than trying to destroy him utterly in a given location then overrun the position. The BEF was still very much wedded to the notion of destruction and would not fundamentally deviate from that policy for about another twelve months. However, whenever the British applied a box barrage to isolate German positions during a raid, the guns fired in more of a neutralising role than one of destruction. Nevertheless, the underlying doctrine in the British camp was that of destruction of the enemy, his materiel and his positions, whereas the Germans had abandoned that approach because they had found it to be unattainable. The weight of firepower that needed to be brought to bear in order to ensure destruction was unrealistic to achieve, whereas neutralisation was always an attainable goal.

The fireplan was set out in some detail by the artillery commander. If the artillery objectives were unachievable or simply unattained during the operation, the assault phase by the infantry and sappers would probably fail. Thus, the artillery held the key to a successful operation. The artillery orders were set out in considerable detail following the agreement on the three objectives for the raid and elucidated how the fireplan was to be carried out. The orders included the number of batteries and how the guns in those batteries were to be engaged during the operation and, hence, the numbers of rounds to be fired by each gun over a given period were also set out. The targets to be hit were allocated according to the batteries, ammunition and the stipulated rate of fire of the guns. A programme of fire was designed to accord with all the factors in the plan. Of all the elements of the raid, more planning and detail went into the artillery fireplan than into any other, reflecting its importance to the success of the operation.

A total of twenty-four field guns, twelve field howitzers, four 3.5-inch and eight 4.7-inch guns, four 5.9-inch howitzers and four Russian 8-inch guns were allocated to support the raid. The ammunition available for the operation included 2,000 rounds for the field guns, 1,150 for the field howitzers, 200 for the 3.5-inch, 200 for the 4.7-inch, 500 for the 5.9-inch and 50 for the 8-inch. These guns were arranged as one heavy howitzer battery, two light howitzer batteries, four field gun batteries, one battery of 3.6-inch guns, one battery of 4.7-inch guns and one battery of 8-inch howitzers. At least four targets were identified, not including the British trench mortar batteries and machine-guns. These were not going to be engaged unless they opened fire on the raiders, in which case, field batteries would engage them independently as they came into action. This implies two things. Firstly that the German artillery was short of ammunition and secondly that the locations of the mortars and machine-guns was not known with sufficient certainty to enable the field batteries to engage them before they opened fire and revealed themselves.

All the batteries were to open fire at 10.40 pm and shoot for 15 minutes. They would then remain silent for a further 5 minutes before recommencing firing, with the exception of the field guns and the 4.7-inch guns, which would continue firing and remain in action throughout. At 11.30 pm, all the guns would cease fire while the field guns lifted to new targets. The nature of the fire, that is to say the type of fuze fitted to the shells, was predominantly percussion (i.e. it detonated the shell on impact) so long as the shells were mostly high explosive. As soon as the emphasis changed to shrapnel for dealing with enemy patrols in no man's land who might pose a threat to the raiders the fuzes were time only. The time-fuzed shrapnel was not supposed to be fired until the cessation of the bombardment at 11.30pm. Neither was no man's land supposed to be fired on at any time during the operation, which rather hindered the use of shrapnel against enemy patrols which by their very nature would be in no man's land, although the caveat only applied to that part of no man's land directly in front of the objective of the raid.

Trench mortars, always indispensable to a raid, comprised one heavy, five medium and five light mortars. The heavy and mediums were used against the earthworks while the light mortars were employed in an anti-personnel role. The New Zealand front trench and the third support line about 100 yards to the rear were the main targets. These were to be hit between 10.45 pm and 11.20 pm with a 5-minute pause at 10.55 pm. A barrage line was to be established 300 yards to rear of the third trench line for 20 minutes starting at 11.25 pm. The point of this was to prevent reinforcements being brought up by the New Zealanders. None of these mortars had a high rate of fire although that was more than compensated by the weight of explosive dropped by the heavies in particular, far more than anything fired by the artillery. The heavies were to fire ten rounds, the mediums fifteen and the light mortars a hundred. Such figures reflected the rate of fire rather than the availability of the bombs they fired. In addition to the artillery and trench mortars, machine-guns would fire a barrage to prevent the New Zealanders following the raiders back into the German lines to create havoc, 'for the British on many occasions had excellently understood how to follow up returning raiders and get into our position without danger, where they then have an easy job'.

The raiders practised the operation over ground that replicated the bastion, their target. However, the regiment was initially undecided about 'whether the raiders should go over the top in a closed body or dispersed, and whether the advance should be made in a skirmish line, single rank or in a "crowd"'. These questions arose because of the influence of the developing stormtroop tactics in which raiders infiltrated forwards as a dispersed group. These raiders were not trained stormtroopers, however. Hence, the regiment decided that the raiders should proceed to the bastion in two groups, each party to attack a flank of the bastion simultaneously but for the party leaders to make the final decisions concerning how each group should proceed across no man's land.

Four days prior to the date set for the raid, the regimental order for the operation was issued. This differed in some details from the original proposal because of the amendments to the operational plan introduced by divisional HQ. The artillery fireplan was essentially unchanged from what had been discussed at the earlier conference:

Shooting for effect 10.40 to 11.30 pm. From 10.55 to 11 pm there will be a pause in the fire on the front and second trench of the Bastion. At 11.30 pm fire will be lifted so far forward and sideways that the sectors of attack are free from fire.

Shortly before 11.30 pm No Man's Land right and left of the sectors of attack will be cleared of any enemy patrols by time-fuze fire.

Care is to be taken that any enemy trench mortars and machine-guns which may try to enfilade the raid are immediately dealt with.

However, division did not like this scheme and insisted that the fire for effect was reduced by 10 minutes. They did not provide an explanation. As for the trench mortars, the batteries comprised only one heavy, five medium and five light. Apart from their role in hitting the target area, they were also supposed to destroy the British wire to allow the raiders to reach the target. In addition to these mortars, further support was provided by a battery of granatenwerfer. These fired small finned bombs to a range of about 300 yards.

Before the interference by division, the raiding party comprised four officers, twelve NCOs and forty-eight men, plus one engineering officer in command of three NCOs and fifteen pioneers. The engineers in the raiding party were split into three groups, each of one officer and three pioneers. Their task was to identify and destroy enemy mine galleries, mine shafts and dugouts. Other pioneers were given the task of destroying wire to enable raiders to reach their objective. In addition, the raiders were accompanied by an officer from Field Artillery Regiment 50, the artillery unit providing support for the raid. Despite the raid commander's reservations about the viability of maintaining effective contact between the raid commander and regiment by means of telephone, the artillery officer took two telephones with him, connected to the German rear by surface line played out from spools as the raiders advanced. The raid commander used the customary hand signals for issuing orders and maintaining control among his raiders during the operation and consequently was not in direct contact with regimental HQ.

> The raiding party will leave the concrete dug-outs at 11.30 pm and rush out of the front trench against Rue du Bois by the four lanes cut in our own wire. The party must get into the enemy trenches before the enemy notices the lift in the artillery. Right and left flankers and connecting files to the rear must ... be detailed. Advance in skirmish line, right flank on the road by the Dachsparrenhaus, left on Point 232.[2] ...
>
> After penetration into the front trench, the advance will be made up the communication trenches to Points 225, 224, 227 and 206, after blocking the trenches at 226 and 232. There will be a 15 to 20 minutes' halt in the trenches; retirement will take place on the pre-arranged signal.

The German front trenches were evacuated between 10.30 pm and 11.30 pm, then lightly held. These men acted as support for the raiders. Once the raiders returned, the normal garrison strength was resumed and patrols sent out again in the normal way. Neighbouring trench sectors provided the raiders with fire support. This was all intended to overwhelm the New Zealanders and prevent counter-fire and counter-attacks.

After the changes imposed on the raiders by the divisional staff, the plan was finalised and everything from signal flares to ensuring the lanes cut in their own wire were immediately closed after the return of the raiders with prepared *chevaux de frise* was set for the 19 July. What the Germans had not anticipated was the New Zealand raid, which hit the 229th's neighbours barely 2 hours before zero hour of their own raid. The British bombardment in preparation for that raid nearly forced the Germans to abandon their enterprise. Nevertheless, the raid went ahead. The New Zealanders were not anticipating a raid and when the bombardment started, it was so intense and the effect so great, they:

> thought at first the enemy had sprung a mine. One of our light trench mortars was destroyed, and the officer in charge, together with nine men of his section, was killed. Other casualties numbered 38, including three missing.

Although the right-hand (northern) party alone claimed to have killed fifty New Zealanders and to have destroyed two of their dugouts, this was fantasy. Indeed, the New Zealander Rifle Brigade lost only one man killed and the raiders were in and out too quickly to do anything of consequence. There is no question that the raiders spent no more than a few minutes in the Bastion before the signal to withdraw was blown. Indeed, the signal may not have been given at all, despite what was claimed in the post-action report. The time spent in the New Zealand trenches was certainly nothing like the stipulated 15 minutes as set out in the orders. The party suffered several casualties including 'two officers, two men killed; fourteen wounded and two missing'. The party did manage to bring back 'four rifles, steel helmets, greatcoats, cartridge belts, several letters, pay books and identity discs and two prisoners'. While the northern party managed to get into the bastion, the southern party did not and were fought off by the New Zealanders.

The artillery preparation for the 229th's raid on the 2nd Battalion New Zealand Rifle Brigade began before the raiders from the 1st Battalion of the Rifle Brigade had returned from their raid. According to the Rifle Brigade's account of the 229th's raid:

> Some twenty Germans effected an entrance into part of the forward trench known as the Dead End, but were immediately ejected, leaving prisoners in our hands. That the enemy penetration was not more extensive was largely due to the heroic work of Corporal H. Ashton, who, the only unwounded man of the sentry group at the block in the Dead

End, kept the Germans at bay and thus facilitated their expulsion by parties under Lieutenants A.P. Castle and G.K. Dee.

When the German raiders withdrew:

> The redoubtable [Lance-Corporal H.E.] Le Comte, in company with Lance-Corporal W. W. C. Bedgood and Rifleman Muff, followed the Germans across No Man's Land, and brought in mobile charges, bombs and equipment dropped in their flight.

Clearly, as the German post-action report stated, the raiders of the northern party had departed the scene in some disarray. Indeed, they had been thoroughly seen off with their tails between their legs.

Nothing about the German operation went well but worst of all the infantry failed to execute the raid according to the plans. Indeed, it was almost as though an unwillingness had gripped them and rendered them ineffectual. While it is always difficult to gauge just how tough a fight is put up by defenders and how determinedly the attackers press home their assault as there is always a tendency to exaggerate the prowess and strength of the enemy, nevertheless, it is evident that the raiders' hearts were not in their work. Their almost immediate ejection from the bastion, their subsequent headlong flight, along with the wildly exaggerated claims, all suggest these were reluctant raiders. Moreover, the bureaucratic manner of the planning process imposed by division and its interference with the scheme that it had expressly ordered regiment to devise was an exemplar of how not to plan a raid. All in all, the whole affair was something of a disaster.

As a counterpoint to the 229th Reserve Infantry Regiment's raid, the one carried out by the 1st Battalion New Zealand Rifle Brigade 2 hours earlier, was an example of a well-planned and well-executed operation. A crucial difference between them, of course, was the high level of enthusiasm for the enterprise among the New Zealanders compared to its lack among the Germans of the 229th Reserve Infantry Regiment. This was the third raid to be mounted by the New Zealand Rifle Brigade since their arrival at Armentiéres on the night of 22–23 May to begin a first tour of the trenches on the Western Front, taking over part of the trench sector east of Armentiéres from the 2nd Brigade. Two officers and sixty other ranks from the 1st Battalion 'operating from the sector held by the 2nd Battalion, entered the German trenches opposite a point just south of the Rue du Bois Salient'.

The raid was commanded by Captain J.R. Cowles, with Lieutenant N.J. Reed and Second Lieutenant N.L. Macky leading the two assault parties. On this occasion, the artillery did not shoot with the same accuracy as usual on account of the batteries concerned having only set up in their present locations the previous night so had not yet had sufficient time to range their guns. Nevertheless, the bombardment was enough to make the Germans on the receiving end take cover in their dugouts, where they remained throughout most of the raid. That made taking prisoners rather difficult and none were taken. However, the raiders killed thirty-three, mostly by throwing grenades into the dugouts. From the dead, the raiders took items of uniform and various papers and pocket books, which made identification easy: the Germans belonged to the 231st Reserve Infantry Regiment.

The New Zealanders did not quite manage to avoid casualties themselves but the number was minimised by 'the skilful handling of his men by Capt. Cowles, who took full advantage of cover in No Man's Land, both before entry into and after withdrawal from the enemy's trenches.' Only six were wounded and few of the injuries occurred in no man's land or inside the German positions. Most were sustained when the party climbed over their own parapet to enter no man's land. One of the wounded was the battalion commander, Lieutenant-Colonel W.S. Austin, who had taken up a position on the New Zealand parapet to monitor the progress of the raid.

Sergeant Miller had what the brigade's historian described as 'a peculiarly exasperating experience'. Miller commanded a bombing section in the operation but was seriously wounded as he entered the German position.

Notwithstanding this, he led one group of his men to their appointed place, bombing the enemy along the trench as they went, and established a block as planned. This accomplished, he moved to where another group was carrying out a similar task in a branch of the trench and assisted them to complete this work also, thus rendering the flank secure.

He was not yet done. When the signal to withdraw sounded, Miller struggled to bring back a wounded but unconscious 'comrade', despite being in considerable pain from his own wounds. However, when he paused for a 'rest, he discovered that the object of his solicitude was not a wounded comrade, but a dead German'. He left the body there.

The success of the raid also rested on the determination and skills of the scouts who had reconnoitred no man's land and the German wire in the week prior to the operation. The battalion intelligence officer, Second Lieutenant Hudson, had provided much valuable information on such missions but was killed while on patrol only five days before the raid. Much of the reconnaissance was carried out, by day as well as at night, by Lance-Corporal H.E. Le Comte, a 2nd Battalion scout. He acquired an 'intimate knowledge of the ground', which was of considerable help in planning the route to the German line. On no less than four occasions he went out with

1st Battalion patrols. During the raid, he was in command of a group of scouts. When they reached the German wire, they found that the preliminary bombardment had not succeeded in cutting it well enough for the raiders to get through.

> The entanglements being found insufficiently broken, the party proceeded to complete the opening with wire-cutters. Though under heavy rifle fire, they succeeded in their task and returned to the assembly position to report, carrying back with them Rifleman Howell [one of the scouts], who had been wounded. This done, they guided the attacking parties forward to the breach, and so on to their objective.

As the raiding parties returned and while they were still in no man's land, the 2nd Battalion trenches were hit by the German bombardment, the preliminary to the 229th Reserve Infantry Regiment's raid. Captain Cowles kept a cool head and extricated his men from a difficult situation. The assembly area for the raiding parties, before and after the operation, was a couple of 'short lengths of old trench in the middle of No Man's Land'. Cowles had already sent back several small groups of men before the German bombardment started. Realising that his men would now have to pass through this to reach the safety of the New Zealand line, he kept the rest of them in the lay-up position in no man's land until the bombardment decreased. When he judged it safe to move, he withdrew the rest of his men as quickly as possible. In this way, he avoided the shelling of the New Zealand trenches as well as the Germans bombardment in no man's land intended to cover the withdrawal of the German raiders.

The changing circumstances of the 1st Battalion raiders could have resulted in far higher casualties than was the case but the ability of Cowles and Le Comte to think on their feet and react positively enabled the New Zealanders to retain control. Moreover, irrespective of planning, it is evident that the 229th were far from keen about raiding while the New Zealanders were much more aggressive and prepared to fight hard. The reasons for such a different attitude are difficult to pin down but it was not merely a matter of training. And there is no escaping the fact that the New Zealanders along with the Australians and Canadians had reputations for being aggressive fighters.

Chapter 9

July–October 1916

Raiding continued throughout the summer of 1916. On the Somme front, the British used raiding as a means of harrying the Germans and keeping them off balance while elsewhere raiding was meant to maintain pressure on German front-line units and so dissuade the German high command from transferring forces from one sector to another. The idea was to deny the Germans quiet sectors anywhere on the front where weary divisions that had been fighting on the Somme or at Verdun might have some respite to recuperate and rebuild. In addition, the British intended that raiding should discourage the transfer of fresher units to the Somme. Thus, raiding became part of a wider strategy for the Allies.

On the night of 5 July, the 2nd Battalion Royal Welch Fusiliers carried out a highly successful raid on a German salient known as the Warren, near Givenchy. In some ways, this was more than a raid as it involved the entire battalion with the intention of holding the captured German trenches for about 2 hours. Only C Company remained behind to hold the British line while the raid was in progress. The preparatory bombardment was more intense than was customary for a raid and involved artillery, Stokes mortars and rifle grenades fired in a hurricane barrage lasting 45 minutes. Here the intention was not destruction but disruption to enable the raiders to get into the enemy positions with the minimum of opposition. To have shelled the Warren for longer would have been counter-productive since major damage to the German trenches would have made the Royal Welch's brief tenure difficult, if not impossible. Moreover, the element of surprise would have been compromised. More than 10,000 rounds were fired, most of them artillery shells. The bombardment started at 10.30 pm and included 4.5-inch and 6-inch howitzers firing on the known positions of machine-guns.

The operation was supported by the eight Stokes mortars of the Light Trench Mortar Battery belonging to the 19th Brigade, to which the 2nd Royal Welch Fusiliers also belonged, assisted by a half battery of four Stokes from the 98th Brigade, making twelve mortars in all. These batteries had prepared for the raid several days beforehand by digging twelve new emplacements and laying the mortars the day before the raid. The four mortars of the 98th Trench Mortar Battery fired at the slow rate[1] from 10.30 pm until midnight, targeting trenches south of northern craters. Three mortars of the 19th 'fired for 45 minutes on enemy supports behind Northern Craters,' while the other five 'fired for 35 minutes on enemy saps and front line behind Northern Craters'. A total of 2,345 rounds were fired. The raid was also supported by the indirect fire of nine Vickers machine-guns of the 19th Machine Gun Company, which interdicted the rear areas to prevent reinforcements being brought forward.

A Company led by Captain J.V. Higginson approached the German line from the west while D.Company led by Captain P. Moody took a north-west route. They hit the German positions in two places simultaneously. While D Company dealt with the first line of trenches, assisted by 11th Field Company Royal Engineers, who went along as demolition experts, A Company pressed on to the third line. Not to be left out, two parties of twenty from what was left of B Company were attached to A and D Companies, one party to each company. Their task was to help carry the demolition charges and hand grenades for the other two companies and the sappers. The entire raiding party amounted to about 300 men.

The raiders moved off 'like a pack of hounds when the guns opened up. D Company used the rims of mine craters as cover as it moved over the broken ground, which was liberally spread with areas of wire. Once they reached their designated waiting area, they stopped. In the meantime, A Company went across no man's land in single file. The first Royal Welch casualty was a scout who was shot dead almost immediately the raiders entered no man's land. This was probably an unlucky random shot since A Company had no other casualties as it continued 'eastwards for about 600 yards over soggy, marshy ground, through long grasses and bits of barbed wire, across abandoned trenches' eventually reaching 'the steep northern face of the German re-entrant, about 120 yards away'. Here, they lay down in good order and smoked and joked as the guns continued to fire. The artillery was not firing in a regular pattern but shifting targets at irregular intervals of 3–8 minutes all along the front, support and reserve lines. At 11.15 pm, the artillery set up an intense box barrage. Now, the raiders dashed for the German parapet.

When Sergeant-Major Fox of A Company stood on the parapet it collapsed under his weight and he fell into the trench in front of a dugout. He was unhurt but unable to get to his feet unaided because he was clutching a rifle with fixed bayonet in one hand and a Very pistol in the other. Helped up, he challenged the occupants of the dugout to come out but they fired at him. Two Mills grenades were thrown in and the four occupants killed. The four Germans in the next dugout surrendered without the need for Mills grenades. They were relieved of their equipment and sent back to the Royal Welch lines with an escort who 'thought they were going to slip him, so he shot them'. They did not arrive at the British line.

While in the front trenches, resistance was weak because the occupants had been stunned by the bombardment and survivors surrendered quickly, in the support and reserve lines, the Germans fought back with determination. Thus, A Company had much more of a fight than D Company, who remained in the first line. A Company 'fought like demons'. Indeed, even those who were not supposed to take part in the operation wanted to get involved, including D Company's CQMS. After he had brought up rations to the British line, he went across and joined the raiders. The Germans were completely overwhelmed. Some men took coshes and clubs with them and one man, Private Buckley, who helped capture and carry back a machine-gun, armed himself with a billhook, which he apparently used in the course of the operation because 'one of the wounded prisoners appeared to have been chased by him'.

The objectives of the raid included the destruction of German mine entrances, galleries and dugouts, which were known to exist, as well as machine-gun and trench-mortar emplacements. By spending 2 hours in the enemy position, these objectives could be achieved; to place and set demolition charges required a reasonable amount of time to accomplish. One large trench mortar was also destroyed with explosives. Very little of the three lines was untouched in the raid so that, at its conclusion, the position was quite useless to the Germans.

The raiders achieved all they set out to do. They took thirty-nine prisoners from the 241st Reserve Infantry Regiment and brought back four more dead Germans along with a large quantity of identification and intelligence material, including fourteen identity discs removed from dead Germans and various documents and papers. The number of Germans killed and wounded by the raiders was not recorded but it was evidently a large number. Many were probably killed by the bombardment. The raiders also carried back a machine-gun, a trench mortar and a quantity of rifles and other equipment. Rather bizarrely, they also brought back food they found in the dugouts. What form it took is not mentioned in the war diary but presumably it was something more interesting than just bread.

So successful was this operation that the Battalion received messages of congratulation, including one from GHQ which read:

Please convey to 2nd Bn RWFus[rs] the Commander-in-Chief's congratulations on their very successful raid last night. Raids of this sort are of great material assistance to the main operations.

The battalion had a similar message in a telegram from Lieutenant General Haking, GOC XI Corps, General Monro GOC First Army, and Major General Landon GOC 33rd Division who wrote:

> I was delighted to hear of the complete success of the operation last night and warmly congratulate Major Crawshay and the RWF who have got their own back well...

The brigade commander also sent a message to the raiders conveying his delight with their 'splendid work' and stated that 'the attack could not have been carried out better and ... all your arrangements were first rate'. High praise, indeed. Such messages as these were not commonplace and they emphasise just how successful this raid was.

The operation was retaliation for the mine blown under B Company on 21 June; the 'got their own back well' in Landon's message was a reference to that disaster when two-thirds of B Company became casualties in a matter of moments.[2] The Warren was chosen for the raid because a map taken from a German killed in a previous unsuccessful German raid suggested that it would be a prime target. The map was very detailed and included the location of every dugout as well as other features of interest. The opportunity was too good to pass up and division even considered an assault to take and hold the ground but finally agreed to the operation suggested by the Royal Welch, namely a raid.

The 2nd Battalion did not get through the operation without casualties of their own, however. As soon as the British artillery opened up, the German guns responded, striking up and down the British line, including the trenches held by C Company as well as the support and reserve lines. Inevitably, there were losses. Among the raiders themselves, the casualties included one officer killed and six other ranks killed. Most of the wounded came from A Company, not surprisingly, because they had been involved in more of the fighting than the others, but injuries were largely caused by shell and grenade fragments. Few were gunshot wounds. The German prisoners mostly suffered bayonet thrusts, emphasising the importance of the fixed bayonet in this sort of close fighting, not to mention the importance of surrendering immediately. The Germans claimed to have captured a corporal from A Company. They called across no man's land later in the day to announce the fact but there is no mention of this in the Battalion's war diary.

In stark contrast to the Royal Welch raid, on the previous night the 4th Grenadier Guards raided Germans occupying what had formerly been Canadian trenches near a position known as Irish Farm in the Ypres salient. The raid was a complete failure. They were relieved the next night by the

2nd Battalion. A week later, on the 13th, the 1st/5th Glosters mounted a raid near Hébuterne. Three officers and sixty other ranks reached the enemy wire at 11.00 pm and 'two attempts to enter the trench were made but were both driven back by rifle fire and bombs'. The raiding party reached their own lines at 12.30 pm. One officer and five other ranks were wounded but there were no fatalities. The Germans had been well prepared and had had no intention of submitting.

A few nights after this raid, on 18 July, the 1st Bucks carried out what it liked to term a reconnaissance in force but it was, in reality, a raid, hitting the German line south of the Albert–Bapaume road on the Somme. The object of the operation was to reconnoitre six points along the line with the intention of establishing the disposition of the German troops in that area. A and D Companies sent out three platoons to enter the German line at specific points. The platoon under Second Lieutenant B.C. Rigden entered their objective at 2.00 am and proceeded to consolidate their position with barricades. Rigden and his men fought off several determined German bombing attacks and succeeded in holding their ground. Rigden won the Military Cross for the action. Unfortunately for Rigden and his men, the other platoons were prevented from entering the German trenches because of machine-gun fire, which caused several casualties. Consequently, Rigden's platoon had to withdraw. Nevertheless, the objective of the raid was achieved in that the strengths and dispositions of the Germans facing the 1st/5th Bucks were established. This raid was part of the preparations for a resumption of the assault on the German line by the 48th Division on the night of 20–21 July.

Raiding was not all one-sided. Although the Germans did not carry out nearly as many raids as the British and Dominion troops, nevertheless, they were not idle. Indeed, they raided for much the same reasons as the Allies. After all, taking prisoners was an ideal way to gather up-to-date intelligence about the enemy as well as apply pressure on him so that he could not relax. While the Germans were not nearly as successful with their small enterprises as the British and Dominion troops were with theirs, they still mounted some effective raids. On 21 August, the 1st Royal Irish Rifles were raided at 3.30 in the morning while they were in trenches in the Quarries sector south of Loos. Around twenty Germans rushed the Royal Irish after a 10-minute bombardment by heavy trench mortars and 'aerial darts'.[3] They 'entered our trenches at Sap 98A. This party proceeded down our front-line trench, visiting Sap 99 en route, & left by Sap 99A'. Each of these saps was garrisoned by one NCO and three men, except Sap 99A, which had an additional man. Saps 99 and 99A were attacked from the rear, the raiders approaching by stealth and completely surprising their garrisons. The trenches between Saps 98 and 99A were largely blocked with spoil from two mines that had been blown a few days earlier, one by the British, one by the Germans, and consequently were not occupied as front-line positions. The firing of these mines had also partly filled in the saps and wrecked the wire in the area.

A spoils party from the Northamptons was working in the disused trench when the raiders struck. They were unarmed because of the work they were doing. The Germans had been forced to advance along the trench in single file and when the Germans encountered the Northamptons, some confusion ensued as the spoil party further blocked the trench as they fled from the raiders. A couple of Royal Irish riflemen tried to put up a fight but were hindered by the Northamptons. They were killed along with one of the spoils party. The Germans were in and out in 5 minutes, departing with eight prisoners. They also killed two Royal Irish of the trench garrison, two sappers from a mining company and one man from a spoils party. Several men were wounded. One of the Northamptons who was taken prisoner managed to escape.

Several somewhat conflicting accounts of the events were hastily written up soon afterwards. The one written by the Lewis gun officer, Second Lieutenant W.V. Cecil Lake, shows just how confused trench fighting could be and illustrates how an observer may completely miss some aspects of an action:

The raid was evidently carried out by a working party which had been at work inside the enemy crater. This was preceded by a trench mortar bombardment lasting about 15 minutes. The trench mortars fell in front of the line on the left and right of Sap 99 and amongst the wire in front of RABBIT RUN.

One Lewis Gun was posted to the left of Sap 99. The team was made up as follows:- no.8176 L/Cpl. Scott, no.1570 Rfn. Dixon, no.9003 Rfn. Norris, no.7453 Rfn. Black, no.9017 Rfn. Murray. The two men on sentry at the time were Rfn Norris and Rfn. Black. For some reason L/Cpl Scott appears to have been round the next traverse to the left and the remaining two men were asleep in a disused mine shaft in the same bay as that in which the gun was. The two men on duty could not have kept on the look out during the short bombardment. The men asleep in the shaft had just been awakened for "stand-to" when two or three Northamptons and the two men on duty crowded in front of them because the Germans were coming along the trench from Sap 99. Rfn Norris and Rfn Black were dragged out & made prisoners as also were the Northampton men. A scuffle ensued and L/Cpl Scott came round the traverse & fired two or three revolver shots. He was then wounded and taken prisoner. The enemy then shouted down the shaft to find out if there were any more men but Rfn Nixon & Murray lay low & did not answer as they were unarmed. Immediately the enemy had gone these two men came out & manned the gun but could see no sign of the enemy.

Another Lewis Gun was posted at Sap 98A. Owing to the repair work going on in the sap, the team had to post the gun in the trench about 6 yds to the right of the sap, where it could command the wire in front of RABBIT RUN equally well. There is no fire step at this point which makes it difficult for the men to pass along the trench when the gun is mounted there. During the bombardment several men congregated here and forced the gunners still further to the right. L/Cpl Manson who was in charge of the team was actually knocked over by the onrush of men & had his knee cut. Rfn, Garraghy of the team was buried by a trench mortar and had to retire. Otherwise the team is intact. A look-out was kept on the wire at RABBIT RUN the whole time but owing to the black smoke & white chalk dust, observation was difficult. From this point it is not possible to see Sap 99 owing to the pile of sand-bags in the trench. This team saw nothing of the enemy.

Evidently, the raiding party quickly slipped over the near lip of the crater into Sap 99, thus exposing themselves for a very few seconds. A whistle was sounded when the party retired. This sound was not thought to be unusual as it is often blown when friendly trench mortars fired.

Similarly, a report by Lance-Corporal Hunter presents a picture of confusion. In it, Hunter stated:

I was in charge of the Sentry Group in RABBIT RUN (Sap 98) which consisted of 2 Rfm, 1 L.Cpl & myself.

This morning between 3.30 AM and 3.45 AM the enemy sent over several heavy Trench Mortars, two landed on my own front & the remainder to my left.

The sentry reported that the smoke caused by the T Mortars prevented him from seeing, when the smoke cleared away a little he reported that he saw a German's Head disappearing into C Coys sap. I ordered the remainder of the Group to man the parapet and ordered 7712 L.Cpl Dunn to take charge until I warned the NORTHERN CRATER. When I went to return to my post I saw the two sentries and L/Cpl Dunn coming towards the Crater. The Officer on watch ordered us back to our post again.

The staff at 8th Division HQ, to whom reports of the affair were submitted, were less than pleased when they realised that the men garrisoning the saps had not put up a fight and disciplinary charges against the NCOs was considered. The intelligence officer noted:

> The first line between the saps is ... [largely] blocked by mine spoil. It was also partly occupied by a spoil party at the time. The narrowness of this part of the trench would inevitably cause a block if there was any confusion, and ... [hinder] the efforts of a fighting man should a few men less courageous than himself happen to be in between him and the enemy.
>
> On the other hand the enemy could only come along the trench in single file, with difficulty in getting out over the parapet or parados.
>
> Two riflemen of the R I Rifles appear to have stood up to them, but were killed, being as is reported, knocked on the head.
>
> It is reported that the garrison of the saps do not appear to have stood up to it as they should have done, and charges are being preferred against two NCOs.
>
> The strength of the raiders is unknown, but is stated to have been 20. They left no casualties behind.

What appears to have taken the Royal Irish by surprise was the brief trench mortar bombardment that preceded the raid. The random firing of trench mortars was a common practice by both sides. Neither the British nor the Germans were stoical about being on the receiving end of these 'hates'. However, they were usually of short duration and while they were intended to cause mayhem, they were not usually the preliminary to a raid or any other action. In this instance, the raiders took advantage of the absence of expectation of further action following the hate.

It is also clear that the Germans had garrisoned at least one of the craters – that is to say, the rim of the crater, not its interior – since a Royal Irish patrol 3 hours before the raid had been treated to a barrage of grenades when it came too close. On the night following the raid, the Royal Irish decided to deal with them, partly as retribution and partly to avoid a recurrence of the assault.

The confusion and the lack of response by the men in the saps was a serious matter and prompted an enquiry by the 1st Royal Irish Rifles, in the course of which, Private Taylor of the Northamptons provided a statement and answered a series of questions about the operation:

> The first I heard about the raid was when a man came running down the trench saying that the Germans were coming. I was between two parties 3 RIR & 3 58th [Northamptons]. [T]he 3 58th got down the mine & I was following when a German officer pointed his revolver at me & told me to come out. I came out & they beckoned to me to get up over the parapet. I

got up & one man followed me. [D]irectly I was over I ran along between out parapet & our wire. The German fired at me but missed. I got back into our trench near the NORTH BORDER CRATER.

Q1   How many Germans did you see [?]
[A]   officer 12 men
Q2   What were the Germans doing?
[A]   They were standing still in the trench. They all had revolvers in their hands.
Q3   Did anyone shoot at or attack the Germans?
[A]   The only shots fired were 6 that were fired at me. None of our men fired.
Q4   How long were the Germans in our trench?
[A]   Less than 5 minutes. Nobody saw them until after they got into our trench.
Q5   Were you & your party armed?
[A]   We left our rifles just outside the mine.
Q6   What did you do when you got back into our trench?
[A]   I went and told an officer of the RIR that the Germans were in our front line.
Q7   Did you see the Germans leave our trenches?
[A]   No. When I was in the open I saw a party of about 6 men in our wire. I could not see who they were.
Q8   Did you hear any one shout at all [?]
[A]   No. When the Germans caught me they put a revolver against my head & said Ssh. Ssh.

That was the end of the questioning. Taylor's account reinforced the confused nature of the business. In all fairness to the men in the saps, the Germans quite clearly took the Royal Irish completely by surprise, which was a reflection on the skill of the German raiders rather than on the ineptitude of the defenders. The outcome of the enquiry is not recorded, nor is the fate of the two NCOs up on charges for their failure to lead their men in a resistance to the German raiders.

Three days later, the Germans again attacked the Royal Irish, this time in the area of the Northern Crater. With the benefit of a feint to divert attention elsewhere, a party of twenty to thirty Germans tried to enter the Royal Irish positions at about 10.50 pm. This time, they were not successful because, despite the diversionary bombing attack, the raiders were spotted when they were less than 20 yards away. The Royal Irish opened rapid fire and threw grenades at them, dispersing the raiders in quick order.

During the continued fighting on the Somme in August, the Germans attempted to the raid the 2nd Royal Welch Fusiliers a day after they took over trenches from the 2nd Argyll and Sutherland Highlanders at High Wood. At 9.00 am on 19 August, the Royal Welch were suddenly subjected to a short but intense artillery bombardment. A raid quickly developed as the shelling stopped. It was repulsed but not before the Royal Welch had suffered fourteen fatalities and ten other casualties. This raid was part of a series of assaults mounted on the Royal Welch by the Germans over three consecutive days, all of them preceded by bombardments, two of the attacks occurring at night. They were all beaten off but with steadily mounting casualties. These assaults were more than raids yet not quite conventional seize-and-hold operations.

While some raids were major operations that resembled battles in miniature with all the preliminaries of a full-scale offensive, others were much smaller operations and depended on speed for their success. Typical of such small-scale raids was the one carried out by the 2nd Lincolns towards the end of September 1916. On the night of the 19th–20th, two parties of fifteen, led by an officer, supported by a party of eight, led by an NCO, raided German trenches in the infamous Hohenzollern sector of Loos.[4] Second Lieutenant H.J. Dickinson was in command of the left-hand party, while Second Lieutenant Wreford commanded the right-hand party. At , Dickinson and Wreford went out into no man's land to mark out with white tape the route to the assembly position, which was about 20 yards from the German wire. Having done this, they returned to their own line. Half an hour later, the two raiding parties set out with a Bangalore torpedo, with which they proposed to blast a route through the German wire. They reached the assembly position at 11.00 pm. Five minutes later, the Bangalore torpedoes were being set in place and by zero hour, 11.15 pm, everything was ready. The artillery opened up and put a box barrage round three sides of the target area. In the meantime, the support party waited in a sap.

Unfortunately, as so often happened with the Bangalore, it became obvious to Dickinson that their torpedo had failed to detonate. Nevertheless, he ordered his men to advance. They managed to penetrate the ragged wire and reach the parapet. Sergeant Biggs and four men of the party jumped into a strongly held German trench. This led to a 'bombing fight', in which both sides tried to out-bomb the other, a very deadly game, in which luck and numbers always played unwelcome roles although determination and raw courage were also important. It was always possible in this sort of engagement, which so deviated from the training model of grenade fighting, that no one would emerge as victor. After about only 5 minutes in the trench, Dickinson decided that numbers did not favour them and blew the signal to withdraw. At least half of the party had been seriously injured in the exchange of grenades. Briggs told Dickinson that another member of the party was still in the German trench so the officer went off in search of him despite the continued bombing and shooting by the Germans. After some time, Briggs was concerned that Dickinson had not returned. He looked over the parapet into the trench but saw no sign of him. He and his party were forced to return to the British line. The next morning, Dickinson's body could be seen lying next to the German parapet.

The other party under Wreford fared no better with their torpedo. Indeed, because of the unevenness of the ground they found it almost impossible to push the Bangalore into position; it's nose kept snagging on things. It took them 20 minutes to do a job that should have taken no more than two or three. When at last they managed to fire the Bangalore, Dickinson's party were in the process of withdrawing. Not surprisingly, the Germans were fully alert by then and they responded with heavy rifle fire and grenades. None of Wreford's party succeeded in getting into the German trench and several of them were wounded. Wreford was himself badly hurt as he helped the wounded withdraw.

The raid was a failure in every respect other than confirming how strongly the Germans held the line. The German wire was in a poor state of repair but that availed the Lincolns nothing and, while the Germans mounted neither a counter-attack nor a retaliatory bombardment of the Lincolns' line, that was no compensation for their own losses: two killed, both officers wounded and seven other ranks wounded, a third of the raiders. Although the raid showed the strength of the German garrison opposite the Lincolns, they must have already had some idea that the enemy was holding the line in strength. The raiding parties were too small and insufficient training had been provided in the use of Bangalore torpedoes, which clearly required some expertise to manipulate and fire correctly. Nevertheless, the battalion CO, Lieutenant-Colonel R. Bastard, concluded that the raid failed because Dickinson signalled his party to withdraw too soon and that success would have followed had the raiders persisted. He did, however, concede that 'some very desperate fighting would have taken place, as the trench was strongly held' had the raiders pressed on.

Two nights earlier, on the 18th, the Middlesex, who had been holding trenches at Agny near Arras, had raided a German sap. The 9th Royal Fusiliers relieved the Middlesex the next night and the night after that relief the Royal Fusiliers mounted a raid of their own on another German sap. This was the same night as the 2nd Lincolns' raid. The Royal Fusiliers' operation was no more of a success than the one mounted by the Lincolns. The two operations were on a similar scale although the Royal Fusiliers sent out only one assault party instead of two. This comprised one officer and about twelve men. They set out at about 9.30 pm and soon reached the

German wire. This belt was 45 feet wide, made more impassable by shell holes 'full of balls of barbed wire'. They spent the next 4 hours cutting their way through about 30 feet of it. By now, dawn was beginning to come up and they stood no chance of completing the last 15 feet in sufficient darkness to avoid detection, let alone then carry out the raid. They had no choice but to abandon the enterprise and returned to their own trenches having achieved very little. They had started cutting the wire about 10.00 pm, which had alerted the Germans in the sap and, although they saw no one, they heard footsteps and someone blew a horn.

On the same night, the 8th Battalion also tried their hand at a raid and that, too, was a failure. The object of these raids was the taking of prisoners for identification purposes. Neither had the benefit of artillery preparation. And as far as the 9th Battalion was concerned, at least, the raid lacked the benefit of adequate reconnaissance that might have alerted them to the thickness of the wire, which would have suggested an artillery bombardment of the wire at some point prior to the operation was necessary in order to make the operation feasible. The very idea of cutting through 45 feet of barbed wire with hand cutters was somewhat ridiculous. There was an evident lack of preparation for this operation in a sector that was known to be strongly defended by the Germans.

On the evening of the 21st, undeterred by their lack of success the previous night, the 9th Royal Fusiliers set about completing what they had started. A raiding party of one officer, one NCO and twelve men with a covering party of one officer, one Lewis gun and ten men 'left the E bay of the SUNKEN ROAD G8 at 8.15 and 8.30 pm respectively, with the Enemy sap X as their objective'. They reached the wire 90 minutes later and the point of entry into sap X at midnight. In the meantime, the raiders had been detected and were fired on by snipers from the flanks and a machine-gun, positioned where the sap joined the trench, opened up on them. Nevertheless, they finished cutting a lane through the wire to the sap. This was discovered to be in some disrepair and clearly was not being used. However, it was blocked every few yards by concertina wire.

The party was in the sap for about 5 minutes when a trench mortar fired several rounds at them from about 50 yards to their left. The Germans were constantly firing Very lights to illuminate the raiders. Clearly, the Germans knew the Royal Fusiliers were in their line but were uncertain about their exact location. Moreover, if the Germans were going to launch a counter to the incursion, such as it was, the likelihood of this happening increased with each passing minute so the party decided to withdraw. Thus, this raid, too, was not a success. And again, lack of preparation and lack of a plan were to blame. The 9th Royal Fusiliers did not try to repeat the exercise on a third night.

Another failed raid was the one attempted by the 2nd West Yorkshire Regiment on the evening of 15 September in the area of Vermelles in the Quarries sector. The orders to carry out the raid had only been issued four days earlier, giving the battalion little time to plan, prepare and rehearse. Nevertheless, the volunteers who were to carry out the raid spent the 13th, 14th and 15th – the day of the raid – rehearsing every aspect of the operation using a taped-out ground plan of the enemy trenches. To enable them to devote all their time to preparing and training for the raid, the party was temporarily withdrawn from front-line duty. This was made more complicated by the need to remove the tapes as quickly as possible every time an enemy aircraft appeared in case photographs of the layout were photographed and correctly interpreted, forewarning the Germans of the impending raid. Enemy photo-reconnaissance flights were always a problem as, indeed, were Allied flights over German-held territory.

The objective was to 'secure prisoners for examination by the Intelligence Officers at Divisional Headquarters' and by so doing find out how the Germans were withstanding the fighting on the Somme. The raiding party was kept as small as possible. The reasoning behind this was simple: if the Germans were taken by surprise, a small number of men would be more than capable of carrying off the operation successfully but if surprise was not achieved and the Germans responded hard and casualties ensued, fewer would result from a small party, whereas a larger party would inevitably suffer more losses. In addition to rehearsing the operation, when not interrupted by enemy reconnaissance aircraft, the raiders studied the German positions through periscopes and binoculars. Small patrols were also sent out to take a closer look.

At 9.30 pm on the 15th, the raiding party of twenty-four, led by Second Lieutenant G. Smailes and Second Lieutenant Fisher, assembled in the front-trench ready for zero hour. Fifteen minutes later, they filed out of the British line, passed through a gap cut in the British wire and entered an area of several small mine craters in the middle of no man's land. The leader of the party was now only 30 yards from the gap in the German wire they had to enter in order to reach the German trenches. However, the raiders now discovered that the Germans had put out more belts of wire since their last reconnaissance. The party could not go forward. Smailes crawled back to the British line to report the impasse. This presented Major James Jack, the battalion CO, with a dilemma. He instructed Smailes to withdraw but he now needed to consult brigade by telephone. However, to explain the situation quickly, he would have to speak in the clear, which, because he was in the front line observing the raid, he could not do on account of the possibility of the Germans tapping the line. Such laxity was forbidden. The dilemma was made worse because the raid had been ordered by GHQ.

Abandoning the enterprise seemed like an unacceptable option in the circumstances. Jack did not want to have to reschedule the operation for another night although the Germans did not seem to have noticed the activity. No doubt the long grass in no man's land had helped to conceal them.

After discussing the problem with the raid officers, everyone agreed that they should try an alternative entry point into the German wire. This was made possible only because those involved in the reconnaissance had had the foresight to find such a location in case of problems with the preferred entry point. Sometime later that evening, the raiding party, now reduced to fifteen, set out for a second time. They took a Bangalore torpedo with them to blast a way through the German wire. The bright moonlight was unhelpful and every time the moon emerged from behind the cloud, the party had to remain absolutely still. Eventually, they reached the desired location and pushed the Bangalore under the wire. Then, they realised that the wire was too deep at that point for the Bangalore to reach to the other side and so would not cut a lane all the way through when detonated. They needed more lengths of torpedo than they had with them. Smailes decided to try somewhere else. For a third time, the Bangalore was pushed under the German wire, this time at a location where the belt was not so deep. It was not their night, however, because a sentry heard them and raised the alarm. The Germans in the front trench immediately open fire on the raiders who had no option but to withdraw as quickly as possible.

Unfortunately, that was not the conclusion of the sorry business. Just as the party reached their own lines, two of their number became casualties. Private Standish was killed and sergeant Mellor was wounded when going to his aid. The two raid officers helped by the medical officer, Captain Fayle, eventually managed to bring in the two men despite continuing fire from the German trenches. By now, it was 2.00 am on the morning of the 16th and the raiders had achieved nothing. Despite the failure, their determination and tenacity were never in question and, indeed, were noted by division.

The 1st Royal Irish Rifles mounted a raid in the early hours of 9 October. At 3.00 am, Lieutenant G.J. Palmer and twelve riflemen climbed out of their trench just east of where it joined another trench known as Gordon Alley in the Hohenzollern sector. They made their way to one of the craters using their knowledge of the area and intelligence gained from a recent photo-reconnaissance flight. This was about midway across no man's land. They found no evidence of German occupation. The raiders then approached the German front trenches. The wire was in a poor state of repair and presented no obstacle. Indeed, in places, it was in such disrepair that it was for all practical purposes non-existent. Clearly, the Germans had made no effort to reinforce or maintain it for some time.

The party got to within 5 yards of the German parapet before they were spotted. The German garrison was not, however, in state or readiness to deal with the raiders, who could hear the enemy talking and laughing as they went up and down the wooden boarding in the trench. By a stroke a misfortune, one of the Germans happened to look directly at the raiders even though they had been quite silent as they approached. He could not help but see them in the light of the moon, which was very bright that night. Or so the raiders thought, especially as the observer immediately ducked down below the parapet. Palmer was not prepared to assume otherwise and ordered five of the party to throw grenades into the trench, then rush the parapet. In their haste, the bombers misjudged the distance and threw their grenades too far so that they exploded harmlessly on the other side of the trench.

The raiders had seen about eight Germans in the trench and there were probably more. These men were armed with rifles. Palmer decided that, in view of the small size of his party, it was imprudent to attempt a further sally as it was evident that others were making their way up the trench. The party made a hasty withdrawal under German rifle fire and detonating grenades. The Germans had been rattled by the sudden appearance of the Royal Irish party and believed that they were part of a much larger group. Even after the raiders had reached their own trenches, the Germans continued to throw grenades at random, an indication of their nervousness.

The raiders had miss-timed their enterprise by a considerable margin. They had arrived at the German trench at about 4.30 pm and the German activity they noticed was due to the Germans standing-to. Had the raiders arrived even half an hour earlier they would have probably succeeded in getting into the German positions and taken prisoners as they had intended. As it was, Palmer and one man were slightly injured in the encounter and everyone returned to the Royal Irish line, but empty-handed. It had been a close call as they might all have become casualties.

At the beginning of November, the 1st East Surreys sent out a patrol to reconnoitre the German trenches in the region of Guinchy with a view to mounting a raid the following night. However, after nearly 3 hours in no man's land, the patrol was discovered by a searchlight. A machine-gun then opened fire on them. They had no choice but to withdraw. The raid was cancelled. The East Surreys next attempted a raid about three weeks later in the same area. At about 10.00 pm on the 24th, Second Lieutenant Gunning led out a party of thirty, including bombers and a Lewis gun team. They were supposed to have been a patrol but ended up acting as a two-group raiding party with the Lewis gun section acting as a flank-covering party in no man's land. When the patrol approached the Embankment Redoubt, which Gunning had wanted to enter to capture a prisoner, he found it too well defended with little prospect of getting in unnoticed.

Gunning and two other men approached a known saphead, while a group of eight guarded the 'root of the same sap' where it joined the main line. The saphead was unoccupied when they got into it but there was plenty of evidence to show that work was still continuing and a digging detail would return to it at some point. They then went back along the side of the Embankment looking for a way in. The Germans were too alert and there was no possibility of effecting a stealthy entry. So Gunning and his patrol waited in the hope that the German garrison would relax their vigilance. The whole business was ended by the arrival of a German fighting patrol, which tried to outflank the East Surreys. A bombing contest then ensued. The East Surrey's withdrew and returned to their own line at about 2.50 am. While this enterprise was not strictly a raid, it had raid-like qualities and had Gunning been able to find a way into the Embankment Redoubt, fighting would have inevitably developed and the whole business would have been transformed into a raid. Sometimes, there was little to differentiate a patrol from a raid.

Active patrolling and raiding became the mainstay of the offensive spirit of the V and XIII Corps as the energy of the Somme campaign blew itself out in the rain, fog and mud of autumn. On the night of 31 October, a patrol in the XIII Corps area south-east Hébuterne discovered 50 yards of the German front trenches were empty. The following night, two V Corps patrols in the Serre area penetrated the German positions as far as the support line without meeting anyone. A week later, the 31st Division carried out a raid south-east of Hébuterne, took four prisoners and killed thirty for only four wounded raiders. It seemed that the enemy was losing his will to fight on that part of the Somme.

Chapter 10

Bomb, Bayonet and Pistol

Raiding was very much a cat-and-mouse business, each side attempting to overwhelm or surprise the other yet avoid being themselves being overwhelmed or surprised in the process. Make a mistake, prepare badly or make assumptions and the consequences could be disastrous. This was well illustrated by what befell the 2nd Rifle Brigade on 3 September in the Quarries sector. One of the brigade's night patrols had been captured the previous night and no one had considered the possibility that the Germans would gain knowledge of the impending raid from interrogation of their prisoners. The battalion-sized operation went ahead despite the fact that the raid had been compromised. When the raiders reached the enemy trenches, they found them completely deserted. Almost as soon as they entered the German line, an intense artillery bombardment hit them and they suffered 50 per cent casualties. The Germans, of course, lost not one man.

Raiding sometimes served but one purpose: harassment of the enemy, usually at night, in order to keep him under stress and prevent him from relaxing. These sorts of raids were a way of establishing dominance over the enemy but sometimes provoked retaliation, which rather diminished the point of the exercise. On the other hand, depending on the morale and disposition of those raided, such enterprises provoked no response at all. They tended to be regarded as tiresome but inconsequential. The tip-and-run style of raid was, of course, in the finest tradition of raiding going back thousands of years, almost guerrilla warfare in their conception, except that on the Western Front the perpetrators or their friends could be made to pay according to how much of a nuisance had been caused. For nuisance value, they scored very highly but little intelligence was gleaned from tip-and-run raids, although, of course, that was not their purpose. The raiding parties varied in size from only two – on rare occasions, even a single man – to about half a dozen. They were organised at no higher than battalion level but often at company level and they might be inspired by rivalry or some trivial matter such as an enemy whistling too much, although they were mostly against outposts beyond the front trench line.

Such ambushes at these might be carried out by men armed only with pistols but more often than not the raid was what was usually referred to as a bombing attack. On the night of 11 September 1916, two Germans approached a trench held by the 2nd West Yorks, having crawled through all the wire in no man's land without making a sound. They shot two sentries and escaped into the darkness like ghosts. Not surprisingly, those who had to do sentry duty in trenches and outposts were very nervous and jumpy for some time to come after that, which was no doubt the object of the attack. Quite often, though, the fear of such an attack, or worse, one in which the attackers struck with knives so that death was silent, was worse than the reality. It was shared by troops on both sides but was largely an irrational fear born of the primordial dread of the darkness or rather of what lurked menacingly within it. Although such attacks did occur, as did larger scale raids, the fear of them was not in proportion to their frequency.

Small–scale bombing attacks would often occur in clusters, periods of quiet being followed by periods of greater activity. As with raids by a couple of men with pistols, the aim was to kill and disrupt in order to cause disorder and fear, although they could also serve a greater purpose when attacking a saphead or an outpost that was too close to friendly positions. Bombing attacks by the British became a feature of raiding from about the late summer and early autumn of 1915, when the No. 5 Mills grenade became the standard British hand grenade. The Mills was the first British grenade to have a mechanism that automatically lit the fuze. All previous grenades had used hand-operated lighters, which were not only unreliable but often highly visible. The Mills made night bombing attacks much more feasible. The Germans, on the hand, entered the war with grenades that employed friction lighters that were more reliable than the British and unlikely to show up in the dark when fired.

The British did carry out bombing attacks at night before the late summer of 1915, but not as frequently as during the last quarter of the year when they became something of a novelty for a while. The 9th Royal Fusiliers carried out several 'bombing patrols' in September that were meant to harass the Germans and establish the dominance of the Royal Fusiliers. On 3 September, the enemy was evidently very quiet at Houplines, a state of affairs the Royal Fusiliers were about to upset. 'A patrol of ours went over to the German wire and threw 6 bombs in their fire trench, but only 4 shots were sent in reply.' The following night, the enemy remained quiet, the previous night's activities having failed to arouse them. At 9.00 pm, after the enemy wire had been cut to enable the bombers to get closer to the German trench, a patrol threw ten grenades over the parapet, which 'caused much

A raiding party from the 1st/8th (Irish) King's Liverpool Regiment. This photograph was taken on the morning after the raid which took place on the night of 17/18 April 1916. Many of the men are wearing knitted cap-comforters, balaclava-like headgear and dark sweaters. One or two have blackened faces, notably the man front and centre who is holding a revolver. A couple of them are wearing gloves and several sport Pickelhaubes, souvenirs of the operation. (IWM)

Landwehr assault troops, December 1917. Although this particular unit served on the Eastern Front rather than in the West, they are a good illustration of Stosstruppen. This photograph was clearly taken on a training ground as the men are armed with practice grenades (as indicated by the apertures in the grenade cylinders). Of particular note are the grenade bags each man wears and the fact that the rifles do not have fixed bayonets, unlike photographs of British raiders. It is significant that the rifles are slung, not carried. (Brett Butterworth)

Raiding party from the 23rd Northumberland Fusiliers Brigade (4th Tyneside Scottish), posing some time after the event and well behind the lines. They mounted a successful raid on the night of 30 September 1916. The eighteen-strong party includes two officers and a sergeant.

Three Canadian raiders from the 25th Battalion after a successful operation carried out on 25 December 1916. Left to right: Captain William Livingstone, Lieutenant John Clifford Trainor, Lieutenant Francis McKider Shirriff. Livingstone won the Military Cross for his actions during the raid. Shirriff was killed on the first day of the Battle of Vimy Ridge, 9 April 1917. They are holding captured German 98 Mausers. Note that Livingstone is armed with a revolver and a semi-automatic pistol. (Alan MacLeod)

Some of the men of the 7th Bavarian Landwehr Regiment who raided the US 16th Infantry Regiment on the night of 2/3 November 1917. Nine miserable-looking US prisoners of the eleven taken by the raiders are visible in this photograph (marked by the original owner with crosses). Several of the raiders are still wearing white armbands. The pile of equipment in the foreground is booty taken during the operation on the US positions near Bathelemont in the Luneville sector. (Brett Butterworth)

Four German raiders and three British prisoners pose after a successful operation in February 1917. The raiders wear white snow coats which a couple of them have tied round their thighs. Their helmets are whitewashed. They carry various items of booty, including SMLEs, gasmasks, haversacks, webbing and a water bottle. The German on the left has a trench knife on his belt. (Mike Welch)

Captain Papineau, July 1916. As a lieutenant, Papineau led a bombing squad during a raid carried out at 4.30am on 28 February 1915 by No. 4 Company of the Princess Patricia's Canadian Light Infantry. The raid was against a German sap at St Eloi in the Ypres salient. (Canadian Archives PA-000434)

German officers posing with trench clubs. Note the loophole shield on the parapet. There is a distinct lack of danger in this casual tableau, suggesting that this is nowhere near the front line. (Mike Welch)

A group of German raiders in an informal pose after a successful operation against the French. Some of the men are showing off French equipment, including kepis. The soldier fourth from the left has a bandaged face. The group includes pioneers (note the black shoulder straps worn by several men) as well as infantry. The man kneeling on the right has a trench knife on his belt. (Mike Welch)

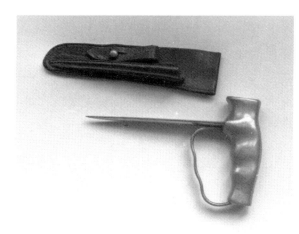

A punch dagger made by Robbins of Dudley, Yorkshire. The handle was held in a fist so that the blade projected from the enclosed knuckles. This could only be used for stabbing. (author)

Trench clubs. Left to right: cast lead head; looped iron head; hobnails hammered into a wooden shaft (probably German); cast flanged head made at Royal Engineers Workshops to fit the haft of the entrenching tool; heavy metal band. Note the wrist loops which helped to prevent the user losing his weapon in a melee. (IWM)

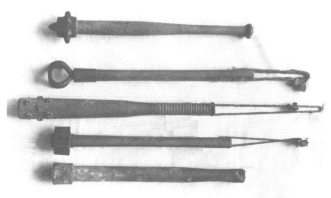

US Model 1918 trench knife. This had a 9-inch triangular-section blade which could only be used for stabbing. (author)

Canadian raiders returning from an operation against German positions near Avion in July 1917. Their faces are still blackened, probably from burnt cork, as are their hands. They have been back long enough for the man in the front to have had his injured arm bandaged which suggests the photograph was taken some distance behind the front. (CWM 19920085-595)

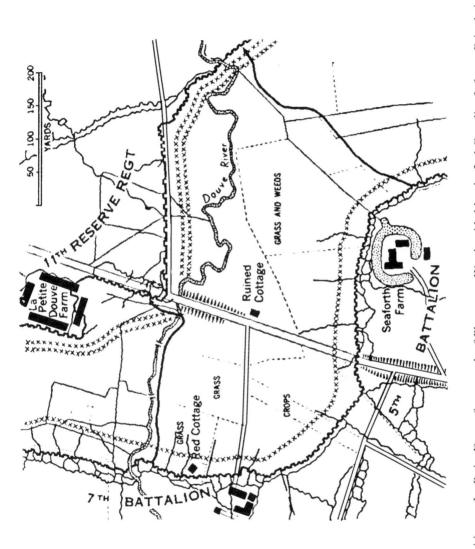

Map showing German positions at La Petite Douve farm, north of Ploegsteert Wood, raided by the 2nd Canadian Infantry Brigade in the early hours of 17 November 1915. No-man's-land lies between the lines of crosses which show the positions of Canadian and German barbed wire entanglements.

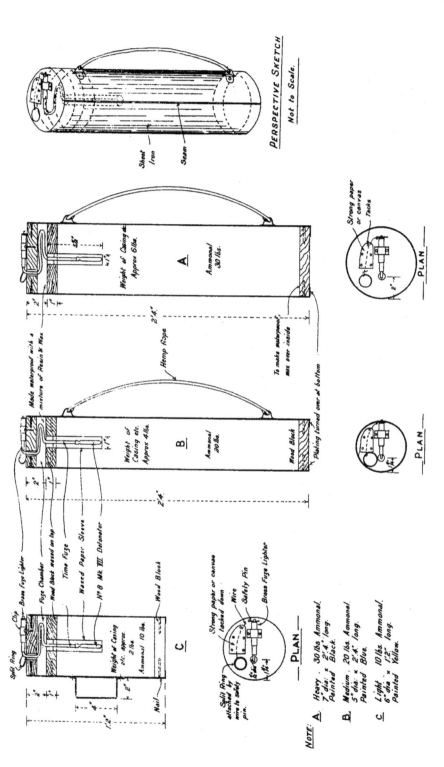

Demolition charges used by Royal Engineers to destroy German dugouts, machine-guns and trench mortars. They came in three sizes: A, 30 lb of ammonal (heavy); B, 20 lb of ammonal (medium); C, 10 lb of ammonal (light). Each was fitted with a friction lighter and a time fuze. Each had a carrying strap. The charges were made by the First Army Workshops from these drawings.

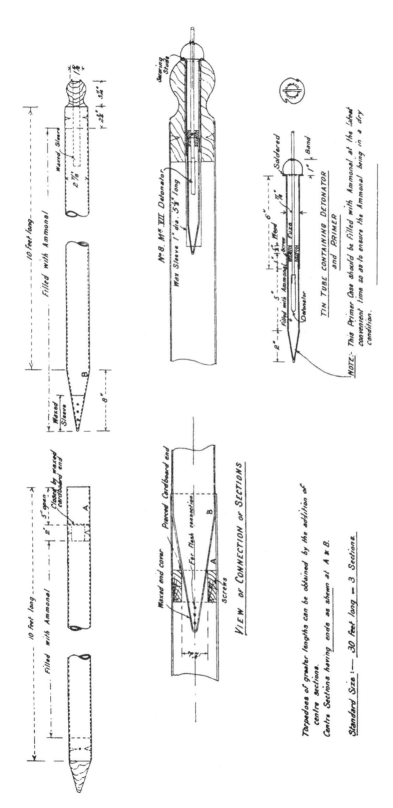

Engineering drawings for the Bangalore torpedo made by the First Army Workshops. The torpedo was made from combinations of 10ft sections: a centre section which had a hollow end to take the pointed end of another centre section; and a detonator/handle section. Any length of torpedo could be made up from these sections. The standard length was 30ft made up from three sections. The pointed end of the centre section was a perforated cardboard cone. The perforations allowed the detonation flash to travel down the ammonal explosive in one tube to the next.

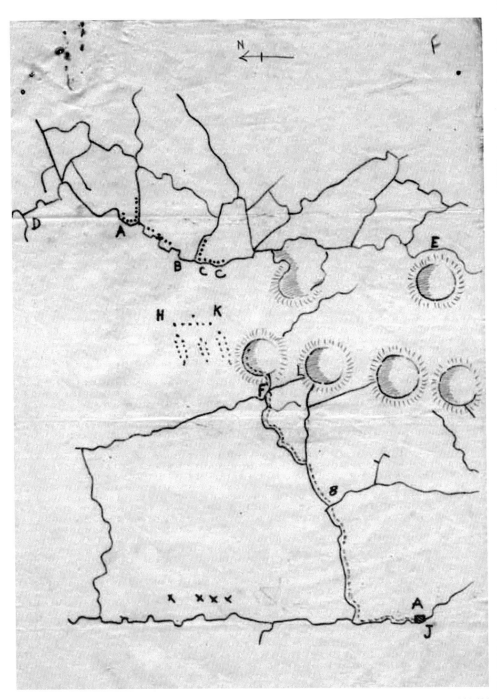

Sketch map of a raid carried out by the 2nd/14th Londons (London Scottish) on the night of 29/30 September 1916 against German positions near Roclincourt. The round features are mine craters. The party comprised two officers, nine NCOs and thirty-one ORs. From the forming-up positions at H–K , the raiders entered the German trench at the point marked B. Blocking parties were set up at A and C. A support party was positioned along the British trench F–L to give flanking fire. Prisoners were escorted down the trench F–8–J. The raiders returned to dugout J for a roll call after the operation. Although the raid was a success, the raiders suffered a number of casualties, including two missing. (McMaster University)

Company Sergeant-Major Edward Brooks, VC, of the 2nd/4th Oxs & Bucks Light Infantry. Brooks had been a pre-war regular in the Grenadier Guards but was a labourer when war broke out. He enlisted in the Oxs & Bucks in October 1914 and first saw action during the fighting on the Somme in July 1916. He won the Victoria Cross during a raid on 28 April 1917 at Fayet, near St Quentin. He captured an enemy machine gun single-handed, turned it on the enemy, then brought it back to the British line.

A tough-looking group of stormtroopers or raiders from the Landsturm Infanterie Regiment Nr 13, May 1917. Most of these men have their unit number embroidered on their collars which, should they be killed or captured, would provide evidence of their identity. These men are armed with Gew 98 rifles fitted with 20-round magazines (so-called 'trench magazines'). Normally, the rifle only had a 5-round magazine. (Brett Butterworth)

Successful raiding party from the 6th Seaforth Highlanders who carried out a trench raid on the Railway Salient near Armentières on 15 September 1916. The board is chalked with 'The Spirit of the Troops is Excellent' and 'Hun Snatchers'. In front of the board are several No. 5 grenades. Several men carry trench clubs with the cast flanged head made at the Royal Engineer Workshops.

Riflemen from the New Zealand Rifle Brigade who successfully raided the Germans near Hebuterne on 21 May 1918. They display their trophies captured during the operation, including ten MG08/15 machine guns and a heavy MG08 on its mounting.

confusion, but evoked no reply'. Yet, when Royal Fusilier snipers engaged a German working party a couple of hours later, the Germans replied by firing two shells at the British trench. Nevertheless, the Germans were not prepared to tolerate a third night of bombing attacks. They fired machine-guns all through the night of the 5th, effectively preventing a repetition had anyone in the Royal Fusiliers taken it into his head to have go. Nevertheless, two nights later, another 'bombing patrol' went out at 9.00 pm and threw another ten grenades into a German trench. After a pause, the patrol threw another four into the same trench but the only response was a yelled 'English pigs!'

That same night, the 9th Royal Fusiliers were relieved but six days later they were back in the line. The enemy remained 'very quiet' and clearly expected to be left in peace by whichever British battalion was facing them. For the next four days, the Royal Fusiliers left them alone but on the 17th, with the 'enemy quiet' still, two bombing patrols went out. They reached the German wire, 150 yards separating them, and each then tossed eight grenades at the German parapet, some of them going into the trench before exploding. This time 'much scuttling was heard' but still not one German responded by throwing grenades at the intruders. A sentry fired two shots widely in their general direction. The following night, German artillery fired a half a dozen shrapnel shells and a dozen whizzbangs at a trench junction without effect. Unlike the Germans, the Royal Fusiliers responded to this and 'at 10 pm we fired Rifle Grenades effectively at German fire trench opposite trench 83 [the German's target]'. The 9th Royal Fusiliers were much aggressive and intended to dominate whoever was on the other side of no man's land.

In April 1916, the 1st Bucks were in trenches at Hébuterne. A little before dawn on the 23rd, an isolated post manned by men from B Company was attacked by a small party of German bombers who threw several grenades at the garrison, then disappeared into the night. The Bucks suffered six casualties. The German bombers executed their task and withdrew before the Bucks knew what had hit them. This was the epitome of the bombing attack, the archetypal tip–and–run raid. Apart from constant vigilance, there was very little anyone on ether side could do to prevent such attacks. It was this sort of attack that made sentries and those manning isolated posts very nervous at night. These sorts of attacks served only one purpose, and that was to harass.

A reconnaissance of German positions carried out by two companies of the 2nd Argyll and Sutherland Highlanders on the night of 21–22 June 1915 'came in contact with a large body of the enemy' when the patrol was in the German lines. However, the Highlanders did not engage in bombing but relied entirely on the rifle and revolver. This operation was, in all but name, a raid that had the objective of 'procuring information' about which troops were garrisoning the trenches opposite them. The operation was also mounted because an aerial photograph from a few days earlier had shown up a sap that the Germans might have been intending to join up with other works. It's purpose was not obvious from the photograph. Orders stipulated that two parties, each one of no less than fifty men, were to enter the German line, assisted by guns of the 11th Battery of the Royal Field Artillery and a machine-gun operated by the 5th Scottish Rifles, all of which were to hit the enemy parapet to suppress the enemy. Serious opposition to the incursion was expected from the Germans, hence the size of the two parties and the support preparations.

The right flank reconnaissance was conducted by fifty men of B Company under Captain Clark, divided into three parties. These met no opposition to speak of until one of the parties reached the sap in question. Here, the left party were challenged, then fired on by Germans in the sap. However, the centre and right parties managed to move round the saps and this established that the sap in question was no bigger than indicated by the photograph and no work was being done to extend it. Unfortunately, the three parties lost touch so that the intention of their entering the sap had to be abandoned.

In the meantime, the left flank reconnaissance was being carried out by fifty men of D Company under Lieutenant Aitken, who had the task of investigating a German listening post garrisoned by eight men, discovered by a patrol the previous night. Dividing into two parties to approach the post from both directions simultaneously seemed like a good idea at the time but events did not play out as anticipated. They were supposed to make the occupants of the post aware of their presence, then run off to await the German patrol that would be sent out to investigate, then ambush it. While the left party concealed itself, the right party ran into a large body of Germans who attacked and easily surrounded them.

Sergeant Macpherson, who was in command of the party, fought his way out and brought his party to safety with only two men being wounded. Macpherson then armed himself with two revolvers and took two sections to find Aitken and his party. He fought his way through the Germans surrounding Aitken, who had already sent out two scouts to locate Macpherson and his party. When Aitken realised the Germans were withdrawing, he 'wheeled his party to the left and fired on the Germans who made off for their trenches with Lieut Aitken's party in pursuit'. In the process, Aitken picked up a German helmet and coat that had been discarded by the Germans in their haste to get away. These provided the identification the raiders needed.

German reinforcements were assembling on both flanks with the intention of surrounding Aitken and Macpherson, who had now combined their parties. Lieutenant Buchan took two sections to act as a rearguard to the cover the withdrawal of the rest of the patrol. The Germans were 'eventually driven off and opened a heavy fire from a position in front of their wire.' By then, the Highlanders were back inside their own lines. In the course of the action, Macpherson was 'known to have accounted for seven'. The enemy certainly came off much worse than the Highlanders, who fought fiercely.

For the loss of one man killed, another severely wounded, one slightly wounded and one missing, the Highlanders killed several of the enemy and obtained the information they sought. This successful operation very nearly went very badly wrong, however, but it demonstrated that grenades were not necessarily needed when engaging the enemy in trench warfare and that raids could be mounted successfully when the men were armed with rifle and revolver. This was June 1915, and as far as the BEF as a whole was concerned, grenades were still very much a specialist weapon and in short supply. Within the next few months, not only would the supply of grenades start to increase exponentially, but proper training schools began to be established in each Army as well as in Britain. Better training, which was derived from trench warfare experience as well as experience of raiding, and better grenades in greater availability ensured that 'bombing' as a skill would become more widespread during 1916. Before mid-1915, grenades were not generally available to the British and the rifle and revolver were the principle weapons. Few men had even seen a grenade let alone handled one. The grenades most British soldiers had seen before the last few months of 1915 were all German.

By mid-1916, moving about in no man's land had become much more hazardous than hitherto because of the greater use of deep belts of barbed wire and the greater vigilance of sentries who were on the lookout for in-coming raids. Surprise was much easier to achieve in 1915 than subsequently. It became increasingly more difficult to accomplish in 1916 and 1917. Nevertheless, surprise was essential for bombing attacks as they could not be preluded by an artillery or trench mortar bombardment, which would forewarn the enemy thereby making the attack redundant. Moreover, such preliminaries meant that for a raid to be effective, a reasonably large body of men needed to enter the enemy trenches.

For a bombing attack to be effective, the enemy had to be in his post, trench or sap and he had to be taken by surprise. It had to be an attack that came suddenly out of the dark, silent night. This principle held equally true for the Germans, the British and all the Dominion troops. The increased use of artillery during 1916 to support raids because of the increased use of wire and the greater alertness of the enemy, helped to make bombing attacks difficult to pull off. The opportunity to make such attacks diminished during 1916, although they continued to be made in 1917 and 1918, but with increasing rarity. To some extent, they reflected the derring-do nature of many of the early raids, a quality that was rather out of place as raiding became more akin to fighting a small battle, requiring a great deal of planning and plenty of rehearsal, the antithesis of the ethos of the bombing attack.

Different types of raid required different sorts of weapons and as warfare on the Western Front evolved, so did some of the munitions with which the infantry was armed. Most noticeable was the evolution of the hand grenade and the development of tactical schemes for their use. The evolution of infantry tactics was heavily influenced by the experience of raiding on the Western Front. As far as the BEF was concerned, that was dependant on the development and supply of effective and reliable hand grenades. This had less of an influence on the German Army because, although it was very short of hand grenades during early 1915, as were the British and the French, they already had a reliable grenade in 1914. Neither the British nor the French possessed a reliable grenade in 1914. As far as the British were concerned, the BEF had to make do with a series of stopgaps until the autumn of 1915 when the supply of the new No. 5 Mills began to increase significantly. In 1915, the British had twelve types of explosive hand grenade, all of which needed different handling procedures and all of them in short supply. Until mid-1915, there were no training schools to train bombing instructors. These were hardly circumstances conducive to the development of the bombing attack as a tactic.

The No. 5 Mills hand grenade was invented in January 1915.[1] The process of taking the prototype and transforming it into something that could be mass produced by small engineering firms, none of which had any experience of munitions work, proved to be more difficult than anticipated by the Ministry of Munitions. Until the engineering firms learned how to manufacture the components and assemble them to a high enough standard, the rejection rate was huge. It was not until the late summer of 1915 that the rejection rate began to be significantly reduced. Then, there was the problem of filling the bodies with explosive, a process that could not be undertaken by the firms who made the components. In 1915, for the British, only two places could fill grenades, the Royal Arsenal and a commercial firm called the Cotton Powder Company. The Ministry of Munitions had to build new facilities and new manufacturing processes had to be devised to enable the Mills to be produced in the numbers required. By the autumn of 1915, 300,000 No. 5s were being produced each week. The No. 5 was the standard British hand grenade from mid-1915 until 1917, when it was superseded by an improved version, the No. 23. By the end of the war, this had been superseded by the No. 23 Mk III, later re-designated the No. 36 but this saw little service in the First World War. By the end of the war, 75 million Mills grenades had been manufactured.

The invention, manufacture and supply of hand and rifle grenades required a huge intellectual and engineering effort without which the BEF would have had to rely on munitions devised and manufactured at the Royal Engineer Workshops in France but these did not start producing munitions in quantity until mid-1915. Although Royal Engineer Field Companies improvised grenades from late autumn 1914 onwards, they could do no more than supply individual companies or battalions with a very limited number of grenades. These were mostly the so-called jam-tin bombs. Many of the stopgap grenades produced in Britain were re-engineered jam-tin bombs. Some of the Workshops grenades were produced in very large numbers but each Workshop supplied only one army within the BEF. In 1915, there was only the First Army Workshop, the so-called Béthune Bomb Factory, and the Second Army Workshops. The two hand grenades that these two facilities produced in the greatest numbers were the Battye Bomb, devised by Captain Battye, produced at the First Army Workshop; and the Newton Pippin hand grenade,[2] devised by Captain Henry Newton, commander of the Second Army Workshops. Until the British had a plentiful supply of the No. 5, an insufficient number of men were trained in its use so that the grenade did not figure prominently until the latter part of 1915. Indeed, no grenade figured prominently in British operations until the latter part of the year.

One of the problems faced by British troops when encountering Germans armed with grenades was that the Germans had a bomb that could be thrown a long way because it had a handle. German bombers could usually out-throw British bombers although the skill lay not so much in throwing to a specific distance but in doing so to a distance that the bomber had accurately judged so that the grenade landed exactly where he intended, namely at the feet of the enemy. Accuracy was as important as range. The Germans entered the war with a friction-lit, time-fuzed spherical grenade, introduced in 1913, called the *Kugelhandgranate*. This was superseded in 1915 by the *Stielhandgranate*, or stick grenade. This was superior to all the British stop-gap grenades as it was far more reliable and much simpler to use. Like most grenades, it had a time fuze, and was fired with a friction lighter operated by pulling a cord connected to a wire inside a friction tube located in the top of the handle. In the first type of German stick grenade, the cord, which passed down a narrow bore in the handle, came out through a small hole in the bottom.

The friction lighter used on many British grenades of the period could not be relied on to function correctly. Indeed, the friction lighter of the Nos 6 and 7 Lemon grenades (a re-engineered jam-tin pattern designed by the Royal Laboratory, Woolwich) was almost impossible to pull, while that of the

Nos 13 and 14 Pitcher pattern was positively dangerous. The bomber could dislodge the entire fuze assembly when he pulled the lighter so that the detonator exploded outside the grenade. The No. 15 Oval pattern was lit in a similar way to striking a match. The top of the fuze had a bead of match composition that the bomber rubbed hard against an arm brassard to ignite the fuze. As the fiasco at the Battle of Loos was to demonstrate, the fuze would not light when wet. More than half of the grenades issued for the attack at Loos failed to work, with disastrous consequences. The Mills system did not require a friction lighter. Instead, a spring-loaded striker hit a percussion cap, which ignited the fuze and fired the detonator. This system made the grenade much less susceptible to water damage.

While the hand grenade eventually became the archetypal weapon of both trench warfare and raiding, that was not the case for much of 1915. Perhaps the most common weapon for raiders was the revolver, which was a handy, short-range weapon that was quick and easy to bring to bear in confined spaces. Hand guns were not issued to private soldiers for routine trench duty so raiders had to return their side arms after a raid, although some men bought their own guns in France or in gun shops and department stores in the major cities of Britain. Shops such as the Army and Navy Stores, Civil Service Stores, Selfridges, Gamages and Harrods all sold trench warfare equipment, including hand guns, periscopes, trench coats, trench knives and all sorts of other paraphernalia associated with life in the trenches.

A variety of semi-automatic pistols and revolvers saw service in the trenches on both sides. Revolvers were preferred over pistols because they were more robust and less susceptible to the effects of mud and dirt and were much easier to strip down and keep clean. Pistols could be temperamental in the trenches and, hence, tended to be less reliable in a crisis. On the German side, 9mm pistols such as the Luger, Mauser and Browning saw extensive service. The advantage of the pistol over the revolver was the larger number of shots that could be fired before reloading. Typically, a revolver had six chambers, while a pistol such as the Luger had an eight-shot magazine and it could be fitted with a so-called snail-drum that held thirty-two rounds. The Broomhandle Mauser was a heavy but popular gun among some German troops. The British Webley revolver saw widespread use on the Western Front. About 300,000 were manufactured during the war by the Birmingham gun makers, Webley and Scott. It fired a large .455-inch calibre bullet, which was capable of knocking a man down when hit, a British Army requirement born of nineteenth-century colonial wars.

The problem with all hand guns is the recoil, which, unless the shooter is trained to shoot the weapon, can result in missing a man-sized target at less than 10 feet. The Webley in particular had a hefty recoil, which made it hard to shoot accurately so its use needed a certain amount of practice for it to be effective. Because of the high demand for revolvers, Britain imported Colts and Smith & Wessons from America and some of these saw service on the Western Front. Some Germans used nineteenth-century military revolvers such as the M1879 and M1883 *Reichsrevolvers*. The French had a choice of several nineteenth-century MAS revolvers as well as a number of semi-automatic pistols manufactured in Spain during the war. However, hand guns were not a priority for trench raiders and most men on a raid did not carry one.

Some British raiders might have armed themselves with sawn-off shotguns. Clearly, each gun would have been bespoke, the modifications being carried out at Royal Engineer workshop facilities or possibly ordnance repair workshops and such a weapon would have been used by the officer who owned it. Major Stephen Midgley of the Australian 5th Light Horse Regiment certainly used a double-barrelled shotgun in Gallipoli until told to stop. The British and Australian use of shotguns was unsanctioned and it is likely that higher command were unaware of their use. While it is true that the US military used shotguns to some extent on the Western Front, there is little to suggest that they were employed specifically on trench raids in 1917 or 1918. Nevertheless, the German troops feared these 'trench guns'. The American weapon was not a locally modified civilian gun but a weapon specifically adapted by Winchester for trench warfare, with a pump action and a bayonet attachment. It had a shorter barrel than a civilian shotgun and a six-round magazine. The cartridges contained 7–9 pellets of hardened 00-gauge shot, devastating at short ranges.

The Canadians experimented with shortened SMLEs but it was a short-lived idea. They were carried by men of the 42nd Battalion on a raid on 1 April 1917. The idea was that a shortened rifle would be easier to handle in the confined space of a trench. However, the SMLE was not a long rifle compared to the service weapons used by the other belligerent nations and certainly, by 1917, training had evolved to enable the rifle to be manipulated very effectively in bayonet work despite its apparent unwieldy length. British bombers were trained to throw grenades with the rifle slung and, indeed, wearing a gas mask. And bayonet men in the British Army were not concerned by the length of the rifle.

The carrying of unconventional weapons by raiders was not uncommon. Some men went so far as to carry things like billhooks, crude spears made from knives fixed to poles, and knuckledusters. Both British and German manuals recommended that raiders and bombers should be armed with some sort of knife or dagger. While the British soldier had to provide his own, the German Army had at its disposal a wide range of *Nahkampfmesser*, close-combat knives, all made specially for trench fighting. Many were purely utilitarian with pressed-steel or plain wooden handles and a simple crosspiece hilt but some were more ornate with bone or horn handles, although these were commercial products bought privately rather than official issue. These knives usually had single-edged or double-edged blades of between about 4.5 inches and 6 inches in length, all capable of killing a man through winter clothing. The French, the Belgians and the Americans all supplied their troops with trench knives. The US Model 1917 trench knife was unusual in that the blade was a long triangular-section spike with no cutting edges, which could only be used for stabbing. It was not unique as a number of French knives had similar blades made from Lebel bayonets, the blades of which were cruciform in section.

Many knives used by British troops were either hunting knives bought locally or in Britain, or improvisations made by Royal Engineers using whatever materials were available locally. The latter included the so-called *Clou française,* or French Nail, forged from barbed-wired piquets by Royal Engineers. Others were made from broken bayonets, even files. A number of commercial firms produced trench knives in Britain, including a firm in Dudley in Lancashire called Robbins. Their knives and daggers were made to their own designs and could be bought in the major department stores. Robbins daggers proved to be quite popular although whether they were well suited to trench fighting is perhaps questionable as some of the designs had a little too much emphasis on the aesthetic rather than the practical. Knuckleduster-hilted knives produced by other makers were also popular.

Generally speaking, the British were not as keen on knives as the French and the Germans. In Britain, there was a feeling that killing someone with a knife was 'un-English' although such a view was not necessarily shared by those who had to use the weapon in earnest. And there is no question of the utility of a knife in the melee of close combat in a trench or no man's land in the middle of the night. Frank Richards of the 2nd Royal Welch Fusiliers described the death of an officer killed by 'a dagger … driven up to the hilt in his belly.' The question of knives in British hands provoked strong feelings. In November 1915, Sir John Macdonald, a retired brigadier general, wrote to *The Times* about the BEF's lack of combat knives and the apparent unwillingness of the Army to provide them. He had been pestering various generals in Britain about it for about a year without success. He wrote that a trench knife was sorely needed because the confined space of a trench did not allow the proper use of the rifle and bayonet – on which point he was quite wrong – and emphasised that:

Everything points to the advisability of a short knife or dirk being at instant command … not for thrusting forward as in striking a blow, but for back-handed action, the arm being swung with the blade projecting – a dagger action in fact, which is much the quickest and most effective way of dealing with an enemy who is close up to you.

Macdonald did not approve of the commercial designs, of which there were quite a number on the market, as he did not consider them to be sufficiently robust for the rigors of trench fighting. He certainly maintained the view that the knife was 'distasteful to the British character' but thought that such thoughts should be put aside when dealing with a deadly and dastardly enemy like the Germans. He advocated that the knife should be swung 'into the face of the nearest man, and as rapidly as possible into the faces of as many men as can be reached – no stabbing at the body'. He believed that stabbing a man in the face was more of a shock than stabbing him in the body, rendering an enemy incapable of offering further resistance. Getting stabbed in the belly was very disturbing, not to say disabling, and often fatal.

The trench club was another ancient weapon revived in the trenches. They went by various names, including knobkerrie, cosh and mace, and came in many forms. The head was weighted and often given spikes or lumps so the whole force of the blow was delivered through a small point of contact, thereby maximising the energy of the impact. Everything from hobnails to metal spikes and cast knobs were used for the business end of the club, which was often given a long leather or rope wrist loop so that the weapon would be less easily lost in a melee. If there was one weapon that was easy to improvise it was this medieval instrument. It was highly effective, despite the reservations of some Australian officers.

One reason the mace was used in medieval warfare was its ability to penetrate steel armour. It was still effective in this regard when it came to steel helmets. The British Brodie steel helmet had a padded liner, which acted as a spacer. This meant that the metal of the shell was some distance away from the wearer's skull, which allowed the steel to deform quite substantially without making contact with the head. That the steel deformed rather than broke when struck was due to the use of manganese steel for the shell. German helmets did not have the same sort of liner so that the shell was much closer to the skull. Moreover, the steel in German helmets was silicon steel, which tended to break when struck. Hence, a blow from a trench club was more likely to cause serious hurt to a helmeted German soldier than to a helmeted British one.

There is no question that clubs were intended for patrols and raids. They served no other purpose. As Stephen Graham of the Scots Guards put it, raiders would be issued with clubs to fight 'like savages' and 'one sharp blow on the head' would render a man senseless, if not kill him. Graham did not arrive on the Western Front until April 1918, showing that such weapons were in use even at the end of the war. Siegfried Sassoon, who served with the Royal Welch Fusiliers, wrote about using his 'nail-studded knobkerrie' on a the raid. Robert Graves, who also served in the Royal Welch, noted that before a raid, 'Some of the officers were going to carry clubs with spikes on, which were very handy weapons at close quarters in a trench.'

The adoption of weapons such as knives and clubs by raiders attested to the brutal and personal nature of close-quarter fighting that often developed during a raid. The importance of these weapons was their shock value although some were particularly lethal at close quarters. Moreover, the diversity of weapons carried by raiders, from grenades to revolvers, from rifles to clubs, showed not only the savage nature of the fighting but the determination of the raiders to achieve their objectives at the cost of the enemy. It also showed that raiders needed a wide range of skills beyond those usually associated with the infantry at the start of the war in order for them to accomplish their objectives. Raiding helped to transform infantrymen from rifle and bayonet men into all-arms exponents, skilled in a range of weapons that, in turn, worked in the evolution of tactics to alter the way the infantry fought. The infantry of 1918 was very different from the infantry of 1914. Although the club did not become standardised equipment in any army, the hand grenade certainly did.

Chapter 11

Weather, Moonlight and the Hindenburg Line

Raiding did not come to an end with the closing down of the Somme campaign in the early winter of 1916. Indeed, there was an upsurge in minor enterprises although the weather and ground conditions mitigated against most kinds of operation. Raids were not infrequently cancelled because they could not be carried out with a reasonable chance of success. In March 1917, the 1st/4th Oxs & Bucks in trenches near Herbecourt, south of the river Somme, planned a raid but had to cancel it due to the poor state of their own trenches, recently taken over from another battalion and formerly owned by the French. They had been very badly affected by the weather. One section was almost impassable because it had turned to mud and collapsed. Moreover, snow that month made things even worse. The ground of no man's land was a morass in places. The raid had already been postponed from the previous night because of poor visibility, which compounded the perennial problem of wire entanglements that could not be cut with hand-operated wire cutters.

During the first quarter of 1917, raiding became a noticeable feature of the trench warfare operations of the 9th (Scottish) Division. The division looked upon raiding as a routine rather than an exception to it. Between 1 January and 9 April, the division carried out ten raids. The majority were successful. A large number of the enemy were killed and forty-nine were taken prisoner, yet the 9th Division escaped with few serious casualties, which did not exceed fifty. The outstanding raid of that period was the operation carried out by the 9th Scottish Rifles (the Cameronians) on 14 February. The idea for the raid came from Major M.N. Forsyth[1] of the Rifles, who put it before Brigadier General Maxwell[2], who commanded the 27th Brigade, rather than it being ordered by division. This was to be a daylight operation over ground that was eminently suitable for such an enterprise. The ground by which the raiders would cross no man's land was in a dip, obscured from the flanks, east of Roclincourt, a village just north of Arras. If the raiders were to cross here, they would be unobserved by the Germans. Forsyth wanted to take a large party into the German trenches on a narrow front of about 350 yards after a 1-minute bombardment by artillery and trench mortars, then spend 40 minutes in the German positions wreaking havoc. Maxwell approved the scheme.

Good planning and adequate rehearsal were, as always, essential for success and the raiders practiced over taped-out ground behind the lines so that, by the 14th, everyone knew their tasks and the timings of the operation and were ready to go. The raid was scheduled for 11.00 am. Medium trench mortars cut two lanes in the German wire during the 1-minute shoot, towards the end of which, the two parties of raiders rushed out of the British trenches and entered the lanes. Forsyth led twenty officers and 350 other ranks into the German trenches. They pushed up the communication trenches that bounded the area under assault as quickly as they could and penetrated about 300 yards into the German defences. The plan was to enclose the German garrison by coming round behind it from the third line and pushing towards no man's land. To help isolate the area from the rest of the German line, flanks and rear, artillery put down a smokescreen round the boundary of the raided area. The artillery also fired a conventional box barrage of high explosive.

The sudden assault by the Cameronians came as a nasty shock to the men of the 104th Regiment who were garrisoning this part of the German line. When the raid hit them, it was midday German time and they were about to eat so they were quite unprepared for the raid, which, consequently, overwhelmed them. As the raiders carried out their demolitions of dugouts and hunted down Germans, the medium mortars created a third gap in the wire to facilitate their departure from the German trenches.

In the fighting which followed the 9th Scottish Rifles killed many men, destroyed several dug-outs, blew up two concrete machine gun emplacements and one mine shaft. Two machine guns, one trench mortar and a large number of rifles and a quantity of trench stores were brought safely back together with 43 prisoners belonging to the 104th Regiment. The withdrawal was successfully completed and the whole operation was executed according to plan. The battalion lost two rank and file killed, two officers and thirteen rank and file wounded and one man was missing. About an hour later the enemy bombarded the British Trenches, but there were no further developments.

Other raids mounted by the 9th Division were equally well prepared. An earlier raid carried out on 6 January by a company from the 8th Black Watch with another from the 10th Argyll and Sutherland Highlanders, both of the Highland Brigade, managed to push to the third line of the German defences and stayed in the German positions for 30 minutes before retiring. Only four of the German garrison were found above ground, three of whom were killed by the raiders, the fourth being taken prisoner. The remainder of the 160-strong garrison was sheltering underground in their dugouts when the raiders arrived. Since the dugouts were then demolished with Stokes mortar bombs, which were thrown inside, it is likely that a good many of them died.

Here, as so often, the key to success was not only good planning but artillery. Intense bombardment of the front trenches preceding a raid, followed by a well executed box barrage while the raiders were in the enemy positions, often ensured success. The Black Watch and Argyll raid was also notable because it was executed at short notice. Short notice tended to run counter to all the tenets of a successful raid but in this instance, the artillery saved the day. The artillery was especially effective because of the inclusion of the heavies, which were not always available to support a raid. In this operation, however, they were being tested for their ability to cut wire, particularly the wire in front of the second and third lines. If successful, as indeed they were, the heavy artillery would be employed in a similar capacity during the forthcoming offensive at Arras, which was in the planning stage when this raid took place. The Germans retaliated by hitting Arras with what turned out to be the heaviest gas bombardment of the war.

German attempts to raid the 9th Division were far less successful. Indeed, between 6 December 1916 and 21 March 1917, they tried and failed on four separate occasions to penetrate the 9th Division front trenches. Each time, the German raiders 'were beaten off with loss'. The German efforts were subsequently described as 'feeble' and 'half-hearted', which were ascribed to 'nervousness and consciousness of inferiority'. Whether that was a realistic assessment of German raiding prowess is perhaps moot since those words were written in the immediate post-war period. However, it is evident that German failures were more common than their successes whereas the converse was true of all the national contingents that made up the BEF, including the British, Canadians, Indians,[3] Australians, New Zealanders and South Africans, all of whom were keen raiders, the Canadians and Australians in particular. There certainly seemed to be an element of national pride when it came to the Canadians and Australians, although it was equally true of the Scots and the Welsh. The Scots and the Welsh, especially those from the more aggressive regiments such as the Royal Welch Fusiliers and the Highland regiments, were keen to show they were more than a match for the enemy. That alone could not fully explain the low success rate of the Germans, however.

Timings of raids could have been a significant factor. Certainly, night raids were potentially more problematical than daylight raids, which, perversely, were more likely to achieve surprise. This was especially true when the raid took place at a time of the day when no one in a front-line trench imagined such an operation would hit them. And while major offensive operations launched in daylight were likely to result in high casualties, daylight raids were on a much smaller scale, which allowed them a level of surprise that no major offensive could achieve. There is no question that surprise was always a major factor in success. There is also the point raised by Lieutenant-Colonel W. D. Croft of the 11th Royal Scots, who ended the war in command of the 27th (Lowland) Brigade. He firmly believed that 'no attack should on any account whatsoever take place at dawn' because of the extraordinary physical demands it put on men. Indeed, he noted that the majority of deaths occurred at dawn, which he attributed to the fact that at that time of day, human vitality was at its lowest. While he was probably slightly off on the time of day that sees the human body at its lowest ebb – the early hours of the morning, around 3.00–4.00 am is the worst time – nevertheless, he had a valid point in that time of day was important in a way not imagined when night raids were first proposed. And, of course, that worked equally for raider and defender alike.

Daylight raids had more of a chance of achieving surprise partly because they were less expected and certainly less expected at midday than around dawn. Sentries were more alert at night than in the daytime and they were especially lax immediately after stand-down as this was the anticlimactic conclusion of standing-to. At mealtimes, soldiers were only interested in food. And after eating, most soldiers went to sleep. Patrols were out at night but not during the daytime, as were working parties and wiring parties. Night-time in no man's land could be very busy, especially if everyone was intent on passing through the same area of ground at much the same time. That sort of thing tended not to happen in the daytime as everyone wanted to stay out of sight, below the parapet. There was always a sniper, waiting. Making yourself noticeable in the day was liable to get you killed. Yet, night-time could be very much more stressful than the daylight hours because of the higher level of uncertainty the darkness brought.

When, in March 1917, Croft was given the task of finding out what the Germans were up to around Arras, he chose to go out in the early afternoon because it was an unusual time of day for such an operation. While his reconnaissance in force with two companies was raid-like in that the object was to penetrate to the German second line, the action was unlike a raid in that the purpose of the operation was neither to take prisoners nor destroy dugouts or other positions but to ascertain the enemy's strengths by provoking him into a response. The action was scheduled for 2.30 pm but was postponed for 30 minutes because of German aerial reconnaissance, which threatened the viability of the operation. British medium mortars then fired again at the wire despite their four-day bombardment of it. Even then, when the operation finally got under way, Croft's men found that only a narrow gap had been cut, which meant that his men had to pass through it in single file, making them vulnerable to machine-gun fire, always a serious risk when operating in daylight.[4]

When the two companies of the 11th Royal Scots went over the top and rushed forward they were still subjected to intense fire. Nevertheless, they got into the first line and pushed on to the second. For reasons that were not made clear, the attackers were only armed with rifle and bayonet. None carried grenades, an unusual oversight since bombers usually formed an essential part of any party irrespective of its size or purpose, especially if the attackers expected to enter the German trenches. Nevertheless, the attackers fought their way along the trenches despite the efforts of German bombers to stop them, which also demonstrated that grenades could be countered with bayonets and bullets. Because of the appalling muddy state of the German trenches, the attackers could not move quickly, which rather favoured the bombers, so the Royal Scots climbed out and shot the Germans from about 50 yard range; 'very few got back to their second line'.

Not only were the Royal Scots subjected to machine-gun fire but they were bombed by German aircraft, although the bombs seem to have inflicted no casualties. The Germans were not prepared to allow the incursion to go unchecked and threw in a counter-attack, which prevented the Royal Scots from completely clearing the second line. These reinforcements engaged them with old-fashioned rifle fire, standing on the parapets to take aimed shots despite the heavy fire from the Royal Scots. They suffered badly because of it, not only while in the German positions but also when they attempted to recross no man's land because the German machine-guns were still firing. Croft asked one of his Lewis gunners to engage the German gun from a crater lip and 'calmly mounting up in the face of heavy M.G. fire he deliberately lighted his pipe, put his gun in position, and then proceeded to take on the Boche machine-gunners. It was a fine sight.' This helped more of the Royal Scots cross back unharmed but the total casualties for the enterprise were more than a hundred.

That night, the Germans raided the Royal Scots. First, the Germans bombarded the British trenches with trench mortars and caused considerable damage in a couple of places. The Royal Scots had devised a way of countering the box barrage the Germans put down to support the raid. As soon as the barrage started, they 'side-stepped to clear the strafed area.' By now, the Germans had entered the Royal Scots trench but were counter-attacked. A brutal fight broke out all down the trench and the

Germans were thrown out. While this raid may not have been direct retaliation for the earlier action, the one mounted the next night by the officer in command of the company that had taken the brunt of the raid most certainly was. However, this was a small affair involving no more than a handful of men. They took a few prisoners, all of whom were shot in the course of a melee that developed when the party was set upon by a party of Germans. There were casualties on both sides and all to no real purpose other than revenge.

Preliminary bombardments always forewarned the enemy of an incoming raid. For a bombardment to be effective it had to ensure that the raiders could get into the enemy trenches and a box barrage had then to keep out enemy reinforcements or counter-attacks for as long as the raiders remained in the enemy positions. Otherwise, artillery helped no one. Effective artillery was the key to success of every kind of operation on the Western Front. Indeed, the importance of artillery to all operations cannot be overstated. The way in which it was used and how trench mortars, Stokes mortars in particular, were combined within the fireplan was a decisive factor in how the Allies won the war in 1918. This integration of artillery and Stokes mortars was equally true with regard to raiding.

However, sometimes factors outside the control of anyone intervened. On the night of 4 January, a raid planned by the 1st East Surreys was cancelled due to unexpectedly bright moonlight. While completely dark nights were often avoided for raids simply because the raiders too easily lost sight of each other at very short distances when there was no light at all, and it was impossible to see obstacles, bright moonlight that lit up no man's land like a perpetual flare was equally unhelpful. In bright moonlight, the raiders could not hide, especially if there were more than just a few of them. A whole company on the move was too easily spotted no matter how stealthily they moved. A patrol of seven sent out by the 1st Bucks in strong moonlight in early March was quickly spotted and engaged by a machine-gun. The patrol had to return. Twice more the patrol tried to work their way into no man's land and twice more they were spotted. In the end, the patrol was cancelled.

A month later, a company from the 1st Battalion of the Duke of Cornwall's Light Infantry waited near Le Quesnoy to carry out a raid. Over several days, they practised using Bangalore torpedoes and succeeded in blowing out several windows in many of the buildings in the village close to their practice ground each time they detonated a Bangalore, much to the annoyance of those billeted there since the glass was irreplaceable and the winter was especially cold. They mounted the raid at 8.30 pm on the evening of 5 January and took two prisoners from the 393rd Regiment and inflicted a number of casualties, but suffered thirteen casualties themselves. Worse, the Germans bombarded the British line with trench mortars in retaliation and the Cornwalls suffered further losses. Although the raid was described as a success, it was a costly one.

Three days later, on the morning of 8 February, the Germans carried out a raid with three parties hitting different sections of the British line at Cuinchy. Two adjacent battalions were struck simultaneously, the 1st East Surreys and the 1st Royal West Kents. The raid was preceded at 4.00 am by the customary intense bombardment with artillery and trench mortars, to which the British artillery replied 20 minutes later following an SOS signal. Soon afterwards, a party of twelve Germans entered the British line and attacked a post held by six of the 1st East Surreys but 'the struggle does not seem to have been very vigorous' and they quickly withdrew, neither side having suffered casualties. While this was happening, another party 'tried to work along the front trench northwards but was stopped by bombs of No. 4 Company'. After a brief exchange of grenades, that party also withdrew, apparently unscathed. However, a Lewis gun section caught them as they recrossed no man's land and inflicted several casualties on them. The third party struck the Royal West Kents on the left of the East Surreys. The bombardment had already inflicted some losses among them and they suffered a few more casualties during the incursion. A German captured subsequently revealed that five of the raiders had been killed and another five had been wounded. They took no prisoners. For the Germans, this raid was a complete failure.

Two days later, the Royal West Kents got their own back, hitting the Germans with two companies in the middle of the afternoon of the 10th. The British artillery shelled the German line with a heavy bombardment before the West Kents went over the top, accompanied by Royal Engineer demolition teams. They struck the front trenches on a frontage of about 650 yards to the north of the Red Dragon Crater belonging to the 264th Reserve Infantry Regiment of the 80th Reserve Division and went on to assault the support line. The Royal West Kents stayed in the German positions for about an hour, wrecking the German trenches, dugouts and trench-mortar and machine-gun positions. The Germans suffered high casualties during the operation, including one officer and twenty-four other ranks who were taken prisoner. The Royal West Kents faired much better, suffering between thirty and forty casualties but most of these were relatively minor wounds.

Hardly surprisingly, this provoked retaliation. German artillery fired on the British line but the bombardment was 'feeble'. Such a response had been anticipated and the Royal West Kents and the East Surreys had withdrawn from their front and support lines before the German artillery opened up. Only two men of the East Surreys were slightly wounded. The British guns opened counter-battery fire, which seemed to suppress the German guns quite effectively. However, that was not the end of the business and the

German guns began to fire more intensely from 4.30 pm, when the British counter-battery fire eased off, and continued until 6.00 pm, but it was still largely ineffectual.

The Germans hit the 15th Infantry Brigade twice in the space of one month, once in February and again in March. On 17 February, the 1st Bedfords were raided by a party of thirty or forty, who apparently entered their trenches without warning at about 4.45 am. It was a very dark night, the sentries, although vigilant, spotted nothing unusual and there was no preparatory bombardment by artillery or trench mortars to herald an imminent raid. The Germans got in between 'islands 30 and 28'[5] in the front trench, 150 yards apart, each garrisoned by a Lewis gun team.

> The garrison at 30a were first alarmed by the enemy bombing our wire to the right. They put up lights and saw a party of about 30 to 40 Germans in file getting though our wire between 30a and 30b. (The 30b is not garrisoned). They opened fire with their gun and most of the enemy retired. However an Officer and about six determined men rushed forward and got through the wire. They bombed toward 30a island. The Officer was killed close to this island and the remainder of this party proceeded between 32 Strong Point and COVER TRENCH and entered out breastwork at about Post 33 from behind. Meanwhile the whole Company had stood to and Lieut. G de C. MILLIAS organised a bombing party and kept them out of the Strong Point. Sergeant GROOM was killed here. At the same time 2nd Lieut. A. A. CREASEY mounted a Lewis Gun at the junction of SHETLAND ROAD and COVER TRENCH and so pinned the enemy in the straight piece of breastwork between 32 and 34. Two Germans were killed by this fire and the remainder wounded. The wounded managed to scramble over the parapet and get away.

While this action was being played out in favour of the Bedfords, another thirty-strong party was spotted crossing no man's land in single file, approaching Post 34. A Lewis gun team engaged the Germans when they were about 50 yards from the British wire. Fire from the Lewis dispersed them, killing at least three. Of the party who succeeded in entering the Bedford's trench, three of the dead were left behind. The raid was distinctly unsuccessful and that was down to the 'alertness, personal courage and initiative' of Second Lieutenant A.A. Creasy and Lieutenant G. de C. Millais, whom the battalion CO, Lieutenant-Colonel Butler, singled out for particular mention.

A month later, on 16 March, the Germans had another stab at the Bedfords. This time, the raid was preceded by a bombardment of the front and support lines at 8.00 pm. Two minutes later, a party of thirty to forty Germans were spotted trying to make their way through the British wire. They were immediately engaged with Lewis guns and rifle fire, forcing the raiders to withdraw. In the meantime, two red Very lights were fired by the duty officer, that night's SOS signal for the artillery to respond. However, no one at company HQ saw the flare 'probably due to the intensity of the flashes from the bombardment'. It was a charitable interpretation. However, as soon as the German bombardment had started, company HQ had requested that the Forward Observation Officer have the artillery retaliate by firing on no man's land and the German front trenches. This they did.

The counter-bombardment with the prompt action by the Lewis gun team and the riflemen in the front trench ensured that the Germans got nowhere near the Bedfords. Later that evening, they sent out a patrol to investigate no man's land where they found two dead, one of whom was recovered, but the other one was 'too badly damaged to move' and had to be left. The dead gave up their identities when their pay books and identity discs were taken. There were more dead elsewhere in front of the British line. The Bedfords lost two men killed in the German bombardment with four others wounded. The decisive repulse of the raid was viewed very favourably by the commander of the 15th Brigade, General Turner, who sent Butler a message of congratulations the following day.

Daylight raids, which, by now, had become much more common, were often more successful than those carried out at night. This was partly because daylight raids were always dependant on artillery for success whereas those conducted at night had a quite different dynamic. In this respect, daylight raids resembled small-scale bite-and-hold operations, except that the raiders withdrew and made no attempt to retain ground. Six platoons of the 11th Middlesex raided the Germans near Arras at 8.30 am on the 26th. Artillery and trench mortars supported the enterprise. The operation was also supported by four Vickers machine-guns of the 36th Machine Gun Company, which used indirect fire to interdict the back areas and communication trenches for 70 minutes. These guns fired 13,000 rounds. In addition, a further nine Vickers from three other Machine Gun Companies – 28th (four guns), 46th (two guns) and 76th (three guns) – also contributed to the operation. The raiders killed a number of Germans in the trenches, 'bombed his dugouts' and captured four NCOs and twenty-one other ranks. Once again, the German retaliation was weak.

The next raids attempted by the 15th Brigade, to which the 1st East Surreys and the 1st Royal West Kents belonged, took place at the end of the month and after a couple of British mines had been fired by the 254th Tunnelling Company in the vicinity of the Red Dragon Crater (one was on its northern lip), followed soon afterwards by a German mine. These raids were carried out simultaneously at 12.15 am on the 27th in the Ferme du Bois sector with the aid of an artillery bombardment. This time, however, the Germans' response was much more robust and the guns fired gas shells on to the approach road behind the front line so that respirators had to be used at the 1st East Surrey's Battalion HQ. The wind blew the gas back towards the front but it had dissipated before it reached the companies in the trenches. Although a mixture of lachrymatory gas and phosgene was fired, the bombardment caused few casualties.

What no one realised until about mid–March 1917 was that the German Army in the Somme region was withdrawing several miles, beginning in February, to a prepared line of defences that were to become known to the Allies as the Hindenburg Line. The depth of the withdrawal was about 6 miles at the extremities but about 30 miles at its greatest distance, in about the middle of the line. In effect, the withdrawal removed a huge salient, straightening the German line, which reduced their frontage by 25 miles. In so doing, the Germans gave up more ground than had been fought over between July and November the previous year. However, this was very much a strategic withdrawal rather than a retreat. The new defences needed fewer troops to garrison them. Ten infantry divisions and fifty gun batteries that had previously garrisoned the old front line were now free to be used as a reserve anywhere along the entire front.

These defences comprised up to five lines or zones, instead of the three so far encountered by the Allies. These eventually extended back to a depth of up to 9 miles, which meant that for the Allies to break through into the rear areas and beyond where there were no defences of any sort, they would have to fight through 9 miles of fortifications and defences. These lines were not, in fact, lines at all but belts of strongpoints. Each strongpoint had all-round defence and was protected by wide belts of barbed wire. And each line or zone was up to 1.5 miles deep. From Arras in the north to Soissons in the south, the German front line was no longer a continuous thread of trenches but a series of outposts, thinly held, about 1,100 yards in depth. Nearly 2 miles further back from this outpost zone was the main defensive line of strongpoints, which was up to 1.25 miles deep. This so-called battle zone was designed to break up any offensive so that the attackers became disorganised and weakened. Concrete artillery and machine-gun emplacements arranged to provide fire support to each other, massive ditches and belts of barbed wire up to 60 feet deep that ran on for miles, trenches that were 15 feet deep and 12 feet wide, along with tunnels for the movement of troops from one trench position to another, deep shell-proof dugouts and underground command posts were all intended to make the zones of the Hindenburg Line impregnable, a series of fortress lines that no army could penetrate.

Everything between the old front line and the Hindenburg defences was effectively destroyed. Villages, roads, waterways and railways were all destroyed so that nothing of military or strategic value could fall into Allied hands while at the same time the cleared areas provided clear fields of fire for the defenders. About 125,000 civilians fit for work were evacuated to areas behind the Hindenburg Line but the infirm, elderly and children, about 14,000 altogether, were gathered into safe havens 'exempt from the devastation order' within the defended area and left to get on with it as best they could. The area evacuated by the Germans was effectively a wasteland.

Although aerial photo-reconnaissance had shown building work almost as soon as the construction began, its significance was not fully appreciated until patrols began to enter trenches that had been abandoned. By March 1917, it became clear that the Germans had pulled back. On 17 March, A and C Companies of the 1st/5th Glosters moved from Cappy into trenches in the sector opposite La Masionette farm, south-west of Péronne on the Somme front 'to do a raid' on German trenches opposite them. As soon as the British artillery began its bombardment, the German artillery responded by shelling the British line. However, this was not heavy enough to deter the raiders, who set out at 2.30 am on the 18th. They reached and entered the German trenches without difficulty. A Company led the assault and killed the few Germans they found in the dugouts by tossing in grenades. C Company then passed through A Company heading for the German support line. There was no one there so they pressed on and advanced through La Maisonette and reached and 'took possession of 3rd line & began consolidating'.

It was immediately apparent that the few Germans left in the front trenches were only a token force intended to create the impression of greater numbers and mislead the British into believing that nothing had changed. However, from the front trenches to beyond the third line, those unlucky few found by the raiders were the sole representatives of the Imperial German Army in the entire sector. The rest of them had gone. Their absence was confirmed by patrols that were quickly sent out by division to find just how far the Germans had retreated. This raid meant that the 1st/5th Glosters were the first battalion in III Corps to discover the German retreat and follow it up.

However, a raid attempted by the 2nd Lincolns at Bouchavesnes, south-east of Combles, on the night of 27–28 February was not a success and gave no hint of the impending German retreat. A party of thirty other ranks commanded by Second Lieutenant Middleton of C Company made an attempt to get into the German trenches 150 yards south of the Bouchavesnes–Moislains road in the early hours. Their objective was the usual one of obtaining identification of the troops occupying that part of the German line. Unfortunately, the German wire proved to be too much of an obstacle because it had not been cut well enough by the artillery. The raiders were unable to get through it and had to abandon the attempt. Had they succeeded in penetrating the wire they might have discovered the Germans were already on the move or even caught them in the act.

The following evening at about 7.00 pm, just before the battalion was due to be relieved by the 1st Royal Irish Rifles, Middleton again attempted to raid the German line with a small party from C Company. This time, they bumped into an enemy patrol in no man's land. Middleton and his party managed to fight them off but almost immediately after shaking them, the raiders were fired on by a machine-gun. Further progress towards the German trenches was now impossible and he called off the raid.

The 12th Glosters mounted a small raid on German trenches just to the north of the La Bassée road on 5 March in the Canal sector near Le Quesnoy. The operation began at 5.00 am. The weather was bitter and it snowed. Three minutes after the one officer and twenty other ranks set out from the British line, the British artillery opened up with a bombardment of the German trenches. The raiders took the Germans completely by surprise and they captured two prisoners, killed four others and destroyed four occupied dug-outs with ammonal charges that probably killed several more. The Glosters' casualties amounted to three slightly wounded. At about 11.00 pm that night, a patrol of two officers and two other ranks from the 1st Devons examined the German wire in front of the 12th Glosters with a view to mounting a raid at some future date. However, the moon shone too brightly that night and they had to cancel the patrol before it had got very far. The 1st Devons relieved the 12th Glosters two days later. On the 11th, the Glosters relieved the 1st Duke of Cornwall's Light Infantry and were back in the Canal sector.

Just before stand-to on the 14th, a German from the 16th Bavarian Infantry Regiment came into the East Surrey's lines in the Canal sector. He had become lost and disorientated during a relief and entered a British sap, imaginatively named Death or Glory, which was just north of the canal, in the belief that it was German. When he realised his error, he tried to escape but, faced by a Lewis gun, he surrendered without a lot of fuss. Not only did his presence indicate that a divisional relief was happening on the German side but he had valuable information. This he did not readily give up, however, but, after much questioning, he let slip that the Germans were soon to mount a raid. Forewarned with this intelligence, precautions could now be taken and countermeasures put in place ready to be sprung when the Germans struck. However, on 17th, the 95th Brigade was relieved by 198th Brigade and moved out of the sector before the German raid was due to take place. Presumably, the 95th passed on the unwelcome news that the 198th were about to be raided.

The 1st Devons were back in the line in the Canal sector by the afternoon the 15th. At midnight, they mounted their raid. The aim was to hit the German trenches north of the La Bassée Canal. The party comprised Second Lieutenants J. Wells, E.J. Berry and G.W. Dibble and forty-one other ranks. Although they blew a lane in the German wire with a Bangalore, they came up against a second belt of wire they had not known about. They did not have another Bangalore so were unable to penetrate the second belt. They had no choice but to withdraw, suffering two slight casualties for their pains. The enemy, however, took no chances and fired off an SOS flare 4 minutes after the Bangalore was detonated, which brought down the artillery on the British support lines. These were only 77mm whizz-bangs and a few gas shells. The retaliation was surprisingly weak. Although not known at the time, this reflected the withdrawal of thirteen German divisions all along the front from Arras to Soissons. The retaliation could not be stronger because the guns had being withdrawn from the old front line.

With the realisation that the Germans had retreated to a new line, the location of which was unknown, the BEF set off in cautious pursuit. A number of actions were fought as the German rearguard was encountered. A more vigorous chase was not really feasible because of the devastation of the ground over which the British now advanced and the poor weather conditions, which made the hauling of heavy guns and howitzers a painfully slow process at times. As a consequence, raids during April were far fewer than in preceding months. There were fewer raiding opportunities for the British and Dominion troops in the region of the retreat, while the Germans were too busy withdrawing and setting themselves up in the Hindenburg Line to mount raids.

Chapter 12

Canada and South Africa

On 20 December 1916, the 1st Canadian Mounted Rifles mounted a massive raid against the 6th Bavarian Reserve Division, sending over several parties amounting to a force of 422. The success of this operation was in no small way due to the use of 'specially constructed galleries leading to craters in no man's land', from which the Canadians emerged to take the Germans by surprise. The Mounted Rifles destroyed twenty-six dugouts and at least one machine-gun emplacement, capturing nearly sixty Bavarians before withdrawing. This was the sort of operation that reinforced the fearsome reputation of the Canadians as raiders, a reputation that was further enhanced by an operation mounted in January 1917.

The Canadian Corps undertook a great many raids following its transfer north from the Somme in October 1916 to the Artois and the Souchez sector, next to Vimy Ridge. As the Canadians were not involved in another major operation after the fighting on the Somme until the attack on the Ridge on 9 April, raiding not only became a way to maintain dominance over the Germans but it was also a means by which intelligence about the enemy's positions for the forthcoming assault could be gathered. Raiding was exactly the sort of attrition advocated by Haig and the Canadians took to raiding in a way unlike any other national contingent of the Allied armies. Man for man, the Canadians Corps probably undertook more raids than any other army on the Western Front. And they mounted some big operations.

The biggest and most ambitious Canadian raid of war so far was carried out on 17 January 1917. This was mounted by the 20th and 21st Battalions of the 4th Brigade with 875 troops who had been specially trained for the operation, commanded by Lieutenant-Colonel R.D. Davies. They were aided by sappers of the 4th Field Company who went along as a demolition team. The objective of the raid was to devastate the positions held by the 11th Reserve Division along a section of the German line, 3 miles of east of Lens in the region of the Lens–Béthune railway line, as well as to take prisoners and what was quaintly described as 'booty', that is to say, arms, equipment and any other items of interest. As a diversion, 'parties of the 18th and 19th Battalions carried out demonstrations on the flank as the assault went in at 7:45 a.m.' The timing of the operation was meant to coincide with stand-down by the Germans, which came after the customary stand-to, observed by both sides up and down the line every day of the year, usually just before dawn, as a precaution against surprise attacks. It was reasoned that following stand-down, the Germans would be far less alert as they would be starting the daily routine of trench life and not looking out for a raid.

An operation on such a scale needed artillery support and this was provided by corps and divisional artillery. In addition, machine-gun companies interdicted German support trenches and rear areas. Canadian Engineers also provided support by firing smoke from 4-inch Stokes mortars to conceal the raiders. The operation lasted about an hour, during which time, the raiders destroyed more than forty dugouts and blew up three ammunition dumps. They captured two machine-guns, two trench mortars and wrecked several more. But the biggest prize was the 100 prisoners they took. All this cost the Canadians 175 casualties, of whom forty were fatalities. According to the post-action report by the Germans, however, they repulsed the Canadians for the loss of only eighteen dead and fifty-one wounded, with a further sixty-one missing. The truth lay somewhere in between.

The level of raiding by the Canadians increased during the first few months of 1917 and reached a crescendo in March. On 13 February, the 10th Brigade, commanded by Brigadier General E. Hilliam, mounted a similar raid to that carried out in January. This was against the 5th Bavarian Reserve Division. The raiding party was 800 strong, made up of men from each of the four battalion in the 10th Brigade, the 44th, 46th, 47th and 50th. Each battalion provided 200 men. In addition, the 10th Field Company and the 67th Pioneer Battalion together provided seventy sappers. The raiders captured about fifty of the enemy, who had a further 110 casualties. Dugouts, mine shafts and barbed wire were all destroyed during the operation. The Canadians suffered about 150 casualties. Clearly, the Canadians were very good at this sort of warfare and they always hit the enemy hard but it was at a price.

By far the most ambitious raid of all was carried out on the night of 28 February–1 March by troops from the Canadian 4th Division. The objective was German positions between a feature known as Hill 145 and another called the Pimple. The attacking force was some 1,700 strong and included men from four infantry battalions, 54th, 72nd, 73rd and 75th. Despite the size of the attacking force and careful planning of the operation, the raid proved to be rather more costly than anticipated, with the Canadians suffering 687 casualties, including two battalion commanders, amounting to about 40 per cent of the troops engaged. The operational planners had decided to eschew the customary artillery bombardment in favour of surprising the enemy. Diversionary bombardments sometimes fooled the Germans about the target of a raid but an operation of this size would be hard to conceal this way. However, it was a considerable risk to have no bombardment of either the target trenches or the wire in front of them. Indeed, the lack of artillery support was a mistake. As the Canadian official history later put it, 'The venture was almost a complete failure'.

Instead of artillery, the operation was supposed to be supported by gas, both lachrymatory and lethal, discharged from cylinders dug into the Canadian trenches along the entire front of the 4th Division. While the Germans did not detect the installation of the cylinders, the first discharge of lachrymatory gas did not achieve its purpose and only succeeded in alerting the 16th Bavarian Infantry Division and the 79th Reserve Division that the Canadians were about to attack them. To make matters worse, the wind changed direction, which prevented the release of the chlorine, and German shells then burst some of the cylinders so that Canadians were gassed. German artillery and machine-guns then caught the parties from the 11th Brigade as they tried to cross no man's land and before they were through their own wire. The parties from the 12th Brigade faired better and most reached their objectives. In all, a mere thirty-seven prisoners were taken in the operation. It was a poor return for such a costly enterprise. Many dead and wounded remained in no man's land over the next few days but the Germans helped the Canadians recover some of the dead.

Undeterred by this setback, the Canadians raided the Germans every night from the 22 March onwards until the launch of the attack on Vimy Ridge on 9 April. The raid carried out by thirty-one men of C Company of the 42nd Canadian Battalion against the 3rd Company of the 262 Reserve Infantry Regiment on 1 April was an exemplar of how a raid should be planned and executed, demonstrating the high level of skill that the Canadians utilised on such operations to increase their chances of success, from planning to tactics. There were no guarantees, of course, since the enemy did not necessarily react as anticipated and a great many other factors influenced events but certain elements of a raid could be maximised in order to achieve the objective with the minimum of casualties.

The raid started at 6.44 am, when a Canadian 18pdr battery began bombarding the German front trenches with shrapnel. Thirty seconds later, the battalion rifle grenadiers, twenty in all, started firing volleys of grenades onto the front trenches while a another six fired on the flanks, assisted by Lewis guns. Then, at 6.45 am, Lieutenant R.Willcock, and thirty other ranks split into four parties, moved off from the Canadian lines. The objective of the raid was to obtain identification and inflict casualties. As the parties set off, three Stokes mortars fired on three junctions where communication trenches joined the front trenches and Vickers and Colt machine-guns[1] interdicted suspected reinforcement assembly areas behind the front and support lines.

> They entered the enemy line … between DURAND and DUFFIELD Craters and covered a square of trenches opposite LONGFELLOW Crater, formed by Batter Trench, Bump Trench, front line trench and trench not named. The 63rd Divisional Artillery furnished a box shrapnel barrage with which our Stokes Guns, Rifle Grenadiers, Vickers, Colt and Lewis Guns co-operated. The barrage continued until 7.10 a.m. rate of fire being gradually slackened. The Artillery then 'Stood to' until 7.20 a.m. when the Artillery barrage was put on again for one minute of intense fire, with the object first, of inflicting casualties on enemy who might have come out of dugouts thinking everything over, and second, mystifying the enemy regarding our intentions.

The Lewis gun located at No. 5 post at the north end of Longfellow was observed to make three hits on enemy soldiers during the raid.

Each of the four raiding parties had a specific task. No. 1 party was a blocking party assigned to the north-western and southern sides of the square that formed the area of the assault, No. 2 attacked the German front trenches, No. 3 went round the south-eastern and northern sides of the square, while No. 4 followed No. 3 to deal with dugouts, then proceeded to a specified trench junction to form another block. Willcock, as raid commander, put himself between Nos 3 and 4 parties. Each party had different experiences during the operation.

> Party No. 1 met no enemy and encountered no dugouts. On returning however they destroyed an enemy bomb store by exploding a Stokes bomb in it. Remaining parties all encountered dugouts. In two cases enemy sentries attempted to escape down dugout entrances and were shot; in a number of other cases enemy had been driven into dugout entrances by our shrapnel barrage. They were all killed by the raiding party and dugouts wrecked with Mills and Stokes bombs.

Willcock was knocked over by an explosion of one of the Canadians' own artillery shells just as he was about to follow No. 3 party, led by Lance-Corporal Kelly up a communication trench. The explosion also injured one of No. 3 party, who suffered internal bleeding. This 'somewhat demoralized' the rest of the party but Willcock encouraged them to continue and took control of the party. The wounded man turned out to be the sole Canadian casualty of the raid.

The Stokes mortar bomb was often used for demolition work of this sort but they were heavy and the burden of lugging a load of bombs about in a raid was very trying for whoever was burdened with the task. Indeed, the 'Stokes carrier was in rear [of No. 3 party] and found it extremely difficult to keep up owing to the heavy going through the mud'. He was so far behind that Willcock was unable to say afterwards how many dugouts were destroyed in the raid. One of them was clearly very big.

> Under the parapet of BATTER Trench there [was] a large dugout with numerous entrances ... at least 8 entrances of which two had been blown in but not completely closed by our Artillery.

As the raiders passed each dugout entrance, they fired inside and threw down Mills grenades. Germans were seen on the stairways that led down into the dugout and some of these were hit. Several dugouts had been hit during the artillery bombardment and smoke rose from five or six locations, which observers in the Canadian trenches presumed to be burning dugouts.

The condition of the German trenches was something of a problem for the raiders due in part to the shelling but also because the Germans had apparently neglected to maintain their trenches in this part of the line.

> BUMP Trench was found to be in very bad shape, with no revetting ... The party were prevented from proceeding far along it, owing to our left Stokes gun shooting short. They therefore left the trench and proceeded to the front line. The four parties then returned through the point of entry at 7 a.m. (exactly as planned)

They brought back one prisoner. He 'proved to be very intelligent and very ready to talk, and the information obtained from him provided our Artillery with several new targets'.

Willcock was subsequently praised for his leadership and was awarded a bar to his Military Cross. Lance-Corporal Myles won a bar to his Military Medal, while Corporal Greaves and Privates Gordon and Gates were also awarded the Military Medal. These awards attested to the success of the raid. Despite the muddy state of the enemy trenches, which made movement much slower than it would otherwise have been, the operation went exceptionally well. The only hiccups were the 4.5-inch shell that knocked Willcock down, slightly wounding one man, and one of the Stokes mortars consistently fired short and very nearly caused Canadian casualties. As soon as the Canadian bombardment started, the Germans in the front trenches and subsequently in the support line after the raiders had got into it fired off white flares to bring down a bombardment but neither the German artillery nor their trench mortars responded. Had they done so, the Canadians would have suffered far more casualties than they did. Surprisingly, the Germans seemed to put up very little resistance to the incursion and very little rifle or machine-gun fire was noticeable the whole time.

The operation was also supported by eight of the battalion's snipers who were stationed in several locations in the Canadian front line. They kept up a steady fire on targets as they presented themselves during the raid.

> Sniper Corporal Cave reports that during the first shoot no targets presented themselves, but he saw a Hun in addition to the one who got into our lines making his way towards us … this man went too far to the left and was struck by a Stokes bomb. After the 10 minute interval when the Artillery opened again, a number of men were observed making their way along BATTER turning right up BUGGY towards STAUBWASSER WEG … Sniper Hale fired 24 shots from No. 3 LONGFELLOW. Sniper McGregor has 12 shots from the same post. These men are both expert snipers and had a good view of their targets so there is every reason to believe that a large percentage of their shots scored hits. The Trench being blocked in several places it was necessary for these men to climb out and expose themselves. Corporal Cave reports that the shrapnel barrage on BLURT was particularly good.

Over the two weeks between 22 March and 9 April, the Canadians suffered about 1400 casualties as a direct consequence of the raids. This cost was justified by the official historian, Colonel G.W.L. Nicholson by the 'knowledge which they gained of the enemy's strengths and weaknesses, a knowledge which enabled the Canadians to take their objectives with lighter losses than would otherwise have been possible' in the attack on Vimy Ridge. That was debatable and it was still a very high price to pay. It contrasted with the boldness of the Canadians a year earlier at the St Eloi craters at Ypres. On 29 July 1916, for example, a party of twenty from the 19th Battalion struck the German trenches opposite St Eloi 'in broad daylight'. They killed or wounded about fifty Wurttembergers and found gas-cylinders that the 19th Battalion had suspected were being installed. The raiders suffered only minor casualties. As the Canadians well appreciated at the time, raiding had to be carried out at irregular intervals at different locations if the operations were to be successful and while boldness was a factor in success, overconfidence would almost certainly lead to disaster.

The large-scale raid was not a Canadian innovation, but its development in the early summer of 1917 into a new tactical approach to battle was new.

However, it was forced on the Canadians by circumstance rather than being conceived as a tactical advantage. The success of these operations certainly encouraged the Canadians to retain their belief in the effectiveness of raiding on this scale in a way that neither the British nor the Australians quite shared. It certainly helped to maintain the image of the Canadians as the masters of raiding, despite the high casualties that ensued. After the success of Vimy Ridge, the Canadians became involved in operations near La Coulotte as part of an attempt to break into a German salient between Avion and the western fringes of Lens to the south-east. This was part of a larger combined operation between the British and Canadians to attack on a 14-mile front from Gavrelle, a small village north-east of Arras, to Hill 70, just north of Lens.

Following a Livens bombardment on the German 11th Reserve and 56th Divisions with more than 600 projectors,[2] the 10th Brigade attacked at midnight on 2 June. The 44th Battalion went for La Coulotte while the 50th attacked the power station to the north of the village. Both battalions experienced fierce fighting but took their objectives. Holding them was another matter, however. In the early hours of the following day, the 44th were pushed out of La Coulotte all the way back to their start line. The 50th Battalion managed to retain their positions at the power station throughout most of the day despite very accurate shelling directed by spotting aircraft, but they were forced out that evening by a strong counter-attack. Nevertheless, the brigade took 100 prisoners but suffered more than 550 casualties. Having succeeded in ejecting the Canadians, the Germans failed reoccupy the power station in significant numbers. Indeed, two days later, when the 102nd Battalion of the 11th Brigade attacked the power station, a mere twenty Germans were there to defend it. Not surprisingly, they fled as soon as the attack developed but were cut down by sustained shooting from some of the brigade's Lewis guns.

By now, the Canadians were faced with a dilemma. Having relinquished much of their heavy artillery to support a forthcoming offensive further north, they were devoid of significant artillery support. The guns still available to them provided insufficient firepower for counter-battery fire, which was essential if the Germans were to be prevented from pounding the Canadians out of captured trenches. The solution to this problem was novel. General Arthur Currie, GOC 1st Canadian Division, suggested to General Allenby, GOC 3rd Army, that future Canadian operations should no longer be about the taking and holding of ground but should strike the Germans hard in the manner of a raid but on a very much larger scale. This would avoid the inevitable bombardment by German artillery of trenches recently captured by the Canadians and, hence, a consequently high casualty rate. This raiding approach to forthcoming battles was adopted. Now, the

Canadians would strike with enough force to break into the German positions, cause as many casualties among the defenders as possible, destroy as much of their works as they could in the time available in order to make them unusable, then withdraw, preferably with the help of a protective rearguard.

The first operation of this type was mounted on the night of 8–9 June by elements of the 3rd and 4th Divisions, which attacked along a 2-mile front extending north-west from the Arras–Lens road and astride a railway embankment. The attack of the Royal Canadian Regiment, which straddled the embankment, experienced the fiercest resistance of the battalions in the 7th Brigade. The other two battalions of the 7th Brigade, the 42nd and 49th, had a slightly easier time. These attacked on the north-west of the line while the 87th, 75th and 102nd Battalions of the 11th Brigade advanced on the south-east of the line. In all, the Canadians employed about 3,500 men in the operation. Like so many other raids, those in involved rehearsed beforehand but not over a replica of the German positions, as that would have been too great an engineering challenge and too easily spotted from the air. Instead, the battalions practised on a training ground on which the German 'positions' were taped out. This was the kind of rehearsal that went into any large-scale operation. By 1917, training had become a fundamental element in the development of fighting skills at all levels in the Allied armies.

The operation went well with in excess of 150 dugouts being bombed and several machine-guns being put out of action or captured. One platoon from the 102nd Battalion operating on the north side of the River Souchez captured a concrete pillbox that housed a machine-gun. The raiders took 136 prisoners and inflicted at least 700 casualties among the troops of the 11th Reserve and 56th Divisions. The 7th Brigade claimed to have killed 560 Germans but this was probably an exaggeration, although the Germans had, indeed, suffered considerable losses in the raid. The 7th Brigade put its own losses at 335, with thirty-eight of them being fatal, while the 11th Brigade lost sixty-two killed with a further 312 casualties.

Currie had never been in favour of raiding for its own sake. Provided each operation had a specific purpose, he advocated hard-hitting raids but if a raid was intended to gather intelligence about the enemy that might already be available from another source he was opposed to such actions because of the losses that ensued. On more than one occasion when he was in command of the 1st Division he cancelled raids during early 1917. This rather went against the popular view that British divisional commanders ordered raids irrespective of their value simply because they were part of Haig's policy of attrition. Currie wasn't only the divisional commander to cancel raids, of course, rather than push them at any cost, but his approach stood out all the more because of the Canadian's reputation as master raiders.

The Canadians were inevitably raided by the Germans but not nearly as often as they hit the Germans. However, the Germans showed on occasion that they could be every bit as aggressive as the Canadians. Patrolling and raiding were all part of dominating the enemy on the other side of no man's land, although the strong defensive stance adopted by the Germans from the outset of trench warfare mitigated aggression. They simply had to withstand what was thrown at them until they were ready to relaunch their advance across France. As far as the Germans were concerned, they had no need to dominate in the way in which the Allies tried simply because the Germans were on territory that they had overrun and had gained whereas the Allies were trying to remove them and take it back. And while both sides maintained a strong presence in no man's land in the shape of patrols so that fights often took place in no man's land during the night, the Germans tended to content themselves with that for most of the time. In addition, they shelled the Allied lines and threw mortar bombs at them all the time. However, if the Germans needed to find out more about who was actually occupying the trenches opposite them they had little choice but to mount a raid, although sometimes a raid was in retaliation for an earlier Allied one.

The Canadians were raided in late November 1916 but were not hit again until the end of February 1917. Whereas in November the Germans had managed to get into the Canadian trenches, they failed to do so in February. They were driven off by Lewis gun and rifle fire and artillery. Artillery was always the most effective solution to a raid. Hit the raiders in no man's land and they rarely reached their objective. However, artillery, also worked for the raiders by neutralising the enemy just before he was raided. So six days after the failed attempt, the Germans tried again with much stronger artillery support that before. A hurricane bombardment by the artillery assisted by a lot of rifle grenades, temporarily overwhelmed the Canadians and this time the raiders got as far as the Canadian outposts, which they bombed. Two Canadians were taken prisoner before Lewis gun fire forced the raiders to withdraw.

While the Canadians were raiding the Germans with every increasing frequency during the spring, the Germans began to hit back more often with raids of their own. The Germans mounted two raids in mid-March, one on the 13th, the second on the 15th. Both operations were well supported by artillery and trench mortars. Another raid hit the Canadians on the 21st, followed by a small raid the following day. Although Canadian artillery broke up the attacks in all but the last one, the Canadians manning the outposts were often the losers as they were the most vulnerable. They were either killed or taken prisoner. However, none of these operations were German successes. Not only did they usually fail to the enter the trenches but they also suffered much worse casualties than the Canadians.

Between the end of October 1916 and the end of March 1917, the Canadians carried out more than sixty raids and a high percentage of the parties managed to enter the German trenches. Something like 20 per cent of Canadian raids failed, however, but that was about half the failure rate of German raids. Moreover, the Canadians, who were only a small component of the British Armies on the Western Front, also carried out more than one raid on a given night, although not necessarily in the same area of the front. On the night of 9 December 1916, the Canadians actually launched three raids, a very ambitious undertaking, although these were carried out by small parties, not the company-sized or battalion-sized groups of later raids.

Even smaller than the Canadian Corps was the South African contingent that served on the Western Front from 1916 onwards. Indeed, it was one of the smallest of any of the forces sent to the Western Front from the British Dominions, consisting of four battalions grouped together in a single brigade. This served with 9th (Scottish) Division for most of the war. The New Zealand Brigade with the New Zealand Mounted Rifles Brigade was a somewhat larger contingent than the South African Brigade and had the advantage of serving with the Australians in a single Corps, the I Anzac. Not only was the South African Brigade small in comparison to the rest of the British forces on the Western Front but it could ill afford to lose men. Considering the steady attrition of men that raiding caused, the South Africans proved to be not only keen but very effective in the planning and execution of small enterprises.

The first raid mounted by the South Africans took place on 13 September 1916 in the Souchez sector. Two parties from B and D Companies of the 2nd Regiment, one led by Lieutenant Lilburn, the other by Lieutenant Walsh, crossed no man's land under a bright moon that was only occasionally hidden by cloud. They took a considerable risk as they might have been detected at any stage but they reached the other side of the German wire unnoticed. The artillery fired a bombardment to cover the advance of the raiders who 'doubled across No Man's Land and jumped into the German trenches' just as the barrage lifted from the front trenches. The raiders took prisoners, bombed dugouts, then, at a prearranged signal, withdrew before German retaliation began. The raiders suffered two casualties, one of them so serious he had to be left in the German trenches. General Monro, GOC First Army, congratulated General Henry Lukin, GOC 9th Division, and expressed his admiration for the way in which the raid was conducted, including 'the meticulous care in its preparation, and the gallantry and enterprise displayed in its execution'.

In 1917, the South Africans carried out two raids, one on 3 January, the other on 7 April. These were both 'dashing' successes. The raid carried out on 3 January had a unique element: during the operation, all the raiders spoke only Zulu to ensure the Germans would be unable to understand what was said. Two parties from the 3rd Regiment, one led by Lieutenant B.W. Goodwin, the other by Lieutenant W. F. G. Thomas, entered German trenches at Arras and wrought havoc, although they only managed to take one prisoner. They destroyed dugouts and concrete machine-gun pillboxes before they returned. The preparatory bombardment caused a considerable amount of damage to the German positions, despite their being deep and well constructed. This, no doubt, played a major part in the success of the raid. The raiders had practised hard during the preceding week to ensure everyone knew exactly what they were doing and that, too, contributed to the success of the operation.

The third raid, carried out by 1st Regiment on 7 April, was much more daring than the others. It was a daylight operation with the objective of identifying the Germans facing them, executed two days before the launch of the Arras offensive. The raid was scheduled for 11.00 am but was postponed at the last moment for several hours with a revised zero hour of 3.00 pm. No daylight operation could hope to succeed without powerful support of artillery and this was duly provided. At the appointed hour, Captain T. Roffe and five other officers led fifty men across no man's land and reached the German parapet without incident. They jumped into the trenches held by the 8th Bavarian Regiment, took three prisoners who were found in a large dugout, and immediately withdrew. By now, the raiders had lost one man killed and three others had been wounded. As they retired, Lieutenant Scheepers noticed a private with a broken leg lying by the German parapet. Scheepers and Roffe returned to help the injured man, who clearly was unable to move unaided. However, German shelling of no man's land grew in intensity and they had to take shelter in a shell hole and wait for it to abate sufficiently to enable them to get to the wounded man. They remained in the shell hole until it was dark but managed to bring him back to their own lines. Roffe was awarded the Military Cross for his actions.

In July 1917, the South African Brigade was transferred to the Somme to undergo training. On the 27th, the 9th Division, of which the brigade was still part, was transferred to IV Corps and, on the following day, the South Africans relieved the 174th Infantry Brigade in the Trescault sector along the Canal du Nord, north of Havrincourt Wood, and south-west of Cambrai. This area was at that time a quiet sector, the tranquility only being disturbed by a few minor raids. By now, the sunshine of summer had turned to torrential rain and conditions in the trenches were becoming very unpleasant and did not encourage raiding. Indeed, the South Africans never carried out another raid after those of 1917. The minor casualties they suffered during raids was in stark contrast to the enormous losses inflicted on them at Longueval and Delville Wood in 1916 during the Somme campaign. In October 1918, the South African Brigade was withdrawn from the front line and did not engage in further operations.

The Canadians and the South Africans both demonstrated their effectiveness in the planning and execution of raids. There was certainly an element of national pride in how they raided. Canadians and South Africans alike shared a fierce individualistic non-conformist approach as citizens of their own countries, which was reflected in how they waged war at the small enterprise level. It was inevitable that they would bring that attitude with them to France. The same was true of the Australians and New Zealanders. None of them was prepared to allow the Germans to dominate. They were tough, resilient men who came from backgrounds that applauded such qualities. That kind of attitude tended to engender the courage and selflessness that successful raiding often required. While courage alone could not win battles any more than it could ensure successful raiding, faint-hearted men did not execute successful raids. Neither did they repel enemy raiders when they tried to enter friendly trenches. What served to make men bold in attack made them equally determined in defence. The Germans certainly regarded all Dominion troops as hard fighters.

Chapter 13

How Not to Raid – Celtic Wood

There were times when raids were disastrous failures. None was, perhaps, a greater disaster than what occurred on 9 October 1917. Eighty-five men of C Company of the 10th Battalion of the 3rd Australian Infantry Brigade raided strong German positions at Celtic Wood during the drawn-out Battle of Paschendaele. The raid not only failed but at least 50 per cent of the raiders became casualties. What happened to them within the German lines has given rise to lurid stories of atrocities and conspiracies of silence because of the lack of certainty about the fate of a significant number of the raiders who did not return. However, the events were more tragic than barbaric, made more so by the fact that the raid was hastily conceived, planned and executed. Moreover, it was a bad idea from the start. The Germans were alert to the possibility of such an operation because this raid was not only the second in two days to hit the same target but it was mounted by the same Australian brigade, the 3rd, although the raiders came from a different battalion.

Two days earlier, the 11th and 12th Battalions had successfully raided the German positions in Celtic Wood and gathered useful information. The second raid was, in fact, a diversionary assault to mislead the Germans into thinking that the Australian 1st Division was about to attack as the spearhead of the next stage of the fighting at Passchendaele, rather than the main assault taking place elsewhere along the Anzac Corps' front. The raid and the main assault would begin at the same time. The objective of the raid was to make the German artillery retain reserves in the sector facing the Australian 1st Division for at least an hour or two and so reduce its counter-battery capabilities against the Australian guns supporting the main assault. However, no regard was taken by the Australian 1st Division or indeed the Australian Corps of the high probability that the Germans would be more alert than usual in the region of Celtic Wood because of the earlier raid, especially since it had been an Australian success. The Germans would not wish to repeat their failure.

On the night of 6 October, two officers and sixty men from the 11th and 12th Battalions, raided the German fortified positions on the edge of the wood, which was described as 'a large, broken copse containing many pillboxes' each housing a machine-gun or an artillery piece. The Germans were taken by surprise and fifteen men from the 448th Infantry Regiment, part of the 233rd Division, were taken prisoner. Twenty of the 448th were killed and another thirty were wounded. The raiders also captured one of the machine-guns. The entire operation was completed in 20 minutes and only two of the raiders were wounded, one from each battalion. That same night, the 18th Battalion also carried out a raid and hit German positions south of a main road, taking thirteen prisoners. These men belonged to the 450th Infantry Regiment. Again, the raiders also captured a machine-gun. These operations were highly successful and no doubt persuaded the Australians that another operation could be mounted with similar success.

The 7 October raid was planned and organised in less than a day, which goes some way to explaining the poor artillery support it received, a warning that should have been heeded when another raid was ordered the following day to hit the same German positions. Indeed, none of the raiders from the 11th and 12th Battalions was quite sure when the Australian artillery and mortars began firing in support of the raid. The two machine-guns of the 2nd Australian Machine Gun Company that were scheduled to fire interdiction for the raiders did not open fire at all because the gunners did not realise the artillery shoot had begun. Fortunately, the two trench mortars assigned to support the operation proved to be invaluable. Zero hour was postponed an hour at the last moment, which meant that the raiders had to lie out in no man's land for that hour. Despite the confusion, Lieutenants Vowels[1] and Gudgeon of the 11th Battalion led a party of thirty men from A Company across no man's land at 2 minutes past midnight on the 7th. Despite the uncertainty of the artillery, the raiders entered the wood 'with such vigour that the enemy was completely surprised, and most were caught in their funk holes and killed or captured quite easily' despite the marshy ground, which made the going very difficult.

The failure of the artillery meant that the expected box barrage was not fired. Not only were the German positions not isolated, leaving the raiders open to counter-attack, but the lack of a barrage allowed many of the Germans to escape when they might otherwise have become casualties. Fortunately for the raiders, the Germans were unable to mount a counter-attack so the lack of artillery support had no impact on the operation. But that was down to a German failure, not good planning and execution by the Australians. This was a case of he who makes the least mistakes wins. This time, it was the Australians.

One of the raiders from the 11th Battalion, Private J.A. Saunders,[2] left a brief account of the raid. He noted that 'Everything seemed to go wrong … the time was wrong and we had to lie on the wet ground an hour longer than was intended. The barrage failed us … only one battery firing.' At zero hour, Vowels 'leapt to his feet, and in a loud voice cried: "Come on!" … our men mistook the enemy position and were running round some skeleton pillboxes crying "Come out, you _____!"' He did not record whether anyone complied. The German trenches were another 60 yards away and the raiders took their prisoners there. Another participant in the raid, Private Jim Kirkwood, stated that 'It was a rotten affair but ended well'. This did not bode well for a second operation.

While the 11th were successfully carrying out their part of the operation, Second Lieutenant Davey of B Company, 12th Battalion, led ten men from B Company with another fifteen from C Company into the copse. They had been in no man's land since 10.45 pm, waiting for the delayed bombardment to begin. They penetrated 100 yards into the wood before they saw the signal to withdraw. They bombed three deep, well-constructed dugouts. Davey later reported that they saw little evidence of concrete pillboxes. But they were there, nonetheless. Indeed, one of the raiders reported that he had seen a field gun fire at the raiders from a

> concrete emplacement concealed in an old farm building just on the edge of the wood. It fired through the rafters and was protected by machine guns.

Nevertheless, the wood seemed to be only lightly held and the few Germans they met offered little resistance. The Australians took ten prisoners and captured a machine-gun but did not see or hear the raiders from the other battalion, making this a double raid rather than a single operation.

The orders for the second raid on Celtic Wood stipulated that the raiding party should comprise four groups of two officers, twenty-five other ranks and six personnel from the brigade's Stokes mortar battery. The mortar men were attached to two of the four groups and their job was to carry mortar bombs for demolishing dugouts and pillboxes, each man carrying two bombs. In the event, only three mortar men went on the raid. The objective of the operation was to destroy as many German dugouts as they could find, kill as many of the enemy as possible and take the rest prisoner, destroying machine-guns and other equipment as they went. Each man was to carry a rifle and bayonet, a bandolier of fifty rounds, along with four grenades. Five men in each party would be rifle grenadiers and each of the five would carry eight rifle grenades, which with the rods and spares[3] came to about 12.5–15lb per man. These men were not going in lightly armed but prepared for a more protracted battle. The presence of the rifle grenadiers shows that division expected the raiders to meet more serious opposition than the previous raiders had experienced and that they might have to hold off a counter-attack. However, it is unclear whether the raiding party did in the end include the rifle grenadiers as they do not figure in any of the accounts, fragmentary though these are. Had they been included, their firepower might have proved decisive.

The artillery fireplan set out the bombardment that would be fired to support the raiders, targeting the wood and the brigade front for 10 minutes. A battery of 4.5-inch howitzers would hit the back of the wood, then fire on a broader front. Stokes mortars would interdict a road for 4 minutes, while the 3rd Machine Gun Company would fire on the flanks of the area being raided to suppress enemy machine-guns and deter counter-attacks. However, the agreed plan was subsequently reduced substantially in scope so that the number of batteries was fewer, the time on target was shorter and the rate of fire was slower. This meant that the density of fire was reduced from about 11 yards per gun to about 33 yards. However, when zero hour was reached on the 9th, the artillery fire did not even match this reduced plan. Far fewer shells were fired on to the German positions in the wood than anticipated. Worse, the weight of fire was simply insufficient to achieve the object of suppression or neutralisation. Indeed, it was but a token showing and only served to alert the Germans to an incoming assault.

Brigadier General Bennet, commanding the 3rd Australian Infantry Brigade, who had discussed and agreed what he believed to be the artillery plan with the divisional artillery liaison officer before the operation, was extremely annoyed by the way in which the artillery had apparently reneged on its obligation. After the raid, he complained to higher authority but it got him nowhere. The guns had been needed elsewhere by the I and II Anzac Corps in the Passchendaele fighting and, although no one admitted it, the raid was not important enough to take precedence as far as the guns were concerned. This was not a case of incompetence or callousness but of priorities. Indeed, although a tragic failure for the raiders, the raid achieved its object of diverting attention although not to the extent that the Germans were fooled into thinking a major assault was going to develop from the incursion. For one thing, the artillery support had been too weak for them to interpret the raid as a major assault so that they saw it for what it was, a poorly supported raid. It is highly likely that had there been a sufficient number of guns to hit the Germans occupying Celtic Wood hard, the raid would not have been ordered in the first place as the object of misleading the Germans would have been achieved by a fierce bombardment alone. However, the paucity of guns made an incursion by infantry essential if the deception was to stand any chance of succeeding.

The raid was described in the Australian official history as an operation that 'ended disastrously'. There was a general belief at the time by all concerned with the raid that it had started out well. However, the lack of fire support from the outset meant that such an assessment was not only unrealistic but disingenuous. The early optimism was partly due to the fact that the raiders got into Celtic Wood without meeting opposition but the ease with which this was achieved was deceptive. In fact, the operation started badly and only got worse. It was timed to coincide with the launch of the offensive further north by the II Anzac Corps on 9 October for what was to become the Battle of Poelcappelle. Zero hour was set for 5.20 am. Although the party was well armed, the raid timetable did not call for the raiders to remain in the enemy positions for long as they were due back in their own lines 30 minutes later.

> The raid was to be covered by five batteries of field artillery firing on a front of some 800 yards but the fire appeared so thin that the infantry was uncertain when it began. The troops were fresh from Caestre [reinforcement] camp, and keen, if inexperienced. They advanced by clock-time. and were seen to enter the north-western end of the wood. A party under Lieut. F.J. Scott … worked behind the foremost German posts, which began to retreat, but the South Australians were then attacked from the farther end of the wood.

The full extent of the disaster was not immediately apparent although the fact that only a few wounded raiders returned to the Australian line that night was an indicator of how badly the operation had gone. A few more returned after dark. Five officers had been in the party. Two were known to have been killed, of whom Lieutenant Frank Scott was one. The other fatality was Lieutenant A.N. Rae. Two others, Lieutenants R.P. James and L.U. Laurie were wounded. The fifth, Lieutenant W. Wilsdon was missing. The following day, stretcher bearers went out to look for any wounded who could be brought in. They improvised Red Cross flags to indicate their non-hostile intent but they were shot down. This was one of a number of such incidents on the I Anzac Corps' front in which both sides had shot stretcher bearers carrying Red Cross flags because the bearers were suspected of not using the flag honestly and that their real intent was hostile. It is always difficult to establish how such suspicions arise but rumours always spread quickly and wear a badge of authenticity. The falsehood becomes truth because it is made real by one side or the other meting out what they believe to be just deserts. Then, fancy becomes fact very quickly, a self-fulfilling prophecy.

The Germans in Celtic Wood were from the 448th Infantry Regiment. Their war diary shows no entry that describes this raid. Hence, there is no record of what happened to the other seventy-one men who did not return from the operation. The names do not appear on any list concerning prisoners of war. There is no record of their bodies ever being recovered by either side. They would appear to have gone into the wood and vanished. There is very little evidence to indicate their fate although it is almost certain that they all died in the wood.

Despite the poor artillery support, the battalion's own Stokes mortars, the 3rd Australian Light Trench Mortar Battery, provided an effective bombardment, which allowed the raiders to press on once they had entered the wood. Some Germans were already falling back but this was in accordance with German tactics. These Germans were from the outpost line. The level of resistance the Germans might put up could not be gauged from their withdrawal because the main line of defence was further into the wood and it was to this line the Germans were withdrawing. They were not retreating. The raiders entered the wood in two parties, one from the north, the other from the west, but two parties were too weak to deal with the serious opposition that they now began to encounter. Indeed, the raiders were enclosed on two sides and enfiladed by machine-guns while riflemen fired on them from a ridge that looked into the wood from the eastern edge.

The raiders attempted to carry out what they were there to do, bombing dugouts as they came upon them, but it became apparent that the wood was fortified to a much greater extent than appreciated from the previous raid. Some of the raiders headed off to outflank a trench from which heavy fire was hitting the Australians. This enterprise was already transformed by the Germans from a raid into a fight for survival and was beginning to take on the look of a last stand. German artillery suddenly pounded the battalion lines on the other side of no man's land. Some of the shells were smoke and before long the wood was lost from view. By now, the two parties had been broken into a number of small, isolated groups by the heavy rifle and machine-gun fire. Sections of German infantry began to seek out these small groups and deal with them piecemeal. The Australians were outnumbered, outgunned and outmanoeuvred.

The groups of Australians became further separated when Scott led some of his men to one of the edges of the wood, deeper into German-held territory. German fire prevented them from reaching the far edge and, indeed, drove them back. The fighting became more intense and it is evident that it became close-quarter for all the groups of Australians. They were relentlessly cut down. However, there is nothing to suggest that this was in any way different from the sort of fighting that inevitably developed whenever an enemy incursion occurred, whether it was of the Allied lines or those of the German. In almost every instance of men being isolated during an attack, as happened to the 10th Battalion raiders, the defenders hunted them down and few were given the chance to surrender. Surrendering under such circumstances was very risky as the intention of the man trying to surrender was unclear to the man to whom he was trying to give himself up. Since ruses are not uncommon in warfare, a man given the option of accepting a surrender or of shooting the man trying to surrender will often shoot first as it is the safest option.

Fragments of stories were gathered from the survivors by the CO of the 10th Battalion, Lieutenant-Colonel Michael Wilder-Neligan, and put into a report. Thirty-one men are known to have been killed, seven were listed as wounded and thirteen were officially listed as missing. Add to this the fourteen who returned unwounded, the number of men unaccounted for is twenty. It is likely that some, if not all, of these also died, either at the time or subsequently of wounds. It seems that none of the raiders were taken prisoner as none appear on any list provided by the Germans. There is no definitive account of what happened in the wood and the question of how many were unaccounted for has provoked argument and speculation. However, it is highly improbable that the men of the 448th Infantry Regiment committed some sort of atrocity on the raiders as a reprisal for the earlier raid, then hid the evidence, as some writers have suggested. The evidence shows that the 448th acted in accordance with German tactical doctrine for dealing with an incursion and particularly with attackers who had become isolated from their own lines. That bodies of many of the dead were not found afterwards was not in the least unusual on the Western Front. The Australians never had the chance to look for them and the wood did not fall into British hands until 1918. Even today, thousands are still missing because they were buried in temporary graves, which were then lost or shelled into oblivion in later fighting. Much of the fighting on the Western Front, after all, was over the same small areas of land, and battles ebbed and flowed over it as well new ones being fought subsequently.

Nevertheless, irrespective of whether some of the raiders were unaccounted for after the raid, the fact remains that this operation was a spectacular failure in every respect with a very high casualty figure. The raid had been hastily put together and it lacked essential artillery support because of the offensive to the north, the very reason the raid was ordered in the first place. There is little question that division knew the approximate strength of the German defences in Celtic Wood and yet brigade was not advised accordingly. Moreover, it seems that Division never had any intention of providing the artillery support requested, yet never made this clear to the 10th Battalion. This was an example of bad planning and poor communication. The raid was doomed from the start. It was an example of how not to go about mounting a raid.

Chapter 14

1917

Raids carried out in April and May 1917 provided the British with valuable information about the German defences at Messines prior to the offensive to take the Messines Ridge due to start on 7 June. The British discovered from the interrogation of prisoners and from captured documents, particularly during the Battle of Arras on 9–15 April, that the defences at Messines had been changed in accordance with the same tactical thinking that had given rise to the defences of the Hindenburg Line. By this stage of the war, neither side held front-line positions with strong garrisons as they had done in the past because doing so only increased the number of casualties when the line was subjected to an intense artillery bombardment as a prelude to an assault. Thus:

> the labyrinth of the front-line trench system and the maze of communication trenches had lost their purpose and importance. The defensive battle was now to be mobile and elastic in character, to be fought within zones two thousand yards deep instead of in trench lines.

As part of the preparations for the Battle of Messines, those troops who were to take part in the attack underwent a long period of battle training. This meant that the front line at Messines was only sparsely manned. One battalion was spread along the frontage normally occupied by a division. However, the Germans were given little chance to realise how thinly the British were holding the line because raiding was intensified, partly to harass the enemy, partly to gain information about him and his positions and partly to fool him into believing the line was still strongly held. Moreover, the raids helped to hide the engineering and mining that was taking place in preparation for the assault on the Messines Ridge.

In the sector held by IX Corps, one of the three corps facing the Ridge, nineteen raids were carried out between 16 May and 7 June. The raiding parties varied in size from only twelve men to 300. More than 170 Germans were taken prisoner and a larger number were killed and wounded. The cost was high, however, 172 casualties arising as a direct consequence of the operations. The 3rd Australian Division of the II Anzac Corps was very active and mounted numerous raids between 27 May and 6 June. Not all of them were successful. Sometimes, the raids were used by the artillery to practice the sorts bombardments they would be firing during the offensive on the Messines Ridge. What all the raiders found each time they entered the German front line was how thinly it was being held, which seemed to mirror the British line.

On the night of 27–28 May, seven officers and 214 other ranks from the 38th Battalion, in two parties under the overall command of Captain F.E. Fairweather, raided the German line opposite Anton's Farm. One party of 100 men, led by Lieutenant W.H. McCulloch, suffered serious losses when sixty were hit by friendly artillery fire but the survivors reached the German trenches. The other party, led by Lieutenant W.H. McCulloch, also got into the German trenches but faced resistance. Private Lock worked his way round a party of Germans, killed several of them and caught a corporal of the 5th Bavarian Reserve Infantry Regiment, who turned out to be a valuable prisoner. The raiders lost two officers and twenty-eight men either killed or missing, while another two officers and sixty-three men were wounded. Although the prisoner turned out to be useful and a number of Germans were killed, this enterprise was not exactly a success.

The following night, the 39th Battalion mounted a raid on German positions near La Douve Farm. Four officers and 130 other ranks under Captain P.L. Smith got as far as the German support line but found only three or four Germans, who they failed to capture. German artillery shelled no man's land, which accounted for most of the 39th's losses. Seven men were killed and another thirty-three were wounded. The only positive result was the destruction of one dugout but that was hardly worth the effort and the casualties. That same night, Lieutenant K. J. Campbell led a party of fifty from the 33rd Battalion in a raid on German positions near St Yves. They met practically no resistance, destroyed a dugout and shot the only German they met. For their troubles, nine of the raiders were wounded and another two were missing when they reached their own lines again. In the meantime, the 34th Battalion sent out a patrol of five led by Lieutenant E. Shannon. They got into the German trenches without trouble, had a good look round and shot a couple of the German garrison before leaving.

On the night of 30–31 May, the 40th Battalion sent out a raiding party that attempted to get into the German positions south of the Douve by stealth alone. Although they penetrated the German wire without too much trouble they were met with stronger resistance than their fellow raiders on the previous two nights. These trenches were held in strength and the Germans opened up on the raiders with rifle and machine-gun fire accompanied by the inevitable grenades. The raiders fought back hard but lost fourteen of their number. Only one of the raiders managed to get into the trench, Private W. Kelty. Unfortunately, it availed him little because he was knocked senseless almost immediately. Worse, he had to be left behind as none of the others could get to him. Curiously, none of the Germans seemed to have discovered him or they thought him dead. The following day, Australian mortars fired on the German trenches raided the previous night. One of the explosions 'blew the body of a man out of the German trench into No Man's Land. The man was seen to get up, stagger towards the Australian line, and then collapse.' The man was clearly an Australian and Lieutenant S. Le Fevre of the 39th Battalion 'walked straight over the parapet and brought him in'. The man was Kelty and apparently unscathed despite the blow on the head and being blown out of the trench by a mortar bomb. His was a remarkable escape.[1]

The following night, five parties went out with the intention of capturing prisoners but they all failed. Two parties from the 37th Battalion were kept out of the German line by enemy artillery shellfire that was hitting their own front trenches. Another party from the 42nd Battalion managed to get into the German trenches but discovered after a 10-minute search that they were deserted except for one German. He was not made prisoner. Two parties from the 34th Battalion had slightly better luck although, unlike the other parties, they not only found Germans, but these put up a spirited defence of their line. Nevertheless, Lieutenants Brodie and Shannon got their men into the German front line and forced the Germans to withdraw. The raiders then threw grenades into the dugouts. Shannon was killed during the fighting. Again, not one German was taken prisoner.

After such an intense period of raiding, the next few nights were quiet but on 4 June, yet another raid was carried out, this time by men from the 44th Battalion. With the support of an artillery bombardment, a practice shoot in preparation for the coming assault on the ridge, Lieutenant F.O. Gaze and Lieutenant C.D.W. Lintott got into the German trenches and took four prisoners. A second party from the 43rd Battalion was also supposed to hit the German trenches at the same time but they were delayed. The vehicles bringing them forward were prevented from reaching their drop-off point by a jam at Hyde Park Corner – not the London landmark but a location in the British trench system at Ploegsteert in the Ypres salient. By the time the 43rd Battalion arrived at their starting point in the Australian line, the support bombardment had already ended. Despite the inadvisability of continuing with the operation, nevertheless, Lieutenant F. Colman, described in the Australian official history as 'its keen young commander', decided to press ahead and led his men out. They were immediately met by German machine-gun fire and Colman was killed. Sergeant H.E. Argus then had to extricate the survivors from a difficult situation. The party lost eight men to no purpose.

This period of intensive raiding finished on the night of 5–6 June, a day before the launch of the Messines offensive. Two raids, one by the 42nd Battalion, the other by the 33rd, were carried out but, once again, the raiders were unable to take a prisoner even though both parties entered the German trenches and 'chased the enemy'. For all the enthusiasm for hitting the Germans with raids in the ten days before the launch of the assault on the Messines Ridge, many of the raids counted for very little. More then twelve raids were mounted by the battalions of the Australian 3rd Division.

Elsewhere, raiding continued unabated, although not always profitably. June was quite an active month. The 1st/5th Glosters launched a platoon-strength raid on 26 June led by Lieutenant Rubenstein. Another platoon under the command of Lieutenant Bingham Hall acted as cover for the raiders, 200 yards to the rear and slightly north of them. The artillery provided a 1-minute bombardment to cover the advance across no man's land. The raiders' objective was a German post to the south of a feature called the Spoil Heap, some miles to the south-west of Cambrai. The post was empty so the raiders withdrew and the covering party went to investigate the Spoil Heap. That, too, was unoccupied so they also withdrew. The whole operation was a non-event.

A few weeks earlier, on the 7th, the 1st/1st Bucks had raided a German post in the same sector. One platoon from B Company attacked the post at 12.05 am after a 5-minute bombardment by a section of field guns, with a second platoon providing flank over. The objective was to 'capture enemy positions on the bank of the canal'. The raiders encountered a thick belt of concertina wire but dragged it out of the way without too much trouble. The enemy opened up with rifle fire but it was effectively suppressed by a Lewis gun firing in support of the raid. The party got into the post before the Germans knew what was happening. However, they did not give up without a struggle and a grenade fight ensued for several minutes but the enemy were quickly overcome and an *Unteroffizier* was taken prisoner. The Bucks then consolidated the positions on the canal. In the sense that the raiders took and retained possession of the German posts, this operation was not, strictly speaking, a raid. Nevertheless, in all other respects this operation was, in fact, a raid.

Another small operation was carried out near Monchy, south-east of Arras, by the 8th Royal Fusiliers on the night of the 29th. The objective was to eject the Germans from two posts that were proving a nuisance to D Company. When the raiders from D Company reached the posts, they were unoccupied. However, while the party was still in the posts, the

Germans returned. In the fight that followed, two of the Germans were killed and another two wounded. This feeble attempt to take back the posts was not repeated, suggesting that their garrisons had been just as surprised by the raiders as the raiders had been by them.

On the last day of June, the 2nd Grenadier Guards were encamped at Cardoen Farm, between the Wippe crossroads and Elverdinghe, north-west of Ypres. Here, No. 11 Platoon and elements of No. 10 Platoon made use of a pond while practising for a raid over the Yser Canal. They crossed the pond 'on mats made by the Royal Engineers'. On 2 July, the battalion moved into the line in the Boesinghe sector. They now held positions along the west bank of the Yser Canal for a distance of 1,500 yards. The raid for which the platoons had been practising was carried out the following night. The operation had been ordered by brigade 'with a view to obtaining identification of the enemy and also information as to their territory'. No. 11 Platoon under the command of Second Lieutenant I.F.S. Gunnis, together with Second Lieutenant Lord Basil Blackwood and five other ranks from No. 11 Platoon, with a number of sappers from the Royal Engineers, set out from the Grenadier's lines at 11.30 pm. No. 11 Platoon had orders to capture a prisoner, while the party from No. 11 had the task of reconnoitring 'a definite point'.

The Yser Canal was a major obstacle to this enterprise as the German positions were along the opposite bank. However, the canal was not full of water. It was empty but for what lay at the bottom of it: thick glutinous mud. This was why the Royal Engineers had constructed:

> 5 feet mats, made of canvas and wire netting nailed to wooden slats. Two of these were used and were unrolled by two specially detailed parties.

These acted as a temporary bridge over the mud, spreading the weight of each man and allowing all of them to cross unimpeded. By 11.45 pm, everyone in the party had crossed the canal. So far, the Germans had not detected them. Now that the raiders were on the opposite bank, they were faced with a more impenetrable obstacle of shell holes, barbed wire and knife rests. None of this had shown up on supposedly recent aerial photographs. Somehow, the raiders struggled through but gradually lost cohesion as they went forward.

Blackwood and his party went some distance before they encountered any earthworks. A German began firing on them from a dugout a little ahead of them. Blackwood's orderly was hit in the leg and one of the sappers was killed. The party, already stretched out, took shelter in several shell holes as the enemy continued to fire on them and began throwing grenades. Blackwood's party became even more dispersed and they lost contact.

Blackwood himself was seen to fall in the gunfire. The survivors of the ill-fated enterprise made their way back to the canal, recrossed and got back to the British lines. Unfortunately, to compound the misfortune, no one reported back to Captain C.F. Walker, the Company Commander. He, along with the Battalion CO and his second in command, was awaiting news of the operation. They had no idea anything had gone wrong until Blackwood's absence became apparent. Had anyone from the raiding party bothered to report back, a patrol could have been organised to look for Blackwood and those of the raiding party who were still missing.

If all that was not bad enough, no one was really sure what befell Gunnis and his party. As was customary on raids, one section of the platoon detached itself from the main body and had taken up positions in the German line to act as a block to prevent the rest of the party being taken by a counter-attack. The remainder of the platoon headed southwards to secure a prisoner. They found a trench and 'proceeded down it until an obstruction of wire, etc., made further progress impossible'. This was a trench block put there precisely to prevent raiders doing what Gunnis's platoon were attempting. This block was well constructed and well placed because the trench sides were too steep to allow anyone to climb out at that point. The raiders had no choice but to go back the way they had come. Gunnis's order to turn round and go back was evidently misheard and the party now split in two.

Gunnis and those of his platoon who were still with him entered another trench but after they had gone some way they were fired on at 'very close range' and they had to retire. Having retraced their steps, they then climbed out of the trench and went overground, back the way they had just come, and went beyond the point at which they had been fired on. It is evident that Gunnis lost his sense of direction because he ended up in the place where Blackwood and his party had been shot at. They came upon the dead sapper and Gunnis detailed two men to recover the body. The party now became dispersed. As the party set off again, several grenades were thrown at the two men detailed to bring back the sapper and Gunnis become separated from the main body. Gunnis did not return.

When the Grenadiers were out of the line a few days later, a court of enquiry was set up to investigate the conduct of the raid as it had been a fiasco with the loss of two officers to no purpose. The lack of accurate photographs was key to the failure of the operation. Had an up-to-date photograph been available to the battalion, it is possible the raid would have been cancelled. At the very least, a different plan would have been devised. The raiders dealt with the obstacle of the canal very efficiently, with the assistance of the Royal Engineers, but the rest of the operation simply disintegrated into chaos because the men did not know where they were in the German-held territory.

Just over a week later, on the night of 8–9 July, the 2nd Coldstream Guards mounted a similar raid in much the same place. The bombing section and the rifle grenade section of Nos. 7 and 8 Platoons of No. 2 Company of the 2nd Coldstreams crossed the canal in three groups using the mats. Zero hour was 10.45 pm. Much to the surprise of the raiders, German artillery fired an intense barrage at precisely that moment, the shells landing just behind the British front trenches. It went on for 16 minutes before abating. This shelling could only mean that the Germans knew about the raid. Nevertheless, the raiders were undaunted and proceeded to cross the canal using the mats. Everyone was on the far bank in 12 minutes but the Germans discovered them 3 minutes later. The centre group under Lance-Sergeant H. Harris held the crossing point.

Second Lieutenant T.H. Porritt and the left-hand party worked their way down 80 yards of German trench using hand and rifle grenades. They killed two Germans and a number fled. The right-hand party under Lance-Corporal F. Graham advanced down the trench for 60 yards in the opposite direction and shot another two Germans from whom they took material that identified the regiment. After 15 minutes, the raid commander, Lieutenant W.B. St Leger, positioned at the crossing point, gave the signal to withdraw, firing three green Very lights. The raiding parties fell back in good order and recrossed the canal, the mats being taken up after them. Everyone was back in the Coldstreams' line within 16 minutes of the signal. Remarkably, only one man was wounded in the operation. On 25 July, Porritt was awarded the Military Cross 'for gallantry and good work during the raid'.

This operation was the antithesis of the one carried out by the 2nd Grenadiers. While the German bombardment at zero hour implied foreknowledge of the operation, the Germans seemed quite unprepared for the raid. The availability of up-to-date information about the German positions no doubt played a part in the success but it is evident that the German front line was already being thinned as part of a withdrawal from the northern sector of the line above Ypres.

As part of the preparations for the forthcoming offensive at Ypres, which was to open on 31 July, there was a substantial increase in raiding by the British and Dominion troops in the sector. The artillery preparation started on the 18th with counter-battery fire and bombardments of German positions. Each of the Corps involved in the offensive mounted raids, all of them protected by the now customary box barrage. These raids were interspersed with gas attacks by Livens projectors and 4-inch Stokes mortars, operated by the Special Brigade. The gas attacks were, in effect, a cross between an artillery bombardment and a raid, albeit of a different sort from those carried out by the infantry as the intention was to harass the enemy, not to take ground from him. On the night of 13–14 July and again a week later on 20–21 July, 4,000 Livens projectors, dispersed along the whole Ypres front, fired on specific targets within the forward zone of the German defences. On most nights, 4-inch Stokes batteries hit selected targets with lachrymatory or lethal gas.

Prisoners taken during this period indicated that the morale of the German troops was being adversely affected by the bombardments and raids. In some instances, the Germans in the forward positions of the defence zone were close to breaking point. The raids were also useful in detecting whether the Germans were withdrawing from their forward zone. In late June, awareness of the coming Allied offensive had led Ludendorff to propose a withdrawal from the Pilckem Ridge to the third line of defence, which ran east of the Steenbeek, a minor river. This would turn their second line into the outpost line and would have negated much of the preliminary work carried out by the corps leading the offensive. It would have made a much deeper forward zone as well as husbanded German resources. Ludendorff's proposal was dismissed as an unnecessary precaution. The Germans seriously underestimated the frontage along which the offensive would be launched, however. Nevertheless, along the northern flank facing the Fifth Army, the Germans did withdraw from their front trenches, a fact picked up by patrols, aerial reconnaissance and raids.

On Monday 2 July, 95th Infantry Brigade instructed the 1st East Surreys to mount a two-company raid on the night of 9–10 July. The East Surreys were in the line north of Arleux. Their objective was a German trench that ran west along the edge of Fresnoy Park. Fresnoy had been captured by the Canadians at the end of April but lost about a week later in a German counter-attack. The East Surreys came out of the line and moved to a camp near Roclincourt to prepare for the operation. While the orders had come from brigade, they originated at 5th Division HQ. On the night of the 4th–5th, patrols reported on the condition of the German wire the raiders would have to cross. At that point, it was thin and in need of repair, which German working parties seemed to be in the process of starting.

On the day on which the raid was scheduled, the operation was postponed until the morning of the 14th. Then, on the 11th, it was delayed a second time. Now, it would take place on the 15th. Zero hour was 3.00 am. The reason for postponements is unclear but they allowed several 'excellent air photos' to be studied. These established that the German wire in front of the park was sparse except at the southern end. More importantly, the photographs showed that some shell holes about 50–80 yards in front of the German line had been consolidated. On the morning of the 14th, the raiders went over the practice ground for the last time.

The raid orders were received on the 14th and these stipulated that the raiders would remain in the enemy trenches for half an hour but would 'not penetrate into the Park more than 50 yards'. The purpose of the operation was to 'obtain identifications and inflict as many casualties as possible on the enemy, and destroy dugouts, M.G. emplacements and other works of Military importance'. A timetable for the artillery support was set and the withdrawal signal was agreed. However, events did not turn out quite as anticipated as the raid got off to a bad start even before the raiding party left the camp at Roclincourt. Indeed, it descended into farce.

The GS wagons[2] were supposed to collect the two companies outside the camp at 9.30 pm to take them to the appropriate location behind the lines from where they would go up the trenches for the operation. However, the wagons were not where they were supposed to be. Ten minutes later, they were located 1,000 yards away on the Roclincourt–St Laurent road and facing in the wrong direction. The next half an hour was spent manoeuvring them into the right position facing the right way up the Ecurie–Roclincourt road. By now, it was raining heavily and the raiding party was already more than an hour late. This was not the end of their misfortunes. As they reached the top of a ridge, one of the limbers became stuck in the mud and its passengers had no choice but to get out. The thunderstorm now broke and it rained harder than ever without stopping until the following day. The raiding party eventually reached the trenches only to find that the relentless rain had turned them into canals. Large working parties going in the opposite direction now impeded the progress of the party even more as they struggled to reach the start line before zero hour. The raid was cancelled.

This was perhaps more a stroke of good fortune than any of them realised at the time because there was no way they would have been able to cross no man's land in the 4.5 minutes required by the timetable under those conditions. That was the duration of the covering bombardment. The shell holes of no man's and were awash with water and mud. It would have been foolhardy to attempt a raid under the circumstances. The operation was rescheduled for the morning of 18 July. This was the fourth postponement. The raiding party went back to rehearsing over the practice course. At 5.00 pm on the evening of the 17th, the two companies, Nos 1 and 4, moved up with battalion HQ for the raid. It began to rain. This time, however, the rain did not amount to much and did not impede the raiding party. And this time, they went by rail to the top of the ridge. From there, the party went:

> without hurry to the ARLEUX LOOP via TIRED ALLEY, drew bombs at the junction of Sunken Trench and OAK ALLEY … then moved into position … At 3.30 a.m. the barrage opened and the advance commenced, No. 1 Coy. On RIGHT and No. 4 Coy. On LEFT with the bank as the boundary between them. The objective was reached on the whole front except the extreme right where there was wire and M.G. fire.

One prisoner (10th Bav.Inf.Regt) was captured by the Left Coy. and a number (probably 20) killed as they tried to bolt from a concrete dug-out.

At 4 a.m. Rifle Grenade rockets[3] were fired from our front line further North and the Companies withdrew.

The operation was not exactly a success, however. The cost was high. Four men were killed and a further twenty wounded, including two of the six officers who took part in the raid, while fourteen men were missing. Their fate was uncertain but the author of the post-action report believed that eight of them from No. 4 Company had probably been killed when they pursued the enemy too far into the Park and, hence, into their own box barrage. The other six had probably been shot down by a machine-gun firing from the right. Alternatively, they could have been killed by grenades. The truth was that the author did not know. The wide frontage of the operation had allowed men to become isolated, especially in the dark, and it is likely they were picked off piecemeal. The survivors were rested for the next day. Two days after the raid, a patrol went out to search for the bodies of the missing men but failed to find them. This had echoes of the Celtic Wood raid but without the wild speculations.

The Germans raided the British lines far less often and it was not unusual for the raiders to be foiled in their attempts to enter British positions. On the night of 22 August, a raiding party tried to get into one of the posts held by the Cameronians near Nieuport. Three other ranks were wounded and one killed in the attack but the raiders were kept out and they 'failed to get an identification'. In the Widyendrift sector, the advanced posts of the 3rd Coldstreams were raided twice on successive nights in September, 9th–10th and 11th–12th, and on both occasions the Germans were beaten off without loss. On 20 October, a party of twelve Germans tried to get into the trenches held by B Company of the 2nd Lincolns at Warneton, north-east of Ploegsteert Wood, during a lull in the fighting in the Passchendaele campaign. The raiders threw a great many grenades in the Lincolns' trench. Nevertheless, they were driven off, leaving behind one man killed. The Lincolns suffered no casualties.

The Germans were not always so unsuccessful, however. Indeed, on occasion, they came close to a major coup that could have prejudiced an otherwise well-concealed and well-prepared Allied offensive. On the morning of 18 November, a British saphead at the edge of Havrincourt Wood was raided under the protection of an artillery and trench mortar bombardment. A sergeant and five men from the 36th Division were taken prisoner. Fortunately, none of them knew anything about the offensive that was going to be launched in two days' time. Havrincourt Wood was south of the town of Cambrai and the opening of the offensive would become famous for the successful use of massed tanks to break through the German lines.

About a fortnight earlier, the roles had been reversed as it had been the 9th Royal Irish Rifles raiding the Germans in this sector. At 4.30 pm on the 3rd, C Company successfully penetrated the German line despite serious resistance. The Germans were not prepared to surrender. The raiding party remained in the enemy positions for 20 minutes and 'bayoneted and shot at least forty Germans' and suffered a few casualties of their own, mostly from grenades. Three officers were wounded, one of them badly. An NCO was killed and thirteen other ranks were wounded, while another three were missing believed killed. One of the accompanying Royal Engineers was also badly wounded. The sappers were on the raid for demolition work. Military Medals were awarded to five of the men who had participated in the operation.

At about the same time as the German raid was taking place at Havrincourt against the 30th Division, about 300 men, the majority from the 184th Regiment, were raiding positions held by the 55th Division further south in the region of Gillemont Farm, which was between Lempire and Vendhuile, SSW of Cambrai. This operation was a huge success for the Germans as they inflicted ninety-four casualties, a little over half of whom were missing, presumed captured by the raiders. The following night, the Germans mounted yet another raid, this time on the 20th Division and more prisoners were taken. None of these prisoners knew any more about the forthcoming offensive than those taken from the 36th Division. However, interrogation of the latter made it clear to the Germans that an attack was about to be launched in the Havrincourt sector. Fortunately, the Germans misinterpreted the information and Crown Prince Rupprecht concluded that, 'The British having failed in Flanders, partial attacks may be expected on other parts of the front'. It was a close call.

The 9th Royal Fusiliers mounted a company-sized raid in the Cambrai area of the front on 2 September, striking German trenches named Spoon and Strap. The 36th Machine Gun Company supported the operation by firing a 21,700-round barrage into the German lines. The raid was carried out by Z Company, which had undergone special training at Beaurains. On the night before the operation, the company had moved into the line while the brigade trench mortars set about cutting the German wire. Gaps were also cut in the British wire in preparation. At zero hour, 7.15 pm on the 2nd, the 100 men and five officers of Z Company under the command of Captain G. La L. Baudains scaled the ladders out of the trench and headed across no man's land as the artillery fired on the German line. The raiders reached the enemy trenches without losing a man, taking the 96th Infantry Regiment by surprise. Nevertheless, the Germans put up a fight, killing one of the officers and wounding eleven men, two of them only slightly. The raiders killed about twenty of the Germans and took a further eighteen prisoner. Two machine-guns and a *granatenwerfer* were destroyed and a dugout was set alight. The company was back in their own lines by 7.35 pm. The operation had taken only 30 minutes from start to finish and everything had gone smoothly. The German response was to shell the British line with artillery and trench mortars but not very effectively. The shelling caused some damage to the front trenches, which was repaired the following day, but the bombardment caused no casualties. This was a successful operation.

On 20 November, during the Cambrai offensive, a number of raids were mounted by the 24th Division on the right flank of the main attack. This division held the right sector of VII Corps. The raids were part of a programme of subsidiary operations carried out on both flanks to support the offensive. The 2nd Leinsters, part of the 73rd Brigade, raided north-east of Hargicourt and destroyed two dugouts. The Germans ran away. The 9th East Surreys, part of the 72nd Brigade, carried out a raid east of Hargicourt and ended up engaged in hard fighting. The raid mounted east of Villeret by the 8th Queens, also part of the 72nd Brigade, hit the 440th Reserve Regiment, several of whom were killed during the operation. The raiders destroyed two machine-guns.

Cambrai was conceived as a means of breaking through the German defences using predicted fire, which meant that artillery did not have to register and thereby give away the British intention to attack on a large scale. A crucial part of this scheme was also the employment of tanks en masse. The combined elements of the attack resembled a raid on a huge scale, especially as the original intention had not been to seize and hold ground but to strike hard and inflict so much damage and cause so many casualties that there would be no need to hold the ground because the Germans would be overwhelmed. The tank phase of the operation retained a raid-like quality but the execution of the rest of the plan failed to retain the initiative during the later stages of the assault. The battle became much more of a slugging match than it might otherwise have been.

The tanks of this era were technically not up to the task being asked of them and within days of the opening of the offensive, ever increasing numbers of them broke down or became bogged down on the battlefield while many were knocked out by German artillery. Nevertheless, the concept of fighting not to take ground but to overwhelm the enemy was one that was gaining more acceptance. The Canadians had used this raid-like approach to battle a year earlier and over the previous twelve months it had become absorbed into the evolving tactical principles of a new form of warfare within the BEF, incorporating predicted fire by artillery and infiltration techniques from the infantry, all of which resembled the tactics of raiding. Such principles were not exclusive to the BEF; they were also developed by the French and the Germans.

Three of the first US troops to be killed in action on the Western Front died on the night of 2–3 November 1917 during a German raid on American trenches near Bathelemont, a village east of Nancy in the Luneville sector.[4] They belonged to the 1st Division, the first US unit to see action. It had only been in the front line since 21 October in what was supposed to be a quiet sector held by the French. The Big Red One was attached to the French 18th Division in what was supposed to be a gradual learning experience for the Americans, acclimatising them to trench warfare as fought on the Western Front. The Germans knew of the arrival of the Americans and 213 men of the 7th Bavarian Landwehr Regiment carried out the raid to find out what these new adversaries were like.

The operation was covered by an artillery and trench mortar bombardment of the American line, producing a box barrage around F Company of the 2nd Battalion of the US 16th Infantry Regiment. The raiders were also aided by fog, which concealed their approach. The raiders used Bangalore torpedoes, having adopted the idea from the British, to cut a lane through the wire. No man's land was only about 200 yards at this point and the raiders were in the American trenches in moments. The men of F Company were taken by surprise as they had no experience of this sort of fighting whereas the Germans were accustomed to it. The raiders remained in the trenches for only 3 minutes and although the Americans fought back, they stood little chance. The Germans lost two dead and seven were wounded. When they withdrew, they had eleven prisoners, some of whom were wounded, and a lot of US equipment, 'booty'. Three of the Americans were dead and five others were wounded. The American Expeditionary Force and the 16th Infantry Regiment had been blooded.

Chapter 15

1918 before the German Spring Offensives

With the coming of the new year, all the armies on the Western Front, apart from the still largely inexperienced Americans, were weary from three years of trench warfare. A process of change was taking place in the armies, however, tactically and technologically, while the defences along the Western Front were being changed significantly. The defence zone concept adopted by the Germans during 1917 was adopted by the British and the French. When the Germans launched their spring offensive in March, it broke over defensive positions that were already being changed in type as well as depth but were still in the process of transition. Significantly, the infantry of all the armies were now trained in the use of a wide variety of weapons, from grenades to light machine-guns. No longer were infantry merely rifle and bayonet men but tactical specialists capable of responding to different situations using their own initiative.

Although the Passchendaele and Cambrai offensives had wound down by the end of 1917, the British and Dominion enthusiasm for raiding did not really diminish. As had happened when previous offensives had come to a halt, raiding started to intensify as the main fighting came to a stop. In 1918, this renewed intensity only lasted for a few months, however, as the German offensives made raiding unworkable. So long as the lines were fluid and especially while the British were being pushed back, although resolve stiffened the further back the Germans pushed them, raiding was difficult to execute effectively. However, wherever a measure of immobile stability was restored so that the lines became static again, even if only briefly, raiding was taken up once more. As soon as the German offensives ran out of steam and the Allies began their counter-attacks in the summer, British and Dominion raiding increased again. As before, raiding not only served to harass the enemy but it helped to provide information as well as maintain contact, which was important when he was falling back, something had not really been achieved by the British in 1917 when the Germans withdrew to the Hindenburg Line. The French had pursued with greater drive than the

British on that occasion. From about June 1918, the Germans were constantly falling back until the end of the war in November.

While the ebb and flow of raiding fluctuated for the British and Dominion troops, the situation was rather different for the Germans, whose offensives were spearheaded by soldiers from stormtroop battalions who employed the tactics of raiding. The concept of shock troops to spearhead an offensive proved very effective. However, to consolidate their achievements, equally well-trained follow-up infantry were needed and this was where the Germans did less well. In the BEF, rather than specialist stormtroops who moved from one location on the front to another and were not affiliated to a particular division, entire divisions were trained during 1918 to be shock troops, which not only worked in much the same way as the German Sturm Abteilung but were able to sustain momentum and not have to rely on follow-up divisions. The 9th Scottish Division had the distinction of being very successful in battle but never worked with tanks.

While the benefit of stormtroop or shock troop tactics could provide an opening, which if exploited could lead to victory, infiltration alone – a form of surprise – was never the answer as raiders had discovered many times. Artillery support was the key. Without suppressing enemy fire or isolating the target area from the rest of the line, raids and any other sort of assault tended to end in bloody failure. The well-done raid demonstrated to those ready to take notice that success never lay in reliance upon a single element within a plan but rather depended upon a judicious combination of elements that fitted together cooperatively. Thus, effective raiders were not only skilled in the handling of a wide range of infantry weapons but understood their tactical employment in an all-weapons team. Moreover, without good artillery support and the support of Stokes mortars, all the infantry training in the world would avail them nothing.

Even as late as December 1917, some kinds of raid retained an almost primordial texture, especially where the terrain impeded greater sophistication. The 5th Australian Division was in the region of the Lys, around Warneton, from mid-November, and found that the river tended to flood. The area of unflooded land was uncertain to both them and the Germans 400 yards away, so neither was sure where their enemy's outposts were. As a consequence, each side constantly tried to locate and eradicate the other's outposts in a cat-and-mouse game with neither side gaining advantage over the other. The Germans in particular had a habit of rushing a post and taking its occupants prisoner. The answer was to withdraw the advanced outposts so that they were closer to the main outpost line and could be supported from there. Within a few weeks that line had been converted into a line of strongpoints, each manned by a platoon, the advanced line no more than 80–100 yards ahead, with all the neighbouring posts being mutually supporting. In this way, the threat of tip-and-run raids on the outposts could be effectively dealt with. However, all these changes required a lot of work as new positions had to be constructed and new belts of wire put out and the old ones removed because they were now in the wrong places.

German raiding continued almost unabated, however. The Australians took the view that:

> the general lightness of the German garrison … made it unprofitable to raid in strength except at Warneton and one or two other parts where No Man's Land was narrow and the enemy garrison comparatively dense.

The Australians identified five such locations and struck each of them hard during the winter of 1917–18. At the same time, patrols went out to:

> reconnoitre the enemy's wire … cut out a small post, and, by capturing or killing some of the enemy … identify the German troops then in the line.

The enterprises carried out by the Germans against the Australians in the Messines sector of the front between mid-November 1917 and early March 1918, when the first of the German spring offensives opened, were a microcosm of the raiding along the entire front line. The raids were a mixture of identification and prisoner-taking raids, harassment and cutting out operations. And they were a mix of success and failure, although the Australians seemed to be more successful in driving off enemy raiders than the Germans were in getting prisoners or killing Australians. Some raids were large-scale affairs, such as the one carried out on the early morning of 19 November 1917 by two parties of the 102nd Infantry Regiment, but many were much smaller in scope. At 5.45 am on the 19th, they struck one of the forward posts of the 32nd Battalion near Kiwi Farm. One party got into the Australian trenches but were beaten back with grenades. Another party failed to penetrate the Australian wire. In all, the raiders suffered three fatal casualties, another three being wounded. One of their number was captured and subsequently identified as belonging to a stormtroop detachment. The dead were identified by papers, which they should not have been carrying. The Australians had only four casualties, none of them fatal. This was a costly failure for the Germans.

Three days later, it was the turn of the Australians to make a mistake when a soldier from the 54th Battalion, one of a small garrison manning an isolated post, was heard to cough by a nearby German patrol. The following night, an officer and twenty-six other ranks from the 93rd Infantry Regiment raided the post. Their first assault was thwarted but the party worked their way behind the post and attacked it again. This time, they killed one of the garrison and captured four others, one of whom subsequently escaped. The raiders lost one dead and several others were wounded. In an ironic twist, one of those who had taken part in the raid was himself captured the following night.

The kind of action that typified the cat-and-mouse nature of the German approach to raiding in this part of the front took place at the end of the month when a patrol from 72nd Infantry Regiment went out in search of suitable gaps in the wire through which a raiding party could pass. The object was to attack an Australian post and take prisoners. At 2.30 am on the morning of the 30th, a party of four officers and twenty other ranks made their way through the gaps in the wire and approached a post north of the Blauwepoortbeek held by an NCO and seven men of the 59th Battalion. The raiders were helped by the noise of machine-gun fire, which masked any sound they made. They crawled through the wire protecting the post itself and were only 8 yards from the post when the nearest of the party stood up and rushed it. The Australians did not give up easily. Indeed, they 'fought desperately' and put up an 'extremely stubborn and bitter resistance' because they had no intention of surrendering. A German support party joined the fray and the eight Australians were eventually overwhelmed. The fight put up by the Australians evidently 'so roused the Germans … they could not be prevented from shooting down the whole garrison'.

The raiders suffered casualties themselves with two of their officers and ten other ranks being wounded in this chaotic close-quarter brawl. They withdrew and took captive one slightly wounded Australian. The remaining seven were left for dead. A neighbouring Australian post noticed the German support party and drove them off. An Australian patrol now went forward and found the seven but rather than having killed them, the raiders had only wounded them. They were brought back to the Australian line. The raiders left behind a cap and a number of weapons but nothing that could identify them. This operation was a German success although it very nearly became a costly business as the Australians were preparing to counter-attack by the time the raiding party withdrew.

The events of 17 December turned out rather differently. Sixteen Germans from the 153rd Infantry Regiment and the 4th Pioneer Battalion reconnoitred an Australian post with a view to their regiment mounting a raid the following evening. The post was manned by five men from the 8th Battalion armed with a Lewis gun. The patrol managed to get closer than they anticipated and decided to take advantage of the opportunity and hit the post then and there. They surprised the garrison and took the post. Unfortunately for the German patrol, parties from the 7th and 8th Battalions immediately counter-attacked and took back the post and the

Lewis gun, freeing three of the garrison in the process. In addition, they captured two German officers, one of whom was mortally wounded, and four others of the raiding party, killing another seven.

A small party from the 72nd Infantry Regiment and the 4th Pioneer Battalion, comprising one officer and twelve other ranks, attempted to raid several of the posts near Houthem held by the 3rd Battalion at about 9.30 pm. The Australians repulsed them for the loss of two men injured whereas one of the Pioneers was killed and seven others of the party were wounded in the enterprise. On the 27th, a German patrol managed to get past two of the 3rd Brigade's posts near Kiwi Farm but they were spotted and in the ensuing fight five of the enemy patrol were wounded, which led to the death of the patrol leader, who went back to rescue them. His uniform showed that he belonged to the 226th Infantry Regiment. Two days later, another German patrol comprising twenty men bumped into a 4th Battalion patrol in the area of Moat Farm, which was close to Deulemont. The Germans were chased off for no loss on either side. The last day of January was foggy and a party from the 1st Bavarian Reserve Regiment took advantage of the poor visibility. During the morning they attacked a post near Potsdam Farm held by men of the 14th Battalion. The two men in it were captured. This was one of the few occasions when the Germans managed to discover the identity of the Australians. They belonged to the 4th Division, which had recently taken up positions along the Bassevillebeek.

The next small raid attempted by the Germans was carried out at 5.30 am on 23 February by eight men of the 226th Reserve Infantry Regiment led by an officer. They were unsuccessful. The post was held by men of the 57th Battalion near Kiwi Farm. They spotted the raiders and fired on them, hitting several. On the afternoon of the same day, German stretcher bearers went out to collect the wounded. A quick-witted Australian NCO removed his tunic, which bore the sleeve patch of his unit, and went out to help. In so doing, he was able to see that a German officer and five of his men had been wounded in the skirmish.

The 1st Division relieved the 4th Division on 1 March. During the course of the handover, the Germans took advantage of the Australian vulnerability and raided several of the outposts south of the Ypres–Commines canal. The raiding party was much larger than those of recent weeks and comprised five officers and 120 other ranks from the 17th Reserve Division.

At one point a party of Germans, penetrating between two posts, reached a concrete "pillbox" which Major Henwood, a company commander of the 10th Battalion, had just taken over as his headquarters. Completely surprised, Henwood was captured; but, on its way back, the party which had seized him was seen by one of the posts between which it passed. Fire was opened, men were seen to fall, and a patrol of the 10th which afterwards searched the ground came upon Henwood, dead.

Nevertheless, the raiders took seven prisoners, all from the 10th, which also suffered another eighteen casualties. In addition, the 13th Battalion, which belonged to the 4th Division, had ten casualties, including Lieutenant Luscombe, who was killed. On the other hand, the Australians killed a German officer and twenty-six others in the fighting. They also took prisoners from the 76th Reserve Infantry Regiment and the 9th Pioneer Battalion.

Overall, the Germans did not best the Australians in this sector between November 1917 and March 1918. They had some successes but mostly the Australians countered the German raiders very effectively whenever they tried to strike their forward posts. Over the same period, the Australians of the 3rd Division mounted raids of their own, especially in the region of Warneton. These raids followed no more of a pattern than those of their German adversaries but were on a much larger scale altogether and, hence, had the potential to cause more damage to the Germans than their raids could hurt the Australians. Typical of such operations was the raid carried out by three officers and seventy men of the 39th Battalion on the night of 30 November 1917, followed by a similar operation the following night. At 5.15 am on the 30 November, a 3-minute bombardment was fired on the German front line. Simultaneously, the neighbouring 5th Division artillery fired a smokescreen on the southern flank. Three officers and seventy men hit positions held by the 103rd Infantry Regiment near the railway line to the west of Warneton. The raiders captured two of the enemy infantrymen and claimed to have killed another thirty and suffered fourteen casualties, one of whom was fatally wounded.

This operation was followed up with an almost identical enterprise 8 hours later mounted by the 40th Battalion at 1.00 am on 1 December, which hit the same German positions as the earlier raid. The object was to catch the Germans unawares by a second operation on the same target so soon after the first one. Not only were the Germans taken by surprise but a working party from the 12th Pioneer Battalion was caught in the middle of repairing the damage done in the earlier raid. One of the enemy infantrymen was taken prisoner while another seventy of the enemy were claimed killed. The Germans subsequently confirmed that they lost eighteen dead and another thirty-six were wounded. They captured one of the raiders but found no wounded or dead from the Australian party. A small counter-attack was beaten off. Because of the double raid, the Germans were under the impression that the Australians were trying to take and hold the ground. The success of the raids persuaded the Germans to reduce their strength in the line at Warneton. A comparison between these two operations, separated by only 8 hours and which had the specific objective of catching the enemy as he made good the damage that had been done earlier, and the two raids carried out at Celtic Wood separated by two days emphasises the unrealistic optimism of the second Celtic Wood operation.

The next big raid on German positions at Warneton was carried out on 10 February by nine officers and 195 men from the 37th and 38th Battalions under the command of Captain Fairweather. They penetrated to the second line of trenches and captured thirty-three infantrymen from the 228th Reserve Infantry Regiment and claimed to have killed another 102. The raiders suffered thirty-nine casualties, nine of whom were missing. Germans taken prisoner two weeks later confirmed that an Australian officer and a private, both of whom refused to divulge any information about themselves or their battalion, had been taken prisoner on the raid. The private had been wounded in the legs.

An even bigger raid took place on the night of 3–4 March, when thirteen officers and 225 other ranks drawn from each battalion of the 9th Brigade hit the 228th Reserve Infantry Regiment. Again, the Germans misinterpreted this as an attempt to take and hold the positions at Warneton and reckoned to have successfully beaten off the attack. Ten men and a machine-gun were captured while fifty were claimed killed, although this, like so many such claims, was probably an exaggeration. While this raid was in progress another was taking place to the north, mounted by the Australian 5th Division, who took prisoners from the 17th and 49th Reserve Divisions.

The following night, the 9th Brigade hit the same targets attacked by the battalions of the 10th Brigade on the 3rd–4th. Again, this was a raid in strength, the party comprising ten officers and 225 other ranks. The 228th Reserve Infantry Regiment put up a fierce resistance and mounted a counter-attack as the raiders withdrew. At the same time, German artillery fired on no man's land and the Australian front line. The raiders captured two but these were subsequently killed as they crossed no man's land. The raiders also claimed to have killed forty of the enemy. The Australians lost thirty-two men including Captain B.G. Brodie, who later died of his wounds. Three men were missing.

In early February 1918, no German had been captured for a while along the northern extremity of the Australian line, a sector held by the 4th Division. Its commander, Brigadier General Glasgow, was not happy about this and instructed the battalions under his command to organise a raid to fetch a prisoner. On the night of 10 February 1918, two intelligence officers from two of the battalions in the division, Lieutenant Castles of the 51st and Lieutenant Barton of the 52nd, accompanied by a scout, Private Whitfield, from the 51st, crossed no man's land, 'struggled through the mud of the

Bassevillebeek valley, unhooking the loose German wire there' and with the help of German flares spotted a German machine-gun position behind Hamp Farm, a prime target for a raid. They needed to reconnoitre further to the rear of the post but were prevented by the approach of a German patrol. They now faced a dilemma. If they waited and captured the eight-man patrol, they would gain valuable intelligence and resolve the issue of a lack of prisoners. But against that, they knew they would have a difficult time dragging the men back to the Australian line through all the wire that lay in between.

They decided on a different course of action and when the patrol was almost on top of them they threw grenades and opened fire with their revolvers, killing or wounding four of them. Flares went up and Germans came at them from various directions but they were hidden by the terrain and, remarkably, they escaped detection. They took documents from the dead and injured and cut off their shoulder straps. The straps contained their regimental number. The three now made their escape, recrossed the wire 'by rolling over it' and made it back to the Australian line without mishap. Thus, a raid was averted, which displeased no one. For all the bravado of the Australians, they no more liked raiding than anyone else as they were highly stressful events.

Such enterprises helped the Australians to dominate no man's land by discovering the identities of the German regiments and divisions facing them. Had the Germans realised it, they facilitated the identification process by providing their uniforms with identifying numbers, which could not be removed except by permanently cutting off shoulder straps. The identifying material on the Australians' uniforms was more easily removed and, hence, the Germans rarely managed to get anything from dead or wounded Australian raiders or from prisoners taken on raids. Between 14 November 1917 and 19 March 1918, the Germans left evidence of the regiment to which they belonged during raids or patrols on forty-two occasions but managed to get proof of the Australians' identity on only ten. Australians secured identities of the Germans on fourteen occasions during raids or patrols but left evidence of their own identity on only seven. While these approximate figures are not wholly reliable, nevertheless, they provide an indication of the level of Australian success and of German failure.

The Germans mounted approximately 225 raids against the British and Dominion troops between 8 December 1917 and 21 March 1918, the start of the first German offensive of the spring, Operation *Michael*. Of these, only about sixty-two were successful in obtaining identification of the troops they raided. Thus, less than 30 per cent were successes. British raiding was less intense during the winter of 1917–18 than hitherto as new defensive measures were developed and constructed, particularly from January 1918 onwards, developing a zone defence similar to that adopted by the Germans. Information about the enemy had to be acquired by other means, principally by air reconnaissance. In the Fifth Army area, General Gough emphasised the importance of frequent raids, among other measures, to avoid being surprised by the Germans, who were known to be planning an offensive. Some Fifth Army divisions began a bizarre competition for a cup to be awarded each month to the most successful battalion in each division. Points were awarded according to an agreed scale: one point was awarded for an identification from a dead German; two points for a prisoner or deserter; and three points for a captured machine-gun or trench mortar. This presaged the notorious body counts of the Vietnam War.

On occasion, opposing raiding parties crossed each other in no man's land. At dusk on the first day of the New Year, a 1st Royal Irish Rifles party was almost prevented from going about its business of capturing Germans for the purposes of identification by a party of German raiders who were on their way to attack an A Company post. This was in the Goudberg sector near Passchendaele. The enemy raiders were driven off, with one of them killed and several more wounded. The required identifications were taken from the enemy casualties. To everyone's surprise, another raid hit a C Company post at 5.30 pm. This time, the Germans were equally unsuccessful as five of them were killed and several more wounded by an alert Lewis gunner, Lance-Corporal Hanna. The Royal Irish suffered no casualties in these encounters. There is no similarity between these two raids and those carried out by the Australians to the south, not the least difference being the scale of the raids.

In 1918, the emphasis was no longer on attrition and harassment as in 1916, although such raids still took place. The main point of a raid was to get the identity of the enemy troops on the other side of no man's land rather than to inflict casualties and damage. The evolution of defences from lines to zones with outposts at the outer edge inevitably changed the nature of raiding. Small raids could not expect to attack the main line, partly because it was too strong, partly because it was too far away and partly because the outposts were there to prevent a deep incursion. They were not usually successful in preventing incursions by large raiding parties whose objective was not the outpost line but the main line. The point here, of course, as far as the BEF was concerned, was also to detect substantive changes in the deeper defences of the enemy, especially during the early part of 1918, while the British were developing their own zone system. The Germans, of course, were keen to keep their plans secret so that their intention to mount a decisive offensive in the middle of March remained unknown to the Allies.

On 26 February, the 2nd Grenadier Guards were ordered to carry out a raid in the sector north of the River Scarpe near Arras. Its commanding officer, Lieutenant-Colonel Roach, was informed that 'the battalion would be required to do a raid during its coming tour in the Front line'. In his post-action report he complained that:

> Raids lately have become regrettably fashionable owing to the anxiety of the Higher Command to obtain a constant supply of prisoners who may give them information of the German offensive which is expected.

The target for the raid was selected from the study of recent air photographs with observations from the front trenches, a German position on the extreme left of the battalion's frontage. Here the enemy wire appeared to be thinner than elsewhere and the rising ground on the left provided some protection from flanking machine-gun fire.

The plan was to attack by stealth. A party of twenty-four from one of the platoons in No. 2 Company, chosen because the company had knowledge of the sector from three previous tours, were then sent to Gordon Camp to train for the enterprise in dummy trenches. However, the plan was vetoed by division, who wanted a more robust show of force. The raid had to be on a much larger scale, with artillery and trench mortar support. The number of raiders was increased by the inclusion of eight volunteers from each of the other companies. These men now joined those from No. 2 Company at Gordon Camp. Several additional officers went with them to help supervise the training. However, the number of raiders was subsequently reduced and, in the end, the raiding party consisted of Lieutenant Clarke and twenty-six other ranks, only three more than originally planned. While the raiders trained, the rest of the battalion carried out other preparations, including reconnaissance. The wire was cut by 6-inch Newton mortars.[1] Due to poor visibility, much of the cutting had to be done the day before the raid, which ran the risk of alerting the Germans because of the increased firing. To conceal where the raid was going to take place, the wire was cut in several locations along the divisional front and 'By the evening preceding the raid the wire at the point of entry was very much knocked about though it was not possible to detect a clear path through it.' Whether that was an advantage or a disadvantage depended on your perspective since, while the path was obscure to the enemy, it was equally obscure to the Grenadiers about to carry out the raid.

The raiders were brought up by bus on the night of the raid. Once in the trenches, they proceeded to the Advanced Battalion HQ, where a tot of rum was issued to each man. At zero minus four, the raiders formed up in three parties in no man's land, 150 yards from the target trench, which was about 240 yards from the Grenadiers' line. The left and right parties were eight-strong and led by a sergeant, while the centre party, led by the raid commander, included five other ranks, an NCO and two stretcher bearers. A 1-minute bombardment by 18-pounders at zero hour hit the German front trenches, then lifted to the support line 180 yards further back. Bombardments of both flanks, saps and machine-gun positions was maintained from zero, while communications trenches were bombarded with the 6-inch Newtons and 4.5-inch and 6-inch howitzers. Gas and smoke was mixed in with the high explosive. In addition, machine-gun barrages were fired and Stokes mortars fired interdiction throughout the duration of the operation all along the divisional front.

The raiders negotiated the wire with ease. The Newtons had done their job well. The left and right parties hit the enemy trench at separate points simultaneously, then wheeled outwards along it, while the centre command party remained at the point of entry. The Germans were completely surprised despite the fact that they were aware of the possibility of a raid, as made clear during subsequent interrogations of prisoners. Various dugouts were bombed. Three men from the 10th Bavarian Imperial Regiment were made prisoner and a machine-gun was captured. One of the captives who 'gave difficulty in the withdrawal was shot'. This gun had been mounted on the parapet and aimed at the gap in the wire through which the raiders had passed and would have to pass again to return to their own lines. The crew were bayoneted.

The raid commander gave the signal to withdraw at this point. The raiders and their booty were back in the Grenadiers' lines at zero plus twelve. Although a heavy retaliatory machine-gun barrage was fired at zero plus three, no casualties were reported. Artillery and trench mortars also fired in retaliation but caused no casualties. As soon as the British guns stopped firing, the German guns and mortars did likewise. The raid was a complete success. None of raiders nor anyone in the Grenadiers' line was hurt during the operation.

The situation did not seem to change. On 7 March, the 7th Royal Sussex raided the Germans with artillery support in the Rouge de Bout area in the Petillon sector and took two prisoners for no loss. There was no retaliation. However, on 20 March, a British raid carried out at about 9.00 pm by a battalion belonging to XVIII Corps in the Fifth Army took thirteen prisoners who revealed under interrogation that an attack was imminent. Indeed, they stated that an offensive would open on 21 March, starting with an artillery bombardment at 4.40 am, barely 8 hours hence. This information was immediately telephoned to Fifth Army HQ and GHQ as well as to the corps of the Fifth Army and to neighbouring Armies. Although there had been indications of major movements by the Germans all along the front and hinterland facing Fifth Army, this was the first clear timing of the forthcoming offensive.

Several German raids took place on the night of the 20th–21st, particularly in the early hours of the morning coinciding with zero hour of the German offensive elsewhere. Hill 70, on the outskirts of Lens and in the First Army area, was raided unsuccessfully at 5.45 am. In the Second Army area, another enemy raid was also thwarted. Two raids were mounted against the French in the Champagne region of the front, preceded by heavy bombardments. These were sorties in strength that penetrated the French in 'the Fourth Army area, between Maisons de Champagne and Navarin [where] the enemy penetrated into our trenches, and there was hand-to-hand fighting'. This turned out to be part of an elaborate scheme of feints to divert attention from the area of the main assault.

Several big German raids took place against the British V Corps, part of the Third Army, in the Ypres salient. The object of these raids, which were akin to large-scale local attacks, was to pin down the British forces on the flanks of the main German assault and keep them occupied until the main advance turned the flanks and forced the British to retreat. These operations did not all begin at the same time. The first was at 5.30 am against the right and centre of the 63rd (Royal Naval) Division; the next one at 9.30 am hit the left and centre of the 47th Division; a third at 10.15 am hit the left of the 17th Division. In every case, the Germans penetrated the first line but no further. British counter-attacks and local bombing attacks pushed them out again so that the Germans were unable to fulfil their objectives.

The Germans mounted similar attacks on the 3rd Division, VI Corps, Third Army. These, too, were carried out at different times on the morning of the 21st, the first at 7.00 am in fog. This attack succeeded in taking several hundred yards of the 9th Brigade's line. Counter-attacks forced them out again 3 hours later after fierce fighting. The second raid was against the 8th Brigade at 11.00 am. This was a bloody failure for the Germans. Other raids carried out against the 76th Brigade were also repulsed at considerable loss to the Germans. That was of small concern to them, however. Their offensive broke through the British lines and threatened to sweep the British back to the coast. This was the first of several offensives intended to bring the war to a swift conclusion with a German victory. That was not to be. The launch of the offensive on 21 March brought about change and the Western Front would never be quite the same for the remainder of the war. But that change was not in favour of the Germans.

Chapter 16

End Game

Following the raid on the US 16th Regiment in November 1917, the Americans wanted to retaliate but the French were less than enthusiastic about it because of the inexperience of the Americans. Nevertheless, they were persuaded to allow the Americans to carry out a raid. Lieutenant Archie Roosevelt, son of former US President, Theodore Roosevelt, who was serving with the 26th Regiment, was given command of the raiding party. The raid was a fiasco, not because of heavy casualties inflicted by the Germans but because the raiding party never actually managed to find its way across no man's land to the German line. This inglorious debut was the first belligerent act of the US Army in France in the First World War.

The Americans had to learn from their mistakes and learn quickly. After the shock of the first German raid, a lengthy report was prepared about every aspect of the attack by Brigadier General James McAndrew, Lieutenant-Colonel Stuart Heinzleman and Lieutenant-Colonel H.B. Fiske of the US Army Schools. Their conclusion, not surprisingly, was that the 1st Division had made mistakes through lack of experience. But they were mistakes that need not be repeated. They also finished by stating that:

> There was a lack of intelligence or discipline on the part of some artillery observers, who themselves suffered none of the evil consequences of their exposure, but who precipitated a raid on the trenches that, postponed a little, might have been better met.

The report also blamed the German success on the fact that:

> before this raid the sector had been very quiet for a long period. Everyone concerned had fallen into a sense of false security and the disbelief that the Germans had any intention of strenuous action. This tendency to become careless in quiet sectors in the measures for defense must be continually combatted.

In many respects, the same caveats could have been applied to all the armies on the Western Front. Vigilance, discipline, knowledge of the ground and, above all, adequate training in all aspects of trench warfare, were essential. And while the risks of being surprised by the enemy could be mitigated, they could not be eliminated. Then, the skills of trench fighting and the collective tactical ability of the platoon, company, battalion or division to respond effectively to an incursion decided who won or lost, although weight of numbers applied at a weak point would always favour the attacker. At that point, the counter-attack could change the balance in favour of the defender. A flexible response that gave up the notion of holding onto ground irrespective of the consequences was the key. These lessons had been learned in raids as well as in major battles by the Allies and the Germans. Now the Americans had to learn the same things. The infiltration tactics employed by the shock troops in the van of the German spring offensives had been tested and developed during raids. The raid became a microcosm of battle.

In 1918, the Americans took note of the French experience of being raided and recorded that:

> French comment on trench raiding activity in March and April testified to an increase in the importance of artillery fire both in preparation for and accompanying the raids. Almost all raids had been prepared for by gas shell fire the preceding day on the French batteries and command post.
>
> Important raids were preceded by the usual indications of a serious attack. The preparatory bombardment was characteristically brief; in the case of the raid on Cheppy Wood, April 9, lasting only one minute before the launching of the infantry attack; in that of April 12 it was entirely dispensed with. Captured regimental orders for a raid west of Cantigny on May 27 show that it was to be preceded by a four hour bombardment; two hours against the hostile artillery with gas; and two hours fire of destruction on the trenches. During the raid a box barrage was to be put down on the hostile rear positions.

German raiding tactics were studied by the Americans during 1918 and published in December, by which time, of course, not only had more fluid open warfare replaced the static positional warfare that had spawned the trench raid in the first place but the war had ended. It is unclear whether the AEF benefited from the survey. Except in the details of the command structure and the organisation of the raiders, what the Americans found and concluded about the German system was just as applicable to the British approach to raiding. The major difference was in the development and employment of specialist shock troops. The British developed raiding skills in everyone and turned every infantryman into a versatile technician who was equally at home with the grenade as he was with the Lewis gun or the rifle and bayonet. Moreover, he had the tactical skills for a flexible approach to battle because that was how he was trained in 1917 and 1918. Infiltration stormtroop tactics were not the sole preserve of the German Assault Battalions. The Americans noted that German raids:

> are conducted under general supervision of the Army Assault Battalion, which contributes some of its specialists to the raiding party. The latter is brought up to the strength of a battalion or a battalion and a half by drafts from units in the sector involved. A few days' previous instruction on positions similar to those to be entered is held.

British and Dominion raiders came from the unit carrying out the raid and did not rely on specialists joining them for the enterprise except for Royal Engineer sappers who were the experts in demolition.

Rehearsal and practice was essential for success, principles that had been proved time and again. Indeed, this had been well appreciated in all armies since 1915. It was not a German insight. Replica trench systems were often constructed behind the lines, or their trace taped out, for rehearsing a raid. Familiarisation with the ground over which the raid was to be conducted was essential. Recent aerial photographs and good maps played key roles in acquainting the raiders with the enemy territory. While the enemy needed to be surprised, the raiders did not want to be surprised themselves when they entered the enemy lines so that they became lost in an unfamiliar enemy trench. When that happened, the raid usually ended badly for the raiders. The German raid on Xivray on 16 June had been 'secretly rehearsed in the rear for five days, the last rehearsal being concealed behind a screen of smoke'. However, their intelligence was at fault and the raiders were, indeed, surprised by the Americans of the 103rd Infantry Regiment, who turned the tables on them. Caught by fire from a hitherto unknown machine-gun, they withdrew and tried again from the flank but were again repulsed. The Germans outnumbered the Americans by six to one. They lost fifty dead and another thirty were taken prisoner.

German organisation of their raiding parties did not necessarily follow a strict pattern but in 1918 it was typical for a party to include three detachments. One detachment comprised four squads of pioneers who led the assault, followed by eighty to 100 regimental infantrymen, all flanked by two squads of six men and an NCO. The second and third detachments each included 170 men and two light machine-guns, each preceded by an assault company and eight pioneers. Finally, a small communications detachment accompanied the raiders. This comprised a radio team of an NCO and three men equipped with a set with a range of 3–4 miles. When the raiders secured the first line of the enemy trenches, a signal was transmitted to that effect. Two signallers equipped to give visual signals also accompanied the detachment and four telephone squads, each of three or four men, laid lines from their own trenches to those just captured. Everyone in the raiding party wore a white brassard for identification.

Clearly, this was a complex system. British raiding parties tended to be smaller, no more than about a third the size of German parties, although bigger parties were sometimes used. British sappers performed a similar role to that of the assault pioneers. Their job was to destroy wire entanglements with 'long charges' – Bangalore torpedoes – and demolish dugouts. British raiders tended to be organised along existing platoon and company lines within the battalion concerned and according to the tasks set out for the raid.

Artillery support was crucial to success. It was to be 'very brief but violent' unless the enemy presence in the line was weak, in which case it only served as a signal that a raid was about to fall on that part of the line. The Germans employed infiltration tactics in raiding as in other forms of assault on the enemy line.

> The advance is either in isolated groups, each with bombers, riflemen, pioneers and carriers: or the entire party leaves the lines at the same point in double column of files and does not separate until the entanglements are passed. No particular pains are taken to maintain liaison between groups which 'is insured by the unity of objective.'

In other words, provided the raiders knew their objective and everyone did what was expected of them, contact between the detachments was unnecessary. As the raiders went forward, machine-guns swept the 'enemy area … to disperse troops forming for a counter-attack'; that is to say, German machine-guns fired interdiction as British machine-guns did on British raids.

The objective of the raid was sometimes, by necessity, beyond the first line, which was unlikely to hold much of value. The big prize for raiders was always documents of any kind as these could not only provide information about the battalion or regiment being raided but also about future intentions, training, organisational structures, orders, post-action reports and a wide variety of other intelligence, none of which was supposed to be taken into the front line. To achieve a great depth of penetration of the line, which was necessary in order to increase the chances of getting hold of useful documents, a greater force of raiders was required.

Hence, the increasing size of raiding parties. However:

the practice of evacuating the front zone at night has imposed upon the raiders the necessity of awaiting the counter-attack, in order to take prisoners. This may mean a sojourn of 48 hours in the enemy's position.

Neither the British nor the French adopted this sort of tactic, although the 2nd Coldstream Guards with the 2nd Grenadiers carried out an operation of this sort near Louverval on 27 September 1918, remained in the captured trenches until the following day, and then withdrew. However, the Germans had retreated on that occasion and did not return to their lost positions. Quite clearly, the nature, conduct and purpose of raiding was not quite the same in 1918 as it had been earlier in the war. The increasing complexity of raiding operations in 1917 and 1918 and the greater flexibility needed in countering raids sometimes turned what was otherwise a fairly straightforward operation into an action not dissimilar from one intended to take and hold ground. Indeed, the German raiding tactics were not much different from the tactics they employed in their spring offensives, although it would be more accurate to invert the comparison.

The French approach differed somewhat from both that of the British and Germans. For them, the raid was 'generally made by men from an organization in rear (support or reserve). Captain of first line company provides the material: Grenades, tools, explosives, rockets, etc.' In other words, those who were to undertake a raid were taken out of the line to prepare for the operation. However, the French system made up raiding parties from troops whose battalion was not currently in the line but in reserve or support. A typical French raid was the one carried out at 3.00 am on 20 November 1917 against the 'western salient of PLAINE TRENCH for the purpose of capturing prisoners'. The raiding party comprised 'a lieutenant, 10 hand grenadiers, and 20 riflemen' from D Company, 80th Infantry Regiment, plus two parties of bombers from D Company to protect the flanks.

The raiding party will penetrate the enemy's first line by a frontal attack, capture the defenders of the salient and return directly by the same route. The raiding party will crawl into "No Man's Land" in front of the PLAINE salient until it reaches the enemy's barbed wire and will prepare detonators [French equivalent of the Bangalore torpedo] for the necessary breaches. The signal to explode the detonators and rush into the salient will be given by the leader of the raid by rocket. The raid will last ten minutes.

The artillery bombardment of the flanks and rear of the salient during the raid was the ubiquitous box barrage. C Company, which held the first line in front of the salient provided sixty detonators, 200 hand grenades and three signal rockets.

French raiders were specially chosen for the task, a platoon or half a company in size but sometimes as many as a whole battalion. The French, like the British and the Germans, emphasised the importance of preparation and up-to-date intelligence about the target. Like the British and the Germans, the French constructed dummy trenches and set out the trace of the enemy trenches with tape so that the raiders could familiarise themselves with the target. The raiders had to practice the operation on the model at least five times.

> All the details of the raid are foreseen and provided for. Each man is made thoroughly proficient in his particular part in the raid, so that, in the confusion and darkness, they will be able to reach their objective and carry out their particular function. Each chief of group must be thoroughly conversant with his duties. The leader of the raid personally conducts the most important of these groups.

Speed in the execution of the raid was emphasised. The time spent in the enemy line was supposed to be no more than 5 or 10 minutes. The hours of darkness were preferred over daylight for the operation but zero hour was sometimes dusk or dawn so that the raiders had some light by which to see what they were doing and where they were going. Sometimes the raiding party included a detachment, which the French liked to call 'trench cleaners', who were armed with grenades and knives for the purpose of clearing enemy trenches of resistance and taking prisoners. They also had the job of what the British called blocking, that is to say, preventing the enemy from emerging from dugouts or round traverses or from communication trenches and surprising the attackers. The flanking parties were also supposed to act as blocking parties to prevent a counter-attack developing. With this mind, as with British blocking parties, barricades were erected in the trenches on the left and right flanks. However, considering that the French expected their raiders to be in and out with 10 minutes, any such barricade could only be rudimentary at best.

The French liked their raiders to be ready for zero hour no more 50 yards from the wire they had to cross to reach the enemy trenches. They were supposed to reach their laying-up points by crawling there, sometimes without the benefit of a bombardment to at least mask any noise they might make. They were then supposed to make use of shell holes for concealment. Gaps in the wire could be created in much the same way as the British and Germans made them, by artillery, trench mortars or the French equivalent of the Bangalore torpedo.

The artillery and trench mortar support provided by the French was not dissimilar to that provided by the British and the Germans. Its purpose was to neutralise the occupants of the trench about to be raided, then isolate that trench during the raid with a box barrage and provide cover for the withdrawal by bombarding the front trench again and the flanks in no man's land. The front trench might be shelled with shrapnel several times at irregular intervals after the raiders had returned to discourage counter-attacks and to catch the enemy as he re-occupied the trench just raided. These were much the same tactics as those used by the British and the Germans.

The main assault party was armed with incendiary grenades, trench knives and pistols. It is significant that no rifles were carried by French raiders. The British emphasised the rifle and the bayonet in trench work. And while the hand grenade grew in importance very quickly, it never supplanted the bayonet or the rifle. The so-called 'cult of the bomb' with which the British infantry were supposed to be obsessed, a fear expressed by higher command during the war, was not, in fact, a reality. It is evident that British infantry, far from relying on hand grenades to the detriment of bayonet and musketry skills, came to be less dependent on grenades as the war progressed. By 1917, the emphasis was on bayonet men in fighting down trenches, rather than bombers who were increasingly relegated to a secondary role. Indeed, the British infantryman was very skilled with the bayonet in trench warfare. British raiders were sometimes equipped with pistols and other side arms but only for small-scale operations. Clearly, serious enemy resistance could not be adequately countered with insufficient firepower. Raiders were usually supported by riflemen, machine-guns and rifle grenades.

> The riflemen of the garrison [the battalion in the French line] of the center of resistance stand ready at the firing parapets to receive the groups returning from the raid. The machine guns carry out an intense fire on the flanks of the point raided to prevent the approach of hostile reinforcements. The rifle grenadiers of the garrison execute fire upon special points on the flanks or on the rear of the raided area, such as machine gun emplacements, junction of boyaux [communication trench], etc.

The Americans tended to follow the French model when it came to tactics[1] and the same was true of raiding, although in late 1917 they were interested in the British method, particularly when it came to fighting along a trench. The Americans were hit by several German raids in April, some of them very large, in which the US battalions hit did not fair well, suffering high casualties. Indeed, so badly were they mauled in some of these attacks that concern began to be raised by Haig and Foch about the ability of the Americans to fight. One of the biggest German raids to strike the Americans occurred on 13 April, when two companies of the US 9th Regiment were raided by elements of three German regiments, the 270th, 271st and 272nd, at 30 minutes past midnight. The raiders penetrated the US lines and remained in the American positions for about 90 minutes. Seven Americans were killed, thirty-nine were wounded and twenty-five were taken prisoner. The Germans did not come off unscathed as they lost sixty dead and eleven were caught in the American lines.

On 20 April, the US 102nd Regiment of the 26th Division was hit by a massive raid located at the small town of Seicheprey. Several thousand German troops[2] struck in the early hours of the morning, after an intense artillery bombardment, and overwhelmed the Americans, who were heavily outnumbered. Despite its huge scale, this was, indeed, a raid. The Americans lost eighty-one dead, 187 missing and a further 400 wounded, the Germans suffered in the region of 600 casualties. The raiders withdrew before a counter-attack could be organised. This was a major blow to the AEF as the action again called into question the ability of the US troops to fight the Germans.

The first raids undertaken by Americans were in collaboration with French troops, the first being carried out on the night of 23 February 1918. Volunteers from the 101st Infantry Regiment raided the Germans at Grand Pont and took twenty-two prisoners. This action was noteworthy because it was the first operation to be supported by a creeping barrage fired by US artillery. The Germans raided the 101st again on 27 May when about 400 of them hit the American line at Humbert Plantation, near Flirey. This time, however, the Germans were driven off. On 16 June, the Germans raided the line held by the 103rd Infantry Regiment at Xivray-Marvoisin. Again, they were repulsed with heavy losses. On the night of 30–31 May, the 26th Division mounted a raid of its own. A large raid on the German trenches at Richecourt was carried out by 300 volunteers from the 101st Infantry Regiment.

The Americans learned quickly from their experiences and continued to carry out raids throughout the remainder of the war, mostly successfully. As late as 6 November, the 103rd and 104th Regiments carried out raids on the German positions to take prisoners. The Germans did not give up raiding as their offensives petered out and the Allied counter-offensives began. Indeed, German raids continued into November. On 4 October, fifty infantrymen of the US 6th Division repulsed a raid by more than 300 Germans at Sondernach in the Vosges.

There is no question that the tactics and purpose of raiding evolved during the war. The raid was transformed from a spontaneous ad hoc adventure with no specific military purpose other than to cause annoyance and inconvenience into a tool by which pressure could be put on the enemy or intelligence gained from him. The tactics of the raid became much more sophisticated as the defensive systems also became more complex. Moreover, the tactics employed in raiding became absorbed into the standard infantry training. Raids were sometimes used to test new tactics as the Germans did in a raid against the French in 1915, when they used infiltration tactics with an intense neutralising artillery bombardment. This became the principal of stormtroop tactics in later raids in 1916 and 1917, as well as in the spring offensives of 1918. The British undoubtedly absorbed some of the tactics of raiding into standard infantry training and developed their bombing tactics with raiding.

There is no doubt that by the end of the war, raiding had exerted a major influence on the evolution of the new tactics of deep battle, the means by which the battles of 1918 were fought and the German Army ultimately beaten on the battlefield. And let there be no doubt about that: the Allies militarily defeated the Imperial German Army. Far from being merely a means of attrition, putting pressure on the enemy and dominating him, or of finding out who he was, the raid became a crucial element in the evolution of tactics, a process that was, of course, experienced by all sides. The raid was not an aberration of trench warfare but both a tool and a catalyst in the evolution of tactics.

Notes

Chapter 1: Genesis and Evolution of Raiding

1. The British official history suggests otherwise, however.

Chapter 2: 1915, the Rise of Raiding

1. Figures are for the La Petite Douve party from *Military Operations, France and Belgium, 1916*, the British Official History. The *Official History of the Canadian Army in the First World War* provides slightly different figures of five officers and eighty-five men. The discrepancy may have arisen because the two parties, although broadly similar, were not identical in composition.
2. The Germans persistently referred to everyone in the BEF as English, irrespective of whether they were Scottish, Australian or Canadian.

Chapter 3: 1916 up to the Somme

1. According to their war diary, the raid took place on the 8th. Other sources quote the 9th.

Chapter 5: The Australians: June and July 1916

1. Later a highly successful pilot in the Australian Flying Corps.
2. These fragments are usually misnamed as shrapnel. Shrapnel comprises lead balls, originally the bullets fired by muskets. During the First World War, shrapnel balls were encased in a resin carrier inside a shrapnel shell. The resin produced a white puff of smoke when the shell detonated high above the ground with the nose angled forwards so that a cone of balls was fired downwards on to the target. Shell fragments of irregular sizes and shapes flew in all directions, although mostly forwards, when a shell detonated on hitting the ground. Such fragments were very destructive.

Chapter 6: Wearing Down and Deception

1. Back in England, the rest of his arm was amputated. Jackson died in 1959, aged 62.
2. Such exaggeration is not bravado and is, indeed, commonplace in battle. It is due to the stress of combat, which magnifies the numbers of the enemy.
3. The Australian 7th Brigade was transferred to the British 24th Division, Second Army, on 17 June.
4. This is, of course, why it is used to construct defensive structures.
5. It is not clear when and by whom the issue of gum to front-line troops began or even if this instance was unique.

Chapter 7: The Kensingtons – A Farce in Diverse Acts

1. *The Kensingtons at Laventie* is a painting executed in 1915 by Eric Henri Kennington RA. It is in the Imperial War Museum, Lambeth, London.
2. This was probably Bickford Safety Fuze, which could be lit with a match.
3. The author of the account provided no dates but it would appear the operation was undertaken in the winter of 1916–17.
4. Fred Karno was a British comedian. Fred Karno's Army was a troupe of comedians whose slapstick antics were very popular. At one time, they included Charlie Chaplin and Stan Laurel. The expression Fred Karno's Army was applied to any enterprise that was absurd and chaotic.
5. Since the diarist neglected to put dates into his account, it is difficult to be certain when this took place but it is certainly after the opening of the Somme, probably autumn 1916 or spring 1917.
6. The No. 5 Mills had a 5-second fuze.
7. A whizz-bang was a shell fired by a field gun and had a high-speed flat trajectory; originally a shell from a 77mm field gun, but the term was applied to all shells from field guns irrespective of calibre. The name was derived from the sound of the shell passing and the explosion.

Chapter 8: Operation *Wilhelm* – A German Raid, July 1916

1. Both sides employed listening devices to tap into telephone conversations.
2. A feature marked on the German trench map.

Chapter 9: July–October 1916

1. Six rounds a minute was the standard and could be sustained for long periods.
2. The crater was subsequently named the Red Dragon Crater.
3. *Granetenwerfer* bombs
4. This was the location of Hellfire Corner.

Chapter 10: Bomb, Bayonet and Pistol

1. For a detailed account of the invention and development of British hand grenades during the First World War and the effect on tactics, see the author's *Reinventing Warfare, 1914–18*, published by Continuum, September 2011.
2. The Workshops also produced in large numbers of a rifle grenade with the same name.

Chapter 11: Weather, Moonlight and the Hindenburg Line

1. Forsyth was killed in action on 11 March 1918.
2. Maxwell was killed by a sniper on 21 September 1917.
3. The Indian Corps left the Western Front for the Middle East in early November 1915.
4. The British conducted various experiments during the war to develop night sights that would enable snipers and machine-gunners to engage targets more easily and did see some use on the Western Front.
5. Islands were, in essence, earthwork obstacles in the trench line, each one surrounded by the trench in which it was situated. The trench bifurcated to go round it and rejoined on the other side. Islands could be very substantial or quite small.

Chapter 12: Canada and South Africa

1. The Colt was known to be unreliable as early as 1915. It was replaced by the Vickers, but these were in short supply so the Colt had to be retained until well into 1917.
2. The Livens projector, named after its inventor, William Livens, who was serving in the Special Brigade, Royal Engineers, was a one-shot mortar that fired a large drum of gas. Projectors were used en masse, all being fired simultaneously. They could create a far denser cloud of gas than cylinders or shells and in a very specific area.

Chapter 13: How Not to Raid – Celtic Wood

1. Vowels was killed at Hazebrouck in May 1918.
2. No relation to the author.
3. Rifle grenadiers always carried spare rods in case one or more was bent, damaged or did not fit the bore of the barrel.

Chapter 14: 1917

1. He went on to fight at Morlancourt in 1918, where he lost a leg.
2. General Service wagon; a four-wheeled, horse-drawn vehicle.
3. No. 31 Daylight signal, No. 32 Night signal; they contained parachute flares.
4. Corporal James Gresham, Private Thomas Enright, Private Merle Hay.

Chapter 15: 1918 before the German Spring Offensives

1. The 6-inch Newton replaced the 2-inch medium in 1917. The Newton worked on the same principle as the Stokes and, hence, had a much higher rate of fire.

Chapter 16: End Game

1. This had a long history, going back to before the American Civil War of the 1860s.
2. Estimates vary between about 2,800 and 3,500.

Bibliography

Official documents

CDS74 The Training and Employment of Grenadiers, October 1915

CDS383 Extract from 'Notes on Minor Tactics of Trench Warfare' by 'A Casualty', June 1915

SS98/5 Artillery Notes No. 5 – Wire Cutting by Artillery

SS98/6 Artillery Notes No. 6 – Trench Mortars, March 1916

SS107 Notes on Minor Enterprises, March 1916

SS126 The Training and Employment of Bombers, September 1916

SS139/6 Artillery Notes No. 6 – Trench Mortars, March 1917

SS143 Instructions for the Training of Platoons for Offensive Action, February 1917

SS182 Instructions on Bombing, Part I, British and German Bombs, December 1917

SS182 Instructions on Bombing, Part II, Training and Employment of Bombers, November 1917

SS195 Scouting and Patrolling, December 1917

SS197 Notes on Minor Enterprises, March 1916

SS381 Collection of Information Regarding the Enemy, October 1915

SS398 The Training and Employment of Bombers, March 1916

SS462 German Raid on the British Trenches near La Boisselle, 11th April, 1916

Journals, newspapers

Anon, 'A German Trench Raid', *The Army Quarterly*, vol. XXX, No. 1, April 1935, pp 86–93

MacDonald, Colonel The Rt. Hon. Sir John, 'The Knife in Trench Warfare', *Journal of the Royal United Services Institute*, vol. 62, February 1917, pp 64–8

Messenger, Charles, 'Trench Raiding', *History of the First World War*, vol. 5, 1971, pp 1844–1852

The Times, correspondence, 29 November, 30 November, 1 December 1915

Books

Anon, *A Survey of German Tactics, 1918*, Washington, 1918

Anon, *German Notes on Minor Tactics*, Washington, 1918

Ashworth, Tony *Trench Warfare, 1914–1918, The Live and Let Live System*, London, pbk ed., 2000

Austin, Lieut-Col W.S., *The Official History of the New Zealand Rifle Brigade*, Wellington, 1924

Bailey, Maj-Gen J.B.A., *Field Artillery and Firepower*, Annapolis, 2004

Bean, C.E.W., *The Official History of Australia in the War of 1914–1918*, Sydney, 1929–42

Bertrand, Georges and Oscar N.Solbert, *Tactics and Duties for Trench Fighting*, New York, 1918

Bliss, Tasker A. (ed), *United States Army in the World War 1917–1919*, Washington, 1948

Bond, Brian (ed.), *Look to Your Front*, Staplehurst, 1999

Bonk, David, *Chateau Thierry & Belleau Wood 1918*, Oxford, 2007

Buchan, John, *The History of the South African Forces in France*, London, 1920

Carver, Field Marshall Lord, *Britain's Army in the 20th Century*, London, 1998

Connelly, Mark, *Steady the Buffs, A Regiment, a Region, & the Great War*, Oxford, 2006

Croft, Lieut-Colonel W.D., *Three Years with the 9th (Scottish) Division*, London, 1919

Dunn, Captain J.C., *The War the Infantry Knew, 1914–1919*, London, 1987

Edmonds, J.E., *History of the Great War, Military Operations, France and Belgium*, London, 1925–47

Elliot, Captain F. Haws, *Trench Fighting*, New York, 1917

Ewing, John, *The History of the 9th (Scottish) Division 1914–1919*, London, 1921

Foulkes, Maj-Gen C.H., *"Gas!" The Story of the Special Brigade*, Edinburgh & London, 1934

Graham, Stephen, *A Private in the Guards*, 1919

Grave, L.W. de, *The War History of the Fifth Battalion The Sherwood Foresters, Notts and Derby Regiment, 1914–1918*, London, 1930

Griffith, Paddy, *Battle Tactics of the Western Front, The British Army's Art of Attack 1916–18*, New Haven, 1994

Gudmundsson, Bruce I., *Stormtroop Tactics*, New York, 1989

Hart, Peter, *The Somme*, London, 2005

Hitchcock, F.C., *'Stand To' A diary of the Trenches 1915–1918*, London, 1988

Jünger, Ernst, *The Storm of Steel*, London, 1929

Landers, Rick, *'Grenade' British and Commonwealth Hand and Rifle Grenades*, Dural, 2001

Pollard, Captain A.O., *Fire-Eater, The Memoir of a V.C.*, London, 1932

Nicholson, Colonel G.W.L., *Canadian Expeditionary Force 1914–1919*, Ottawa, 1964

Rawling, Bill, *Surviving Trench Warfare, Technology and the Canadian Corps, 1914–1918*, Toronto, 1992

Richards, Frank, *Old Soldiers Never Die*, London, 1933

Saunders, Anthony, *Weapons of the Trench War, 1914–1918*, Stroud, 1999

Saunders, Anthony, *Dominating the Enemy*, Stroud, 2000

Saunders, Anthony, *Trench Warfare 1850–1950*, Barnsley, 2010

Saunders, Anthony, *Reinventing Warfare 1914–18*, London, 2011

Sheffield, Gary, *Forgotten Victory, The First World War: Myths and Realities*, London, 2001

Spagnoly, Tony and Ted Smith, *The Anatomy of a Raid*, Barnsley, 1998

Terraine, John (Ed), *General Jacks' Diary*, London, 1964

Travers, Tim, *The Killing Ground, The British Army, The Western Front and the Emergence of Modern Warfare, 1900–1918*, London, 1990

Travers, Tim, *How the War was Won*, London, 1992

Willcocks, General Sir James, *With the Indians in France*, London, 1920

War Diaries
19th Brigade Light Trench Mortar Battery

22nd Brigade Light Trench Mortar Battery
36th Brigade Light Trench Mortar Battery
91st Trench Mortar Battery
19th Machine Gun Company
22nd Machine Gun Company
36th Machine Gun Company
2nd Argyll and Sutherland Highlanders
1st Bedfordshire Regiment
1st Buckinghamshire Battalion, Oxfordshire & Buckinghamshire Light Infantry
2nd Coldstream Guards
3rd Coldstream Guards
1st Devonshire Regiment
1st East Surrey Regiment
2nd Grenadier Guards
1st/5th Gloucestershire Regiment
2nd Lincolnshire Regiment
1st/1st London Regiment, Royal Fusiliers
1st/13th London Regiment (Kensingstons)
1st Middlesex Regiment
1st/4th Oxfordshire & Buckinghamshire Light Infantry
8th Royal Fusiliers
9th Royal Fusiliers
18th Royal Fusiliers
20th Royal Fusliers
9th Royal Irish Fusliers
1st Royal Irish Rifles
11th Royal Scots Fusiliers
1st Royal Welch Fusiliers
2nd Royal Welch Fusiliers
7th Canadian Infantry Brigade
Princess Patricia's Canadian Light Infantry

Index